C

D0150117

TAKE A HIKE PHOENIX

LILIA MENCONI

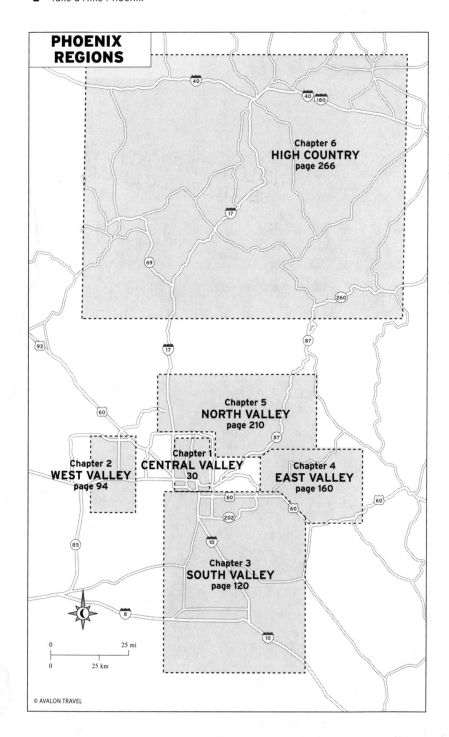

PHOENIX
REGIONS

Chapter 6
HIGH COUNTRY
page 266

Chapter 5
NORTH VALLEY
page 210

Chapter 1
CENTRAL VALLEY
30

Chapter 2
WEST VALLEY
page 94

Chapter 4
EAST VALLEY
page 160

Chapter 3
SOUTH VALLEY
page 120

0   25 mi

0   25 km

© AVALON TRAVEL

Contents

How to Use This Book 6

Introduction 9

Author's Note 10

Best Hikes 12

BEST(Butt-Kickers
BEST(Climbing and Scrambling
BEST(Hikes near Water
BEST(Historical Hikes
BEST(Kid-Friendly Hikes

BEST(Solitude
BEST(Summit Views
BEST(Wildflowers
BEST(Wheelchair-Accessible Trails

Hiking Tips 14

Hiking Essentials 14

Health and Safety 19

Wildlife and Plants 22

On the Trail 25

Chapter 1
Central Valley...29

Chapter 2
West Valley...93

Chapter 3
South Valley...119

Chapter 4
East Valley 159

Chapter 5
North Valley 209

Chapter 6
High Country 265

Resources 313

Index 318

How to Use This Book

ABOUT THE MAPS

This book is divided into chapters based on regions that are within close reach of the city; an overview map of these regions precedes the table of contents. Each chapter begins with a region map that shows the locations and numbers of the trails listed in that chapter.

Each trail profile is also accompanied by a detailed trail map that shows the hike route.

Map Symbols

`-------·` Featured Trail	🚐 80 Interstate Freeway	○ City/Town
`------·` Other Trail	101 U.S. Highway	✗,✗ Airfield/Airport
Expressway	21 State Highway	⚲ Golf Course
Primary Road	66 County Highway	🖑 Waterfall
Secondary Road	★ Point of Interest	Swamp
`= = = = = = =` Unpaved Road	🄿 Parking Area	▲ Mountain
`············` Ferry	🅃 Trailhead	♠ Park
`—·—·—·` National Border	⋀ Campground	)(Pass
`—··—··` State Border	▪ Other Location	✛ Unique Natural Feature

ABOUT THE TRAIL PROFILES

Each profile includes a narrative description of the trail's setting and terrain. This description also typically includes mile-by-mile hiking directions, as well as information about the trail's highlights and unique attributes.

The trails marked by the **BEST(** symbol are highlighted in the author's Best Hikes list.

Options

If alternative routes are available, this section is used to provide information on side trips or note how to shorten or lengthen the hike.

Directions

This section provides detailed driving directions to the trailhead from the city center or from the intersection of major highways. When public transportation is available, instructions will be noted here.

Information and Contact

This section provides information on fees, facilities, and access restrictions for the trail. It also includes the name of the land management agency or organization that oversees the trail, as well as an address, phone number, and website if available.

ABOUT THE ICONS

The icons in this book are designed to provide at-a-glance information on special features for each trail.

The trail climbs to a high overlook with wide views.

The trail offers an opportunity for wildlife watching.

The trail offers an opportunity for bird-watching.

The trail features wildflower displays in spring.

The trail visits a beach.

The trail travels to a waterfall.

The trail visits a historic site.

The trail is open to snowshoers in winter.

Dogs are allowed.

The trail is appropriate for children.

The trail is wheelchair accessible.

The trailhead can be accessed via public transportation.

ABOUT THE DIFFICULTY RATING

Each profile includes a difficulty rating. Definitions for ratings follow. Remember that the difficulty level for any trail can change due to weather or trail conditions, so always phone ahead to check the current state of any trail.

Easy: Easy hikes are 4 miles or less and with an elevation gain or loss of 500 feet.

Easy/Moderate: Easy/Moderate hikes are 4–6 miles long and with an elevation gain or loss of 500–1,000 feet.

Moderate: Moderate hikes are 2–8 miles long and with an elevation gain or loss of 1,000–1,500 feet.

Strenuous: Strenuous hikes are 6–10 miles long and with an elevation gain or loss of 1,000–2,000 feet.

Butt-kicker: Butt-kicker hikes are 8–14 miles long with an elevation gain or loss of 2,000 feet or more.

INTRODUCTION

© LILIA MENCONI

Author's Note

Want to know about Phoenix hiking? Ask a native. Only, that might be easier said than done. Phoenix is a city of transplants.

Fortunately, with *Moon Outdoors Take a Hike Phoenix*, you can experience the best hikes in the Phoenix area, each recommended by me—a gal who was born and raised in Phoenix. Whether you're a newcomer, visitor, or long-time resident, after a quick thumb-through of this guide, you'll quickly see why my home town was named one of the best U.S. hiking cities by National Geographic.

As the fifth-largest city in the United States, Phoenix is a bustling, car-infested grid. Suburban streets, highways, and light rail train tracks make for total concrete coverage.

Except, of course, for our beloved trails.

Phoenix and its surrounding suburbs (locals refer to the 16,573-square miles of metro area as The Valley of the Sun) offer breathtaking views of the Sonoran Desert. This dusty terrain, dominated by iconic saguaro cacti, craggy boulders, and spiky plant life, occurs nowhere else on the planet. And with a quick drive to many trailheads, it doesn't take long to escape the rushing traffic and enjoy the peace of this one-of-a-kind landscape.

The Phoenix Mountains Preserve sits in the heart of the city and invites residents to take advantage of more than 20 well-maintained trails that intersect to create endless combinations. Folks on the south side of The Valley easily access the South Mountain Park, which offers more than 16,000 acres. The trails boast a wealth of petroglyphs made by the ancient peoples of the prehistoric Hohokam society. For those on the east side, the Superstition Wilderness entices thrill-seekers who aim to explore the grounds of the legendary Lost Dutchman, who allegedly discovered a very rich gold mine. (To this day, the mine's whereabouts remain unknown.) To the west, residents explore a whopping 30,000 acres in the White Tank Mountain Regional Park, named for its white granite rock formations, scoured by torrential rains.

And those are just the main parks. Smaller outcrops of buttes and peaks pepper The Valley, so no matter which direction you face, trails keep tempting those of us who can't get enough of the desert dirt.

When the summer heat hits, hikes within the city are typically accessed during the one hour after sunrise and the one hour prior to sunset. Still, even the most acclimated hikers are slowed by constant water breaks and the relentless heat. The Valley's trails are virtually abandoned during daytime hours, when the sun is at its most brutal.

It's the perfect time for residents to head north. Within a two-hour drive, city-dwellers can easily escape the oven-like feel of the summer months and find plenty of trailheads. Hikers can experience the state's high forest areas filled with pine trees and, with any luck, trickling streams.

Prescott, Payson, and other areas to the north assure hikers they can shave off at least 10 degrees from the day's temperature high. And for some of the most stunning views in the state, Sedona is just about two hours away. The mars-like landscape of world-renowned red rock canyons and dramatic spires will stir the souls of even the most conservative. For the best summer temperatures, a trip to Flagstaff is sure to satisfy hikers who are fed up with the heat. With plenty of short trails for the family, it's also the perfect place to set your sights high. Flagstaff's Humphreys Peak offers a summit trail to the highest point in Arizona at 12,633 feet.

I've traveled every trail outlined in this book. And with each trail's profile, I aimed to provide enough information for proper preparation and accurate expectations. It's been an amazing challenge to research, categorize, and explore each of these hikes. I've called Phoenix home for my entire life. When it comes to hiking, this place has something for everyone, and each trail offers a chance to see some of the most soul-moving landscapes on the planet. I'm so grateful to have this opportunity to extend an invitation for others to find out why I love living here.

You in?

Great. Now, let's hit the dirt!

Best Hikes

BEST(Butt-Kickers
Charles M. Christiansen Memorial Trail 100, Central Valley, page 49.
National Trail, South Valley, page 140.
Hunter Trail, South Valley, page 155.
Siphon Draw Trail to The Flatiron, East Valley, page 188.
Humphreys Peak Summit Trail, High Country, page 268.

BEST(Climbing and Scrambling
Echo Canyon Summit Trail, Central Valley, page 75.
Hunter Trail, South Valley, page 155.
Siphon Draw Trail to The Flatiron, East Valley, page 188.
Cathedral Rock Trail, High Country, page 284.

BEST(Hikes near Water
Arizona Canal Loop at Arizona Falls, Central Valley, page 81.
Waterfall Trail, West Valley, page 100.
Butcher Jones Trail, East Valley, page 162.
Bell Trail to Wet Beaver Creek, High Country, page 287.
Fossil Springs Trail, High Country, page 297.
Horton Creek Trail, High Country, page 304.

BEST(Historical Hikes
Waterfall Trail, West Valley, page 100.
Hieroglyphic Trail, East Valley, page 192.
Rogers Canyon Trail, East Valley, page 201.
Sears-Kay Ruin Loop, North Valley, page 219.
Rim Lakes Vista and General Crook Loop, High Country, page 307.

BEST(Kid-Friendly Hikes
Piestewa Nature Trail 304, Central Valley, page 59.
Hole in the Rock Trail, Central Valley, page 84.
Waterfall Trail, West Valley, page 100.
Dragonfly Trail, North Valley, page 216.

Sears-Kay Ruin Loop, North Valley, page 219.
Buffalo Park Loop, High Country, page 274.

BEST(Solitude
Ford Canyon Loop, West Valley, page 96.
San Tan Loop, South Valley, page 148.
Black Mesa Loop, East Valley, page 169.
Rogers Canyon Trail, East Valley, page 201.
Spur Cross and Elephant Mountain Loop, North Valley, page 212.
Highline to Donahue Trail, High Country, page 301.

BEST(Summit Views
Piestewa Peak Summit Trail 300, Central Valley, page 68.
Echo Canyon Summit Trail, Central Valley, page 75.
Siphon Draw Trail to The Flatiron, East Valley, page 188.
Peralta Trail to Fremont Saddle, East Valley, page 195.
Brown's Trail, North Valley, page 261.

BEST(Wildflowers
Sunset Vista Trail, South Valley, page 152.
Siphon Draw Trail to The Flatiron, East Valley, page 188.
Main Trail, East Valley, page 205.
Pemberton and Tonto Tank Loop, North Valley, page 245.
Fat Man's Loop, High Country, page 277.

BEST(Wheelchair-Accessible Trails
Eliot Ramada to Double Butte Loop, Central Valley, page 87.
Waterfall Trail, West Valley, page 100.
Gila to Baseline Loop, West Valley, page 109.
Merkle Memorial Loop Trail, East Valley, page 178.
Fountain Lake Overlook Loop, North Valley, page 258.

Hiking Tips

Before you set out for a day of fun hiking, it's best to know how to prepare for this unique environment. Your bare minimum is a backpack stocked with a handful of essentials and some basic know-how. Good preparation makes for a good experience and that makes for happy memories and more hiking. And that's the whole point, right? Read on for your Hiking 101 lesson.

HIKING ESSENTIALS

Water, water, water. Oh, and don't forget more water.

This will be a recurring theme when discussing hiking essentials. It's a desert out there, folks, and often the only water you'll see for miles is the water you carry. The importance of bringing water can't be stressed enough. So, once you've got the whole water-is-the-most-essential-hiking-necessity thing down, check out the information about sun protection, clothing, general hiking safety, trail etiquette, and all that good stuff.

Water

If you take any advice from this book, let it be this: bring lots of water. Then bring another bottle, just in case. It only takes one water-shortage scare for a Phoenix hiker to wise up. Hopefully, you'll bypass this hard-learned lesson. The rule of thumb for Phoenix-area hiking goes like this: Pack what you think you need. Double it. Then bring one more bottle, just in case.

There are lots of options when it comes to portable water devices. Many hiking backpacks come with water reservoirs (or "bladders") that easily slide into an insulated pocket and deliver cool sips through a connected hose. Any outdoor equipment store will stock water bottles galore in hard and soft plastic. (Heck, even Dad's old Army canteen will do!) As long as it doesn't leak and holds enough water for your day, you should be good to go.

Most experts recommend bringing a minimum of 2-6 quarts (or 1.8-5.6 liters) of water for day hikes, depending on the length and weather. To put that in real-world terms, a large water bladder usually holds up to 3 liters. That should be enough for 2-4 miles on a temperate day. For longer hikes, fill a 3-liter water bladder then bring at least another gallon of water for refills. Each person in your hiking party should carry this much water—you'll rip right through it, especially on a hot or warm day.

To be safe, drink 4-6 cups of water even before you hit the trail and you'll start out ahead of the game. As an extra precaution, stock your vehicle with 2 gallons of water (per person) so you have a stash in case of an emergency. Driving while disoriented due to severe dehydration is dangerous. This may sound excessive, but if you've ever experienced the onset of dehydration (thirst, dark urine, headache, confusion, cottonmouth, muscle aches), you'll soon be panicked for this life-sustaining fluid.

When you're out on the trail, take constant stock of your water supply. Make continued judgments as to whether or not you have enough for your total journey—especially on a warm day and a strenuous trail. When in doubt, turn back and cut the hike short. The trail will always be there.

If your water level gets low, continue drinking the water you've got and return to civilization as soon as possible. Don't be afraid to ask for help; if you come across fellow hikers, ask if they can spare enough water to get you back to the trailhead. Likewise, if you see someone else who's not looking so great, ask if they're okay and if they have enough water. This simple act might save a life.

If you run out of water, immediately take steps to conserve your precious sweat. Long pants and sleeves are your best friends here. Do not go off trail to search for water, especially in the desert where springs or washes indicated on a map are most likely dry. The only place you might see water near the trail is in the High Country, but this water should only be used for hydration in emergency situations (water purifying tablets are handy in this scenario).

Bottom line: Bring lots of water. Especially in the summer months, you're going to drink more than you think possible.

Teddy bear cholla is not to be snuggled.

Sun Protection

It's called The Valley of the Sun. If you're a hiker, you can title yourself The Person with the Sunblock.

Sun protection is a crucial skill to master to have any chance of enjoying these hikes. Your first line of defense against the sun is to stay out of it. For shorter hikes, consider heading out in the morning or evening to take advantage of the long shadows cast by a low-hanging sun. Wide-brimmed hats, long pants, and long sleeves are natural shade-makers that you can carry with you at all times. Take advantage of UPF (Ultraviolet Protection Factor) clothing, which shields skin from damaging rays with its fiber type, dye, construction, and (in some cases) chemical treatment. Just like sunblock, the higher the UPF rating, the better. Coverage is the most effective method to keep those rays off your skin.

And, of course—sunblock, sunblock, sunblock. Grease every inch of exposed flesh thoroughly before you head out and always carry at least a small tube of SPF 30 (or above) in your pack for reapplications (check the sunblock directions for guidance here). Include sunglasses with UV protection and SPF lip moisturizers in your basic sun-protection essentials as well. One way to guarantee a sure-fire bad memory is to feel a raging burn for days after your hike. Not fun.

Clothing

Clothing in the desert can be quite tricky. The desert can dramatically drop its temperature in a 24-hour period (Arizona's record: 120°F to 39°F) and your wardrobe has to fluctuate right along with it. Under the sun, your greatest risk is heat stroke; after sunset, you can easily find yourself in a battle with hypothermia. Your best bet is to dress in cotton or other lightweight fabrics then pack fleece, wool, blended knits, or various high-tech winter fabrics in case you get stuck overnight.

Cotton and moisture-wicking blends work wonders in the heat. Outdoor recreation stores offer a huge selection of high-tech and lightweight nylon pants (look for "convertible" styles that can quickly become shorts with a few unzips). Most survival books will tell you to avoid cotton at all costs because it fails to insulate and actually robs your body of heat. Desert survivalists, however, assert that cotton is your best friend *because* of these features. Old-timers and cowboys swear by loose fitting, long-sleeve shirts and long pants made from cotton.

Most hikers have trouble resisting the urge to strip down during a summer hike. But the more coverage your clothing provides, the less exposed you are to the sun. Conserving your sweat under those longer sleeves can save you from dehydration if you're low on water (but you brought extra, right?). Use your best judgment here and find your comfort zone of protection versus temperature.

For longer hikes in cooler weather, increasing clothing layers is your best bet. Shorts and short-sleeve shirts should be your base layer with heavier pants, a coat, and a jacket on top; opt for winter fabrics like wool, wool blends, fleece, and water resistant or waterproof materials. When you get hot, peel yourself like an onion and then pack it back on to accommodate fluctuating weather and sun intensity. And always pack a beanie to keep that head warm under your wide-brimmed hat.

And now the most important wardrobe item: a bandana. A bandana is an absolutely crucial piece of clothing. With a few clever folds, this square of cotton is a sweatband, beanie, wet neckerchief, fly swatter, sponge, or tourniquet. Take at least one with you on every hike, no matter the distance. Not to mention, it can add a sharp splash of color to any ensemble!

Shoes and Socks

Every hiker has a preference when it comes to footwear. On desert trails, the most common shoes fall into two categories: trail runners and hiking boots.

Trail runners are low-cut sneakers with an intense, cleat-like tread for skilled climbing among Phoenix's rocky trails. A new pair of these puppies will make you feel like Spiderman as the ticky-tacky tread sticks to every surface. These are great for summit trails in the desert and make for sure-footed scrambling up steep terrain.

Traditional hiking boots are heavier, made of leather, water resistant, and offer ankle support. These are best for long, flat trails of six or more miles. For northern Arizona's High Country, heavy hiking boots are much more popular in the pine forest terrain, where you might come across a creek or a muddy path.

For desert hikes, lightweight, moisture-wicking socks with a padded sole or support are king. Also consider hiking shoes that offer ventilation (via breathable mesh) to keep those feet cool. For High Country hikes, consider bringing along a thicker, more heavy-duty pair of socks to protect your feet from the cold climate and elements, especially if you head up in fall, winter, or spring.

In both shoe styles, look for designs with mesh ventilation to keep feet cool during your hot-weather hikes.

Rain Gear

Most desert hikers have been stuck in a rainstorm at least once. Rainstorms come on fast and furious—especially during monsoon season—and will soak you to the bone in a matter of seconds, transporting you instantly from sweating to shivering. It is ideal to carry rain gear in your pack at all times, but at the very least an inexpensive poncho will do the trick in a pinch.

Navigational Tools

A compass, map, and GPS device (or trail-tracking app on a smartphone) are the magic combination to keep you oriented. Even if you've hiked a trail multiple times before, unexpected closures, weather, or animal attacks may require a change of plans to find a different route to safety. In fact, most preventable survival situations occur on short day hikes as a result of an unexpected change and poor preparation.

Every hiker gets a little lost from time to time. Referencing these essential tools can make the difference between "just getting turned around" to "lost for days and presumed dead." Always bring a paper trail map. Never leave home without a compass. And download that app while you're at it. One of these tools does not replace the other, so take them all, every time.

Studying the trail ahead of time is another easy task that can save you. Know your mileage (this is also important for planning how much water to take), the elevation climb, and the general direction the correct trail should take you. Desert vegetation is slow to replenish misleading paths, so it's easy to get off course.

Always let a friend or family member know where you plan to hike and for how long. Sign in at the trailhead when a registry is available. In a search-and-rescue situation, you'll dramatically increase your chances of being found if authorities know where to look.

When on the trail, stop as soon as you get that sinking feeling that you don't quite know where you are. Immediately consult your map and use nearby ridges, washes, and other landmarks to identify your location. If high ground is available nearby (and doesn't stray too far from your current location), climb to a perch and look for the trail, trail markers, or cairns (stacked rocks obviously arranged by people, not nature). If you're still disoriented, place your map on the ground, place your compass over the map, and orient the map to north. Don't move further until you've regained your orientation. Consider marking your current spot with a cairn if you should need to return.

Most important, take your time and stay calm. A clear head for sound judgment makes a huge difference. One rushed or poor decision can lead to a series of cataclysmic events, so take a deep breath and double-check your work.

Food

Hiking is exercise—that means you're burning calories as you cruise through the terrain. For day hikers, a jaunt on the trail can last up to 10 hours, depending on terrain and weather. Your body's energy is a simple equation of calories in, calories out. If you plan ahead for your food intake for longer hikes, you'll never hit the trail hungry.

As you sweat, the water flushing through your system can put you in a sodium deficit. A salty snack—pretzels, trail mix, or salted peanuts—will replace the sodium in your bloodstream. A lack of sodium, essential for maintaining balanced electrolytes, can lead to hyponatremia or water intoxication, which in severe cases is a serious medical emergency.

For hikes longer than 5 miles, pack a heavy snack or a full lunch. Energy bars, dried fruit, carrot sticks, hard-boiled eggs, and beef jerky are all great trail snacks. For hikes that last 6 miles or more, a hefty, mid-hike meal is essential to keep your energy and spirits high. Pack a sandwich with cheese, veggies, and cold cuts and be sure you have plenty of water. (Digestion requires water, so if you're in a no-water situation, get hydrated before attempting to eat.)

Light Source

While perched on a summit during an evening hike, it's easy to stare too long at The Valley's vast sea of twinkling city lights below. Before you know it, the sun has set and you've still got some craggy desert trail to descend. Whoops.

Always carry a small flashlight in your pack for such occasions. Or, consider a headlamp to free your hands for a safer trek down. Don't want to splurge on a headlamp? A popular trick is to clip a bicycle light on the bill of your hat. Brilliant, eh?

Whichever item you choose, check the batteries frequently and pack a spare battery or two just in case.

First-Aid Kit

This is a must-have for all hikes, no matter the length or effort involved. You can pick up a waterproof first-aid kit at any outdoor store for $10-20. Carry it in your pack at all times. A basic first-aid kit should include:

- Ace bandage
- Adhesive bandages
- Alcohol wipes
- Aspirin or an anti-inflammatory
- Athletic tape
- Gauze pads
- Iodine ointment
- Knife or scissors
- Moleskin
- Safety pins
- Tweezers

HEALTH AND SAFETY
Fitness

What better way to stay fit than to hike? You'd be surprised how big a difference just a few good hikes per week can make.

When starting out, be sure the hikes are reasonable for your fitness level. Begin with easy, flat hikes to strengthen muscles and increase your cardiovascular conditioning. If you don't hike regularly, don't take on a moderate, strenuous, or butt-kicking hike. Be sure to stretch before and after every hike to avoid any injuries that might keep you out of commission and off the trail.

Though hiking is a great workout, it's best in combination with other physical activities like biking, jogging, and yoga. The variety of exercise increases muscle condition and strengthens your body's connective tissue.

Hiking Solo

Whenever possible, it's best to bring a partner on the trail for increased safety. However, solitude is something often craved by city-dwelling hikers, and solo hikes are common.

Before heading out on your own, be sure that someone knows which hike you plan to complete, including your start time and end time, and let them know once you've finished. If your regular hiking partner is not with you, consider working out a pre-arranged system in which you keep one another informed of your respective solo hikes. A simple call or text message at the beginning and end of each hike is good practice.

Speaking of cell phones, always take a fully charged mobile phone with you. While in the Central Valley, you'll most likely have reception during your hike. On the outskirts of the city and in the High Country, however, reception is less reliable (that's why a whistle, signal mirror, and other rescue items are on your checklist).

If you should become injured, lost, or overheated, stay calm and assess your situation before making any decisions. In that situation, your brain is your number-one partner. If you find yourself in trouble, remember the acronym for STOP: Stop, Think, Observe, Plan. Your plan might be as simple as waiting in the shade for a hiker to pass by or as complicated as using rope and other supplies to make camp for the night. Either way, take a few minutes to think about your next moves.

Heat Exhaustion and Heat Stroke

Here's a brief explanation of how heat exhaustion and heat stroke (also known as hyperthermia) go down—and take you down with it.

In a heat-stress situation, symptoms of heat exhaustion will come first. This includes clammy skin, profuse sweating, light-headedness, rapid or shallow breathing, and heat cramps. As soon as you feel sickly, seek some shade and rest. Sit on your pack to elevate yourself off the hot desert floor. Remove some clothing to help cool off. Slowly drink water and eat a salty snack to restore hydration and electrolytes. Feel better? Good. Now give it a solid 10 minutes more. It can take up to 24 hours to fully recover from heat exhaustion, so don't push yourself. Seek medical attention if symptoms persist.

Heat stroke is a medical emergency. It means the body is no longer capable of cooling itself and your core temperature can climb to 105°F or higher. Symptoms include a red face, hot dry skin, rapid pulse, and dilated pupils. Evacuation or medical intervention is required. In the meantime, get the victim into the shade and remove their clothing. Wet the victim's skin with cool water and fan it to increase evaporative cooling. Use wet clothing or ice packs and place them on the neck, armpits, and groin. Maintain an open airway if the victim loses consciousness, and get medical intervention as quickly as possible.

Your best defense is prevention. Avoid hiking in the middle of a summer day.

BEAT THE HEAT!

Here's a quick rundown to help you avoid heat stress that may lead to heat stroke, a serious medical emergency:

- In the summer months, restrict hiking to the cooler hours in the early morning and evening, or stick to hikes in the High Country region.
- Pre-hydrate before hitting the trail.
- Wear a wide-brimmed hat and lightweight clothing to protect yourself from the sun.
- Pack a hat, your pockets, and extra clothing with ice-filled baggies.
- Bring water, water, and more water.
- Wet any clothing and a bandana to help with evaporative cooling.

- Take constant inventory of your water and head back to the trailhead if you start running low.
- Munch salty snacks along the way to maintain sodium levels and electrolyte balance.
- At the first signs of overheating, head to the shade for a long break.
- If you start to feel symptoms of heat stress, make your hiking party aware of your condition.
- Offer help to other hikers who look confused or disoriented, and be assertive if necessary.
- When in doubt, turn back and return to civilization...your survival ensures that you can hike another day!

Bring more than enough water and stay hydrated. Keep aware of your physical state and head into shade at the first sign that something is off. Make your hiking partners aware of your condition. And, if you observe a fellow hiker experiencing these symptoms, take the lead and insist that they take a long break in the shade. Do what you can to cool them off. Most hikers feel a little embarrassed to admit that they're overheating, so make sure you've got each other's backs to avoid a more serious situation.

Hypothermia

Desert hikers can become so heat-focused that it's easy to forget about hypothermia. This occurs when the body drastically drops its core temperature. It can be fatal and is the number one killer of people in the outdoors.

Remember that the desert is the land of extremes. Dirt doesn't hold heat through the night, so as quickly as it bakes during the day, it turns freezing at night. Hypothermia can happen when temperatures are in the 50s, and desert temperatures can drop way below that number.

Symptoms include shivering, weakness, loss of coordination, disorientation, cold skin, drowsiness, slowed breathing, and low heart rate. At the first signs of hypothermia, seek medical intervention. While waiting for help to arrive, immediately move the victim out of the wind and cold. Seek shelter in a dry, warm area. Wrap the victim in warm, windproof clothing and material. Start a fire (this is why matches, lighter, and a magnesium spark rod are on your checklist) and encourage the victim to attempt eating something high in sugar. Just as in a heat-stress situation, it's best to be vigilant and assertive when treating hypothermia.

Again, prevention is key here. When hiking in the colder months or in the High Country, always carry a fleece jacket or winter coat, an emergency blanket, and a beanie in your pack. Be aware of your physical state and look for symptoms in other hikers.

Flash Floods

Flash floods are the second leading cause of death in the desert and the first leading cause of weather-related deaths in the United States. This is no joke, people. Check the weather forecast before you hit the trail, be particularly vigilant while hiking in canyons and washes, and plan carefully when hiking during high-risk rainy seasons (from noon to 8pm between July and September). Postpone your hike if the weather looks iffy. Even if the sky above is clear, a micro-burst of rain miles away could send a wall of muddy water (complete with boulders, branches, and dangerous debris) your way. Rarely will you have enough time to react—and if you do, it will only be a few seconds.

Dust Storms

"Haboob" has become a favorite new word in The Valley, ever since 2011 when a monstrous dust storm (called a haboob) covered the metropolitan area. The haboob spread 50 miles across and 10,000 feet high when it rolled through town, causing flight delays and power outages throughout the city.

If you have the misfortune of getting stuck in a haboob, stop and take cover. A nearby rock outcrop is your best option, but if you're caught out in the open, crouch down and keep your back to the wind. Cover your face with a bandana or shirt and do not attempt to navigate your way back to the trailhead—the dust-filled air will completely blind you. Be patient and wait for the haboob to pass. Then have fun saying the word over and over when you share the story later.

WILDLIFE AND PLANTS

In Phoenix, you can step out of your car and right into the thick of the wild desert. No matter how popular the trail or how close it is to the city, you're sharing the environment with all the unique vegetation and specially evolved animals that call the desert home. It truly is alive out there, and after just a handful of hikes, you're sure to see something scurry, crawl, trot, or slither by.

Coyotes

With coyote population on the rise across the United States, you'll be hard pressed not to see (or at least hear) one while hiking. A coyote is a canine species with tan fur that typically hunts in pairs and travels in a pack. They can be seen at any time of day but are mostly nocturnal. If you hear high-pitched howling or yipping in the distance, it means there are coyotes somewhere nearby.

Coyote attacks on humans are rare and, in those few cases, usually occur toward small children. However, coyotes can be confrontational when encountering dogs. If your dog is a small breed, they may target it as a potential meal. As a precaution, keep dogs on a leash and small children close by.

If you do see a coyote, it's best to stop at a safe distance and observe its behavior. If it starts trotting toward you, clap your hands and yell or make some noise so the coyote sees you as a potential threat. Never, ever try to feed a seemingly docile coyote. Usually, coyotes remain disinterested and will move along without bothering you.

Snakes and Lizards

It's inevitable that you will see reptiles during your hike in the desert. All reptiles are cold blooded and will avoid extreme temperatures. On a hot day, they often hang out under rocks or in the shade; be wary of those areas and never, ever, stick your hand in a rock crevice. Walking sticks are useful for prodding the ground ahead.

If you hear a creature scurry along the trail, chances are it's a small lizard trying to get out of your way. Most lizards are less than six inches from nose to tail. Chuckwallas (up to 16 inches) and desert iguanas (up to 17 inches) are rare, but you might get lucky and spot one or two during your adventures. Most lizards are passive, non-poisonous, and fearful of humans—you can usually count on them to book before you even see one. Gila monsters grow up to two feet in length, and while venomous, they are rarely seen and are so sluggish that they represent little threat to humans. As with all creatures in the desert, if you see a lizard, keep your distance and let it be.

Saguaros make for dramatic sunset scenes.

As the sun goes down and the desert floor cools, you're more likely to encounter rattlers and other snakes. In the early morning, it's not uncommon to see a snake sunning itself after a long, cold night. Masterfully camouflaged, rattlesnakes are tough to spot, and you'll often cruise by one without even knowing it. If you do get too close, however, they'll let you know. There are few things in this world that will stop you dead in your tracks like the sound of a rattlesnake rattle. Once you hear that distinct sound, stop and try to visually locate the snake, then back away slowly. Once you've cleared some distance, the snake will move along. It has no interest in you, so if you leave it alone, you'll be fine.

Rattlesnakes typically only bite when provoked. If you have the misfortune of receiving a bite, don't bother with any field remedies—sucking out the poison and using a snake-bite kit have proven ineffective methods, and tourniquets do more harm than good by isolating the poison to one area of the body, creating further damage. Stay calm and return to the trailhead as quickly as possible, then visit a hospital immediately for treatment. The good news is that rattlesnake bites are rarely fatal.

Scorpions and Insects

Bad news: There are more than 40 species of scorpions in the desert. The good news? Only one scorpion's sting—that of the bark scorpion—is fatal, and it's usually fatal only to babies, the elderly, and people with pre-existing medical conditions. If you take off your shoes or discard any clothing while taking a break, give each item a good shake and inspection before you get dressed. Scorpions do enjoy a dark, dank place, and human clothing fits the bill.

Bees are another concern while out in the desert. With so many Africanized or killer bees in the area, be aware of loud buzzing noises that may indicate a nearby nest. (Bee nests can be as large as a basketball.) If you hear or see lots of bees, head the other way. If attacked, cover your head as best you can with a shirt or other clothing and run (and run, and run) to a car or building. If you're allergic to bee stings, carry a prescription Epi-Pen while on the trail.

Cacti, Succulents, and Wildflowers

Desert vegetation is a uniquely beautiful sight on the trail. With more than 3,000 species of plants in Arizona, the state is hardly barren. While the endless spikes of desert cacti can seem menacing, few deny the beauty when each needle catches the waning light during sunset to make the desert glow. These spiky species are often surrounded by soft succulents and stunning wildflowers that smooth the visual harshness of the desert. Spend enough time out here and you'll soon appreciate the slight variations that make each plant a one-of-a-kind survivor.

The general rule when it comes to desert plant life is to look, don't touch. Still, with so many spikes and cholla dropping their prickly pods, it's tough not to accidentally pick up a pokey "friend" via attachment to a shirt, sock, a dog's paw, or straight into the skin. Always carry tweezers or pliers for such an occasion. A good pair of gloves can also come in handy when removing these pesky orbs.

Springtime in the desert is truly a sight. With the help of winter rains and lovely temperatures, the dry brush that covers the desert floor in summer and winter

WHAT'S A PETROGLYPH?

Look for the faint spiral shape of a petroglyph, carved into the rock centuries ago.

Petroglyphs are designs that have been carved onto rock, most often by ancient Native Americans. You'll undoubtedly come across tons of petroglyphs as you hike The Valley's trails. Most take the shape of spirals, suns, or animals and were carved by the ancient native peoples who originally inhabited the Phoenix area.

With time, light-colored granite and other desert rocks become coated with microorganisms, moisture, and minerals. These elements bake in the sun and cover the rock in a dark (sometimes black) patina over the course of thousands of years.

Ancient native societies—including the Archaic People (5000 BCE) and the Hohokam (100 CE to 1200s CE)—made their designs by chipping away at the rock's patina with a hand-held pointed rock called a hammerstone. As the patina was removed the light-colored rock surface beneath was revealed. While no accurate interpretation exists, it's believed that the shapes are to be read as symbols and story-telling signs rather than as a written language.

Petroglyphs are fragile, irreplaceable, and sacred to modern-day Native Americans. Admire petroglyphs from afar and never touch them; the oils in your skin can damage this ancient treasure.

© LILIA MENCONI

suddenly explodes in a rash of fabulous color. Wildflower season typically occurs from February to April and is the most popular time of year to hit the trail.

ON THE TRAIL
Trail Etiquette

You're not the only person who enjoys the trails around Phoenix. And of course you're happy to share, right? Here's the best way to do it.

First, know how to yield. Officially, hikers only yield to horses. When a horse approaches, hikers should step to the side of the trail and wait until it has passed. Mountain bikers should yield to hikers by slowing down, announcing themselves, and then passing slowly.

When encountering other hikers, a friendly hello is often expected. Practice common courtesy and offer to allow other hikers to pass—particularly if a hiker comes

© LILIA MENCONI

Hiking with kids can introduce a life-long hobby.

from behind at a faster pace. Scoot to the right and let them breeze by. On busy trails, it's a good idea to stick to the right side of the trail just like you would in traffic, creating a "slow lane" and a "passing lane." Always yield to hikers who are climbing up—don't interrupt their hard-earned pace. Also, be aware of any signs of overheating, injury, disorientation, or dehydration and don't be shy about offering help. It never hurts to ask.

Respect the trail itself. Stay to the center of the path as much as you can to avoid destroying surrounding plant life. Trailblazing is a huge no-no and is strongly discouraged by park officials and your hiking peers. The desert is a sensitive environment, and certain forms of plant life (like saguaro cacti) take decades to gain a foothold. It's hard to survive out here, so let them do their thing by staying on the trail.

Hiking with Children

Taking to the trails with little ones in tow is a popular activity in Phoenix. It's a great time for adults to ensure that kids have fun adventures on the trail that will keep them coming back for more.

When hiking with babies, use a secure baby backpack to carry the infant. Be absolutely sure to follow proper sun protection and to hike with a partner so another adult can keep an eye on the baby. For toddlers in strollers, the many wheelchair-friendly hikes are a great option.

For children ages three and older, choose shorter trails that offer points of interest. Many trails close to Phoenix are interpretive and include plenty of illustrated plaques for educational discoveries. Hikes that end with a waterfall or spectacular view will keep kids interested and pumped up for future hikes.

School-aged children should carry their own pack with plenty of water, healthy snacks, a compass, and mini first-aid kit. Take advantage of as many teaching opportunities as possible so that they learn proper preparation and trail behavior. Refer to the trail map frequently and provide opportunity for group decisions on navigation. Goal-setting and high-five celebrations for completing trails add to the positive experience.

HIKING GEAR CHECKLIST

- Backpack
- Bandana
- Compass
- Emergency blanket
- 50-ft rope or cord
- First-aid kit
- Flashlight or headlamp
- Garbage bag
- Lighter
- Mace
- Magnesium spark-rod
- Map
- Poncho
- Signal mirror
- Sunblock
- Thermometer
- Utility or pocket knife
- Walking stick or hiking poles
- Water (1 more liter than you think you'll need)
- Water (2-6 quarts or 1.8-5.6 liters, minimum)
- Water (and that extra bottle, just in case)
- Waterproof matches
- Water purifying tablets
- Whistle
- Wide-brimmed hat

With so many trails in town, kids have ample opportunity to take to the trails and continue the hobby for life. All you have to do is lead the way.

Hiking with Dogs

Leash laws apply for most of the hikes in the Phoenix area. For the trails that allow dogs, an on-leash policy is ever-present. (This is expected throughout Arizona, so if you let your dog loose, don't be surprised to get the stink-eye from fellow hikers.) With poisonous rattlesnakes and hungry coyotes in your midst, this is really for your dog's protection. Encounters with wildlife are common and inevitable. Keep your pup close and under control to avoid any skirmishes.

You're also expected to pick up after your pet. Some trails provide plastic bags at the trailhead, but bring plenty of your own, just in case. Carry all pet waste off the trail and into a garbage can. This is litter that most hikers won't adopt, so be courteous and pack it out.

Adopt Trash

There's nothing worse than ugly, busted-up trash littering the trail and robbing hikers of an opportunity to enjoy nature. First and foremost, adopt your own trash by following a strict "pack it in, pack it out" policy. You'll see plenty of evidence that other hikers don't follow the same policy or simply lost track of their trash. Do your good deed for the day by adopting the orphaned garbage and sending it home to the dump via the closest trash can.

CENTRAL VALLEY

The Central Valley has plenty of hikes to keep you on your feet. In the Phoenix Mountains Preserve, hikers create endless combinations of intersecting pathways through 6,000 acres of land. The popular trails on Camelback Mountain are always thick with spry hikers. With the canal system cutting through the city, folks take to the waterways for easy strolls. Many opt to wander the Dreamy Draw Recreation Area with a tangle of trails for every fitness level. Looking back up to the skyline, there's no shortage of high vantage points. Aptly named Lookout Mountain gives hikers an unobstructed, 360-degree view of the Central Valley while nearby Shaw Butte tops out at 2,040 feet. Yes, any hiker will certainly wear out a pair (or two) of boots with the abundant hikes in the Central Valley.

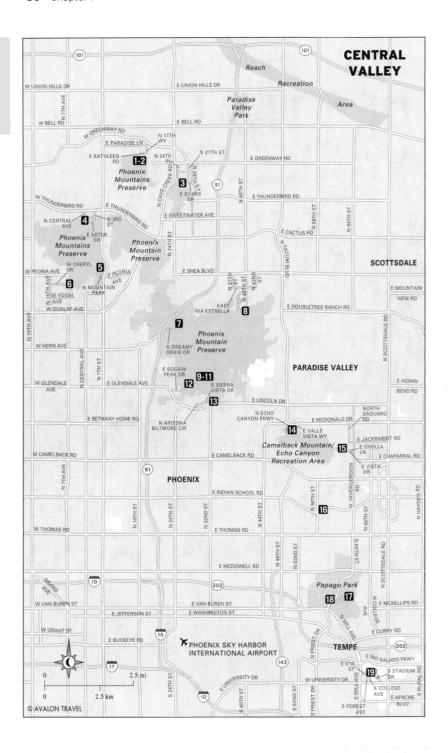

TRAIL NAME	FEATURES	LEVEL	DISTANCE	TIME	ELEVATION	PAGE
1 Lookout Mountain Summit Trail 150		Easy/Moderate	1 mi rt	30 min	400 ft	32
2 Lookout Mountain Circumference Trail 308		Easy/Moderate	2.3 mi rt	1.5 hr	400 ft	36
3 Shadow Mountain		Easy	1.2 mi rt	1 hr	300 ft	40
4 Shaw Butte Trail 306		Easy/Moderate	3.9 mi rt	2 hr	850 ft	43
5 North Mountain National Trail 44		Easy/Moderate	1.4 mi rt	1 hr	575 ft	46
6 Charles M. Christiansen Memorial Trail 100 BEST		Butt-kicker	11 mi one-way	6.5 hr	1,500 ft	49
7 Dreamy Draw Loop		Easy/Moderate	3.5 mi rt	1.5 hr	800 ft	53
8 L.V. Yates Trail 8		Easy/Moderate	5 mi rt	2.5 hr	700 ft	56
9 Piestewa Nature Trail 304 BEST		Easy	1.3 mi rt	1 hr	320 ft	59
10 Freedom Trail 302		Easy/Moderate	3.7 mi rt	2 hr	1,200 ft	62
11 Mohave Trail 200		Easy	1.2 mi rt	30 min	300 ft	65
12 Piestewa Peak Summit Trail 300 BEST		Moderate	2.4 mi rt	1.5 hr	1,190 ft	68
13 Quartz Ridge Trail 8A		Easy/Moderate	2.2 mi rt	1.5 hr	500 ft	71
14 Echo Canyon Summit Trail BEST		Moderate	2.5 mi rt	1.5 hr	1,350 ft	75
15 Cholla Trail		Moderate	3.6 mi rt	2 hr	1,300 ft	78
16 Arizona Canal Loop at Arizona Falls BEST		Easy	3.2 mi rt	1.5 hr	50 ft	81
17 Hole in the Rock Trail BEST		Easy	0.3 mi rt	15 min	60 ft	84
18 Eliot Ramada to Double Butte Loop BEST		Easy	1.6 mi rt	1 hr	100 ft	87
19 Hayden Butte Summit Trail		Easy	0.9 mi rt	30 min	400 ft	90

1 LOOKOUT MOUNTAIN SUMMIT TRAIL 150
Lookout Mountain Preserve

Level: Easy/Moderate

Total Distance: 1 mile round-trip

Hiking Time: 30 minutes

Elevation Gain: 400 feet

Summary: This quick jaunt gets your heart pumping and muscles aching to gain the reward of a 360-degree view of The Valley.

If you want a lot of bang for your buck (so to speak), this is *the* trail. The Summit Trail on Lookout Mountain is for city hikers who are short on time but still want a tough workout. In just 0.5 mile, the trail quickly climbs 400 feet—even the fittest folks will feel a decent burn on the way up.

It's easy to understand how this small mountain range earned its name. Lookout Mountain's summit is by no means the highest peak in The Valley, but it offers one of the clearest views to the city below. Other city mountains live a healthy distance from Lookout Mountain, so nothing gets in the way of this view.

Start hiking the Summit Trail 150 from the southwest corner of the parking lot (next to the posted trail sign). After about 100 feet, the trail splits to the right. Remain on the trail that veers left (southeast) and clearly leads up the mountain. After a gentle slope up, the real ascent begins. Put your head down and start the heavy breathing.

For the next 0.25 mile, the trail is easy to navigate until it hits the saddle at 0.3 mile. Turn left (east) to continue on the Summit Trail and ignore the connecting trails that descend south. The trail seemingly deteriorates, and as you continue, you may have to do some light scrambling. The proper trail is tough to follow; look instead for the white-spray painted dots that lead the way. If you head off the path, don't worry. As long as you're traveling east and up, you can find the main trail.

After the scramble, the trail flattens out. Veer to the left and notice the metal trail marker on the north side of the summit. Soak up the unobstructed 360-degree view and catch your breath.

To return to the parking lot, simply scramble back down to the saddle and retrace your steps to descend along Lookout Mountain's north side.

Options
Incorporate this trail with the **Lookout Circumference Trail 308** (see listing in this chapter). Once you reach the peak (the view shouldn't be missed), turn

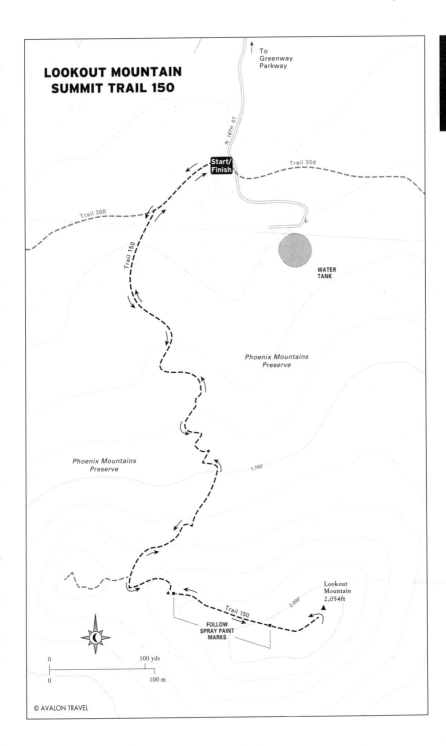

LOOKOUT MOUNTAIN SUMMIT TRAIL 150

To Greenway Parkway

N. 16TH ST

Trail 308

Start/ Finish

Trail 308

Trail 150

WATER TANK

Phoenix Mountains Preserve

Phoenix Mountains Preserve

1,750'

2,000'

Lookout Mountain 2,054ft

Trail 150

FOLLOW SPRAY PAINT MARKS

0   100 yds
0   100 m

© AVALON TRAVEL

Reaching the summit of Lookout Mountain guarantees an unobstructed 360-degree view of The Valley.

around and descend to the saddle. Look for the trail marked by a brown metal post; this leads to the south side of the mountain. Within approximately 0.25 mile, this trail intersects with the Lookout Circumference Trail 308. Choose to hike either east or west; both directions trace around the side of Lookout Mountain and lead back to the parking lot. This option totals approximately 1.8 miles either direction.

Directions

From downtown Phoenix, take I-10 east toward Tucson for approximately 2 miles. Take exit 147B to merge onto AZ-51. Follow AZ-51 north for about 12 miles and take exit 12 for Greenway Road. Keep left at the fork and follow the signs for Greenway Road west. Turn left onto Greenway Road heading west. After 1 mile continue on Greenway Road as it becomes Greenway Parkway. Follow Greenway Parkway for 1.6 miles. Turn left onto 16th Street, heading south for 0.6 mile until the street ends at the Lookout Mountain parking lot and trailhead. The Lookout Mountain Summit Trail 150 trailhead is located at 15800 North 16th Street on the southwest corner of the parking lot (sunrise-7pm).
GPS Coordinates: 33.6269 N, 112.0486 W

Information and Contact

There is no fee. Dogs on leash are allowed. Maps are available online at www. phoenix.gov/parks. For more information, contact City of Phoenix Parks and

Recreation Main Office, Phoenix City Hall, 200 West Washington Street, 16th Floor, Phoenix, AZ 85003, 602/262-6862, www.phoenix.gov/parks.

2 LOOKOUT MOUNTAIN CIRCUMFERENCE TRAIL 308
Lookout Mountain Preserve

Level: Easy/Moderate

Total Distance: 2.3 miles round-trip

Hiking Time: 1.5 hours

Elevation Gain: 400 feet

Summary: Circle the Lookout Mountain and see the city's expanse from every direction.

Hiking the circumference of Lookout Mountain may not offer the sensation of being cut off from the civilized world, but that's okay. In fact, it's really okay if you're looking for a good bit of exercise that's close to home. It also seems to be okay for the packs of coyotes, which take no issue at all with the presence of the surrounding houses. This hike is perfect for a light, midday stroll in spring or an evening/early morning hike in summer.

Due to the proximity of these nice folks' backyards, the Lookout Mountain (part of the Phoenix Mountains Preserve) is wrought with some serious trailblazing. The area maintains only two official trails, but many dirt paths have been carved up, over, and through this tiny outcrop of mountain. This can lead to a bit of confusion when trying to stay on the proper trail, but if you take a wrong turn, it's no biggie. The preserve is small and you can quickly regain your bearings.

Find Trail 308 on the east side of the 16th Street trailhead parking lot, next to the dirt maintenance road that leads to the white water tower. Take the trail heading east (best for evening hikes), following it up and over a small hill, and continue to the southeast as the path curves around the mountain. As the Circumference Trail continues, many trailblazed paths intersect. Stay on the main trail. As the curvature of the trail approaches the south side of the mountain at 0.6 mile, the same rules apply—you should always stay on the outermost loop trail and try to stay off the smaller, inner trails. The Circumference Trail is well-marked with metal posts signed with "308" to keep you on the right path.

At 0.6 mile, the trail heads west and ascends along the south mountainside. Again, many small unofficial trails cross the path. Most of the time, the next trail marker can be seen in the distance, so when in doubt, look ahead to find the correct direction. After passing by the saddle on your right (to the north), you will encounter an unmarked fork in the path at 1.1 miles. Both trails look well-traveled,

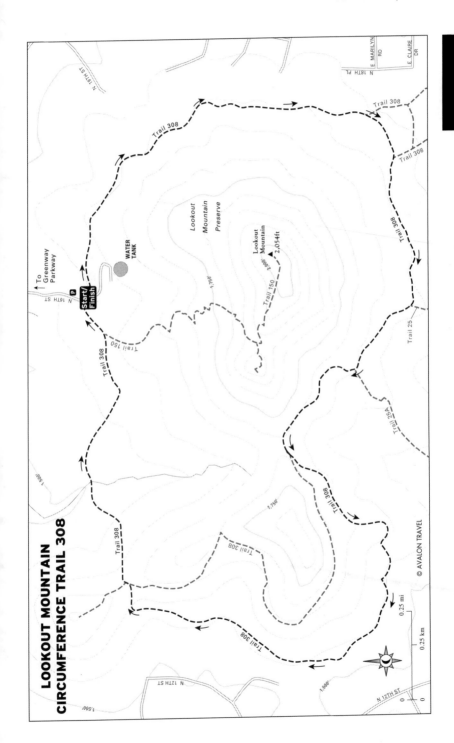

© LILIA MENCONI

This trail offers a little bit of nature—that slams right into the suburbs.

but Trail 308 is the trail to the left that descends a small slope. Follow this trail as it curves around the west side of the preserve.

From here on, keep following the main path as you ignore the smaller intersections, and look for trail markers. After a short climb, you soon reach the flat portion of the trail at 1.8 miles that leads east, back to the parking lot.

Options

To add a tiny bit of a butt-kick at the very end, take a sharp right turn (south) just before you reach the parking lot onto the **Lookout Mountain Summit Trail 150**. This is a hard-earned 0.5-mile up to the top of Lookout Mountain, which will (ahem) top off your workout with a fast and furious cardio session. This option makes a hike of 3.3 miles total.

Directions

From downtown Phoenix, take I-10 east toward Tucson for approximately 2 miles. Take exit 147B to merge onto AZ-51. Follow it north for about 12 miles and take exit 12 for Greenway Road. Keep left at the fork and follow the signs for Greenway Road west. Turn left onto Greenway Road heading west. After 1 mile continue on Greenway Road as it becomes Greenway Parkway. Follow Greenway Parkway for 1.6 miles. Turn left onto 16th Street, heading south for 0.6 mile until the street ends at the Lookout Mountain parking lot and trailhead. The Lookout Mountain Circumference Trail 308 trailhead is on the southeast corner of the parking lot (sunrise-7pm).

GPS Coordinates: 33.6269 N, 112.0481 W

Information and Contact

There is no fee. Dogs on leash are allowed. Maps are available online at www. phoenix.gov/parks. For more information, contact City of Phoenix Parks and Recreation Main Office, Phoenix City Hall, 200 West Washington Street, 16th Floor, Phoenix, AZ 85003, 602/262-6862, www.phoenix.gov/parks.

3 SHADOW MOUNTAIN
Phoenix Mountains Preserve

Level: Easy

Total Distance: 1.2 miles round-trip

Hiking Time: 1 hour

Elevation Gain: 300 feet

Summary: A quick neighborhood hike perfect for a weeknight.

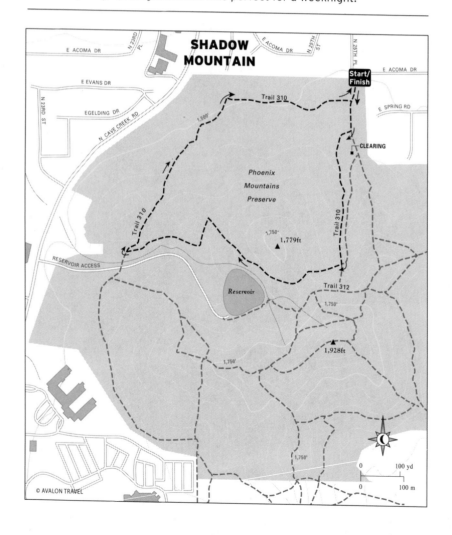

© LILIA MENCONI

Find the Shadow Mountain trail at this residential trailhead.

For folks living in north-central Phoenix, Shadow Mountain is a great hike to include in the weeknight workout rotation. It's short, with just a few opportunities for climbing, so hikers get quick exercise at a convenient location—which is also perfect for families. For Valley-dwellers obsessed with gaining as many bragging rights as possible, Shadow Mountain was named in 2006 as one of the "7 Summits of Phoenix" by the local newspaper, *The Arizona Republic*. Include this summit in the repertoire to complete them all.

Shadow Mountain is a well-traveled area. So well, in fact, that it's often difficult to follow the proper trail. The Phoenix Mountains Preserve map indicates a circumference trail with a summit spur to the southeast, but there are many trails blazed throughout the park. The best strategy here is to stay in and among the established trails as best you can to avoid stomping out any new paths. The trailhead is just a simple entrance to the mountain, tucked away on a neighborhood street without a parking lot.

Start the trail on the north side of the mountain and enter via the unnamed trailhead—a sidewalk surrounded by a short brick wall. The trail is wide and easy to follow south. At just 0.3 mile, you pass a small clearing with a metal water trough.

From here on out, the trails wiggle all over and around. To reach the summit at 1,928 feet, veer to the left (southeast) and start your climb to the highest point on the mountain that sits directly south from the trailhead (it's easy to see and is less than 0.5 mile away). To complete a circumference loop, opt for the trail that curves to the right (west) and leads to a saddle at approximately 1,730 feet. Pass by a large triangular building to the south and then follow the trail as it turns north alongside Cave Creek Road. Before you know it, the trail heads east, back toward the trailhead, for a total of 1.2 miles.

Options

To shorten this hike, once you've reached the summit simply return the way you came, taking the trails north and back to the trailhead for a brisk 0.8-mile option.

Directions

From downtown Phoenix, take I-10 east toward Tucson for approximately 2 miles. Take exit 147B to merge onto AZ-51. Follow it north for 11.3 miles. Take exit 11 for Thunderbird Road and turn left, heading west, onto Thunderbird Road. Take Thunderbird Road for 0.2 mile and take the second right, heading north, onto 32nd Street. Take 32nd Street for 0.5 mile and take the second left onto Acoma Drive. Take Acoma Drive west for 0.6 mile and turn right, heading north, onto 28th Street. Take 28th Street for 150 feet and take the first left onto Claire Drive. Take Claire Drive west for 0.1 mile and then turn left heading south onto 27th Street. Take 27th Street for 425 feet and take the second right onto Acoma Drive. Take Acoma Drive west for 0.1 mile. Park on the street. The Shadow Mountain trailhead is on the north side of the street.

GPS Coordinates: 33.6188 N, 112.0265 W

Information and Contact

There is no fee. Dogs on leash are allowed. Maps are available online at www.phoenix.gov/parks. For more information, contact City of Phoenix Parks and Recreation Main Office, Phoenix City Hall, 200 West Washington Street, 16th Floor, Phoenix, AZ 85003, 602/262-6862, www.phoenix.gov/parks.

4 SHAW BUTTE TRAIL 306

North Mountain Park, Phoenix Mountains Preserve

Level: Easy/Moderate

Total Distance: 3.9 miles round-trip

Hiking Time: 2 hours

Elevation Gain: 850 feet

Summary: A challenging loop that climbs up and around Shaw Butte promises spectacular views to the city below and some stellar dog-watching.

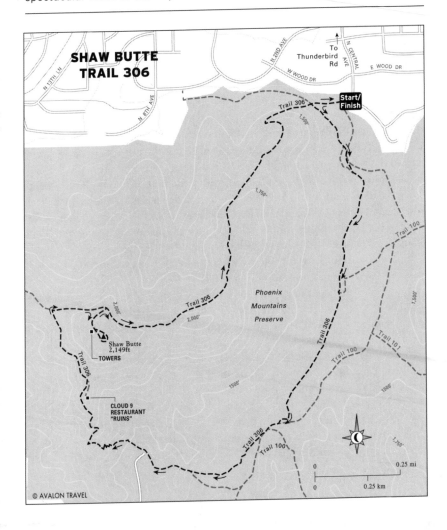

© KRISTINA SMITH

movin' on up the Shaw Butte Trail

Welcome to Phoenix's best hike for dog lovers. On the Shaw Butte Trail 306, located at the northwest corner of the Phoenix Mountains Preserve, hikers are known to have their family pup in tow. Especially on the northeast side of this loop, you're treated to a less-pretentious version of a dog show with breeds of every kind prancing up and down the mountain.

Trail 306 is a favorite hike for humans as well. The loop starts with a decent warm-up on the flat terrain along the southeast side of Shaw Butte and then hauls up the 720 feet heading west to reach the highest point of the trail at 2,149 feet. The loop ends with a lengthy descent along the northeast end (where the dog show happens).

To begin, follow Trail 306 south from the Shaw Butte trailhead parking lot. Ignore any connecting trails to the east. At 1.2 miles, Trail 306 shares a short portion with Trail 100 as the path curves west. Stay to the right along Trail 306 as Trail 100 breaks away and other small, unofficial trails connect from the south. At 1.3 miles, continue west to begin the ascent.

No switchbacks help you here. Keep your head down and your breath steady as you climb, climb, climb. Again, ignore any trails to your left as the climb slowly veers to the northwest. At mile 2, take a minute to explore east of the trail. Find a large cement slab and ruins of rock walls marking the former location of the Cloud 9 Restaurant, a swanky destination for diners in the early 1960s that was destroyed by a fire in 1964 and never rebuilt.

After you've explored the "ruin," hop back on Trail 306 to continue following it northwest, for a 0.3-mile break from climbing as the trail mellows out. At 2.3 miles, ignore a spur trail to the west and make a right turn, heading east to pick up the climb once more. The trail is now paved as you ascend for the final 200 feet up to the highest point of the hike—a small spur toward radio towers south of the trail at 2,149 feet. Check out the stretching urban streets that abruptly end at the McDowell Mountains to the north.

Now, let the dog show begin. As you complete the final leg of Trail 306, it's easy to breeze by on the partially paved service road as you see other hikers and their leashed friends climbing this popular side of the loop. Follow Trail 306 for the remaining 1.3-mile descent, which leads north, curves east, and ends at the Shaw Butte trailhead and parking lot.

Options

For the short version of this hike, take the trail counterclockwise and end it at the towers to experience the most popular portion of Trail 306. From the Shaw Butte trailhead, veer right (west) and follow Trail 306 (this side is a wide service road) as it traces the northeast tip of Shaw Butte. As it turns south toward the radio towers, enjoy the views of McDowell Mountains to the north. At 1.3 miles, you reach a fine stopping point at the radio tower trail spur. Turn around here and retrace your steps back to the Shaw Butte trailhead for an up-and-back hike that totals 2.6 miles.

Directions

From downtown Phoenix, take I-17 north for 11 miles. Take exit 210 for Thunderbird Road. Follow the exit ramp for 0.2 mile and merge onto Black Canyon Highway, heading north for 0.1 mile. Turn right onto Thunderbird Road, heading east for 0.8 mile. Turn right at Central Avenue and follow it south for 0.3 mile. The small Shaw Butte parking lot (open sunrise-sunset) is on the right. The Shaw Butte Trail 306 trailhead is on the northwest corner of the parking lot.
GPS Coordinates: 33.6034 N, 112.0742 W

Information and Contact

There is no fee. Dogs on leash are allowed. Maps are available online at www.phoenix.gov/parks. For more information, contact City of Phoenix Parks and Recreation Main Office, Phoenix City Hall, 200 West Washington Street, 16th Floor, Phoenix, AZ 85003, 602/262-6862, www.phoenix.gov/parks.

5 NORTH MOUNTAIN NATIONAL TRAIL 44

North Mountain Park, Phoenix Mountains Preserve

Level: Easy/Moderate

Total Distance: 1.4 miles round-trip

Hiking Time: 1 hour

Elevation Gain: 575 feet

Summary: This short and mostly paved trail is perfect for little kids and dogs.

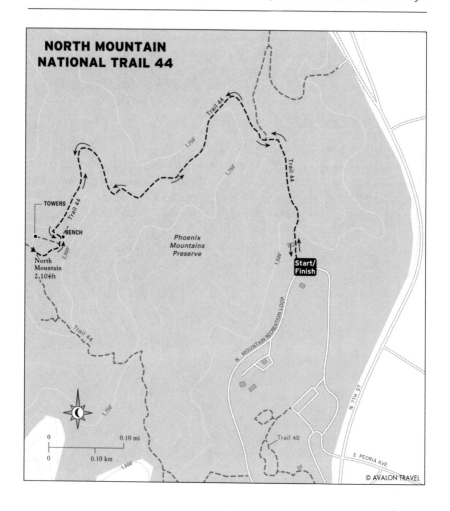

© LILIA MENCONI

A hiker climbs the final paved ascent toward the cellular phone towers.

There are many different ways to skin this cat...or dog (considering the heavy population of pups on the trail). But for those looking for a quick workout or family-friendly hike, the most popular route begins with a short, rocky jaunt that eventually meets up with a wide paved trail that climbs to the North Mountain summit.

Start this route from the National Trail 44 trailhead on the north end of the parking lot. The workout begins right away as you climb 300 feet in a measly 0.2 mile along the unpaved portion of Trail 44. Just when your lungs feel like fire, the trail whips to the left, up a short flight of steps, and onto the paved road. Phew!

But this is just the beginning, friends. Don't be fooled by the luxuriously paved trail, because the remainder of Trail 44 is a steady incline to the summit. Follow the wide path as it wiggles its way west, steadily climbing the remainder of the elevation gain. Once the trail turns south at 0.5 mile, you see the unmistakable metal towers that mark the summit. Push ahead; it's almost over.

At 0.6 mile, pass by a large clearing and continue straight, ignoring the tempting benches to your left. On the south side of the paved clearing find a narrow dirt path. Follow it for a quick 0.1 mile to reach the summit at 2,104 feet. This small, rocky summit is at the foot of the tall metal towers. Check out views of the Phoenix Mountains Preserve and Camelback Mountain to the southeast. Take a peek west to see Mountain View Park, where Trail 100 starts. And, of course, there's South Mountain Park and the Sierra Estrella Mountains to the south.

Once you're ready, just turn around and head back down to the National Trail 44 trailhead parking lot.

Options

This trail to the summit is part of a loop. If you're interested in extending the hike, simply continue south along National Trail 44 after the summit. The trail soon becomes rugged and unpaved as you make a steep descent. After 0.5 mile from the summit, notice a split in the trail. Turn left (east) for 0.2 mile to a small trailhead on the south end of National Trail 44. From there, turn left (north) to walk along **North Mountain Recreation Loop**, which quickly leads to the National Trail 44 trailhead parking lot. This option totals approximately 1.6 miles.

Directions

From downtown Phoenix, take 7th Street north for approximately 9 miles through Dunlap Avenue. Turn left (west) on Peoria Avenue and then follow for 0.3 mile as the road turns right (north) and becomes the North Mountain Recreation Loop. The National Trail 44 parking lot and trailhead are on the north end of loop, at the Maricopa picnic area in North Mountain Park (10600 North 7th St.), on the right side of the road. The parking lot is open 5am-7pm.

GPS Coordinates: 33.5859 N, 112.0660 W

Information and Contact

There is no fee. Dogs on leash are allowed. Maps are available online at www.phoenix.gov/parks. For more information, contact City of Phoenix Parks and Recreation Main Office, Phoenix City Hall, 200 West Washington Street, 16th Floor, Phoenix, AZ 85003, 602/262-6862, www.phoenix.gov/parks.

6 CHARLES M. CHRISTIANSEN MEMORIAL TRAIL 100

North Mountain Area, Phoenix Mountains Preserve
and Dreamy Draw Recreation Area

BEST **Butt-Kickers**

Level: Butt-kicker

Total Distance: 11 miles one-way

Hiking Time: 6.5 hours

Elevation Gain: 1,500 feet

Summary: You can't call yourself a true-blue Phoenix hiker until you've done Trail 100.

You live in Phoenix. You like to hike. You just fulfilled the prerequisites to hike the Charles M. Christiansen Memorial Trail 100.

Trail 100 travels from 7th Avenue and Glendale Road (ish) to Tatum Boulevard and Doubletree Ranch Road (ish). When you finish those 11 miles (no ish about that), you feel like a true Phoenix city hiker, having traveled through the main artery of the Phoenix Mountains Preserve.

The 11 miles may seem daunting, but fear not—Trail 100 cleverly wraps, twists, and wiggles its way around Shaw Butte, North Mountain, and Piestewa Peak, making for a pleasant, all-day stroll with little elevation gain. The trail is masterfully planned and offers a flirtatious play with the urban surroundings. One minute, you're trekking through tunnels that pass under major roadways like 7th Street as you hear the overhead thunder of rushing cars. The next minute, you're enjoying miles of desert trail in which all you hear is the dry breeze and the crunch of rocks underfoot. Sounds lovely, doesn't it?

Okay, let's get going. For this review, Trail 100 is described end-to-end, from west to east. Arrange for a pickup or parked second vehicle on the east side to avoid a ridiculously long hike back.

The Charles M. Christiansen Memorial Trail 100 trailhead is on the northwest corner of the Mountain View Park parking lot. A boulder with an embedded metal plaque introduces Trail 100 and sets you on your way.

Follow Trail 100 north for a few hundred feet across some vacant terrain. Continue as the trail veers northeast and then straightens out to the north once more. At approximately 0.5 mile, you find the first (of many) brown metal trail markers. For the next 1.5 miles, continue to follow this wide, well-worn, and well-labeled trail as it curls to the south side of Shaw Butte and passes along the north side

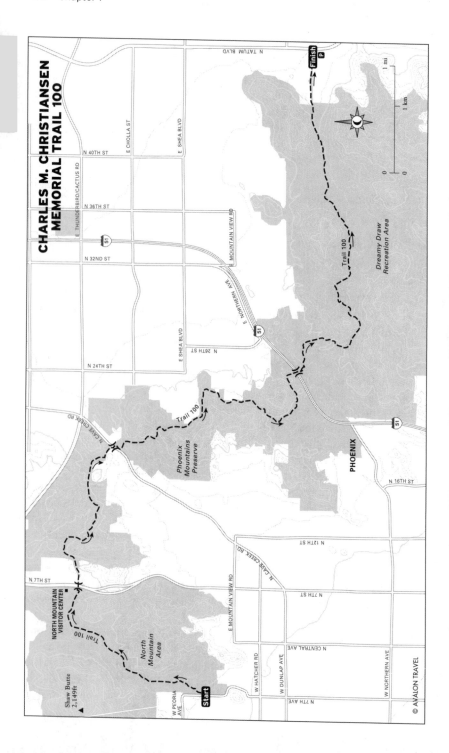

© LILIA MENCONI

This is your view as you travel the home stretch.

of North Mountain. At 2 miles, you reach the North Mountain Visitor Center, where a restroom and water are available. Follow Trail 100 heading east through the tunnel to cross under 7th Street.

Emerge on the other side of the 7th Street tunnel to start a gentle ascent. Avoid any unmarked trails along this stretch, and when in doubt, always opt for the widest, most well-traveled trail option. At 2.3 miles, the trail curves north, then briefly south. Generally speaking, however, you're heading east until you reach the second tunnel at 3.8 miles, which passes under Cave Creek Road.

Once through the Cave Creek Road tunnel, pick up Trail 100 heading south. Cross the paved Cortez Road and continue south as the city melts away once more. At 4.5 miles, climb 185 feet (your first "intense" climb of the day). Once at the top of this small hill, follow Trail 100 to the right (south) and ignore the deceptive turnoff to Trail 100B on the left. Descend and follow Trail 100, which keeps moving south as you march along the east side of this small range in the Phoenix Mountains.

At 6.5 miles, cut through yet another tunnel. This time, you're cruising under AZ-15. When you emerge, continue east; you have now entered the Dreamy Draw Recreation Area. Bathroom facilities and water are available to the south of the trail (visible after the first few feet beyond the tunnel). In this area, keep a vigilant eye for Trail 100 trail markers. Everything is well-labeled, but the tangle of Dreamy Draw trails can quickly take you off course.

After heading east from the tunnel for 0.3 mile, Trail 100 turns south. Follow signs carefully for the next 0.7 mile generally continuing south. When the trail turns to the northeast, you've successfully cleared the confusion of the Dreamy Draw area trails. By this time, you've accomplished the second big climb of the day—a mere 110 feet over 1 mile. Follow Trail 100 to the northeast and don't forget to look south so you can catch glimpses of Piestewa Peak.

Once the trail straightens out and heads east, the tough part is over. Merely continue along the flat, desert basin sitting on the north side of the Phoenix Mountains for the remaining 2.3 miles of the hike. The McDowell Mountains and Four Peaks are now visible to the east.

The final 0.6 mile stretches along a shady wash that runs behind private residences. Stir up a quail flock or two and enjoy this final little bit of your hike. Before you know it, *pop!* You stumble out onto a very small parking lot on the west side of Tatum Boulevard.

Oh, do you feel that stinging sensation? It's not sore muscles. It's pure Phoenix pride washing over your cells. (But you might want to stretch, just in case).

Options

To cut this hike, the **Dreamy Draw Recreation Area** is a convenient and popular stopping point. After emerging from the AZ-51 tunnel, simply turn right (south) when you see the parking lot. This makes for a hike that totals 7 miles.

Directions

From downtown Phoenix, take I-17 north for approximately 9 miles. Take exit 208 toward Peoria Avenue for 0.2 mile. Merge onto Black Canyon Access Road, heading north for 0.2 mile. Turn right onto Peoria Avenue and follow it west for 1.9 miles. Make a slight right onto 7th Avenue and follow it south for 0.2 mile. Take a left into the Mountain View Park parking lot. The Charles M. Christiansen Memorial Trail 100 trailhead, marked by a boulder with an embedded metal plaque, is on the northwest corner of the large parking lot.

GPS Coordinates: 33.5647 N, 111.9785 W

Information and Contact

There is no fee. Dogs on leash are allowed. Maps are available online at www.phoenix.gov/parks. For more information, contact City of Phoenix Parks and Recreation Main Office, Phoenix City Hall, 200 West Washington Street, 16th Floor, Phoenix, AZ 85003, 602/262-6862, www.phoenix.gov/parks.

7 DREAMY DRAW LOOP

Dreamy Draw Recreation Area, Phoenix Mountains Preserve

Level: Easy/Moderate

Total Distance: 3.5 miles round-trip

Hiking Time: 1.5 hours

Elevation Gain: 800 feet

Summary: This hike may challenge your navigation skills, but if you do it right, you reap some serious rewards.

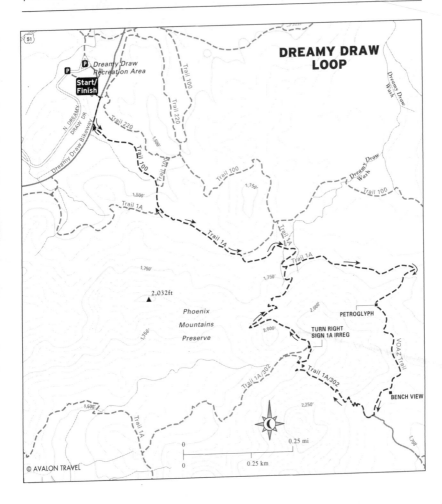

© LILIA MENCONI

Viewing sunset from the saddle is a rewarding treat for any hiker.

Dreamy Draw Recreation Area is what some call a "Choose Your Own Adventure" set of trails. The tangled web of marked and unmarked trails can make for a satisfying and aimless meander through flat desert, foothills, and mountain saddles. It's all a part of the larger Phoenix Mountains Preserve, and if you know where you're going, you can hook into the trails that lead to Piestewa Peak.

With so many options, following this loop can be tricky. It's a combination of the Perl Charles Memorial Trail 1A and the VOAZ (Volunteers for Outdoor Arizona) Trail that will, without a doubt, test your trail-reading skills. If you should succeed, however, you get to experience one of the least-known viewpoints this area has to offer—and a close-up encounter with a beautiful spiral-shaped petroglyph. You in? Of course you are.

To find the trailhead, head to the southeast corner of the Dreamy Draw Recreation Area parking lot. Continue heading southeast to pass the volleyball court, ramada, and bathroom, then follow the paved bike path south until you see a large kiosk on the east side of the path. Enter the trails at this trailhead (marked by the kiosk), which enters via Trails 1A and 100 and heads southeast. At approximately 0.6 mile, ignore signs for Trail 1A heading south/southeast. Instead, you'll veer right at 0.8 mile to follow the 1A Trail.

At approximately 1.3 miles, turn right to follow the VOAZ Trail heading south. Remain on the VOAZ Trail as you climb 190 feet in 0.5 mile to an unnamed saddle. Notice the dirt as it turns from powder gray to rich red (this means an increase of iron). As you turn on a switchback at 1.4 miles, be on the lookout for a lone, spiral-shaped petroglyph carved into a large boulder among the paloverde trees. At 1.8 miles, climb up and over the ridge to discover a beautiful view to the vast Phoenix Mountains Preserve to the east with Piestewa Peak to the southwest (you can see teeny, tiny people walking on the summit in the distance).

Descend 50 feet or so and you soon hook into a three-way trail juncture of Trail 302, Trail 1A, and VOAZ Trail at 1.9 miles. Turn right (northwest) and climb. And climb. And keep climbing. The switchbacks here are a little brutal, but after gritting through it, you pop up to another unnamed saddle at 2.1 miles and get your second reward of the day, with a breathtaking view to the west valley and the White Tank Mountains in the distance.

Work your way along the trail as it descends and wiggles north (you're still on the 1A/302 combo). At 2.2 miles, follow the sign for "1A Irregular" heading northwest. Continue along the trail until you plow into a fork at 2.4 miles. Veer right (northeast) to remain on the 1A Irregular Trail. Then, at about 2.6 miles, turn left to follow the clearly signed 1A Trail as it curls and bends west, back to Trail 100.

From here on, it's cake. Retrace your steps back to the trailhead located on the east side of the paved bike path. Then pat yourself on the back because you just successfully navigated the toughest trail-finding hike of this book.

Options
To add an extra 1.3 miles to the loop, ignore the first turnoff for the VOAZ Trail and continue east along Trail 1A. Trail 1A turns south around the mountain and joins Trail 304 for a short 0.15 mile until it splits off into the 1A again. After just 0.2 mile, it hooks into the 1A/302 combination trail. Follow it as described to return to the trailhead. This option totals approximately 4 miles.

Directions
From downtown Phoenix, take AZ-51 north for approximately 7 miles. Take exit 7 (Northern Ave.) and turn right on Dreamy Draw Drive, heading east. Follow Dreamy Draw Drive for 0.6 mile until the road ends at the Dreamy Draw Recreation Area parking lot (2421 East Northern Ave., 5am-7pm). The Trail 100/1A trailhead is southeast of the parking lot, up the stairs from the volleyball courts, past the restrooms, and on the east side of the main walkway.
GPS Coordinates: 33.5624 N, 112.0287 W

Information and Contact
There is no fee. Dogs on leash are allowed. Maps are available online at www.phoenix.gov/parks. For more information, contact City of Phoenix Parks and Recreation Main Office, Phoenix City Hall, 200 West Washington Street, 16th Floor, Phoenix, AZ 85003, 602/262-6862, www.phoenix.gov/parks.

8 L. V. YATES TRAIL 8

Phoenix Mountains Preserve

🔭 🐎 👪

Level: Easy/Moderate

Total Distance: 5 miles round-trip

Hiking Time: 2.5 hours

Elevation Gain: 700 feet

Summary: If you haven't yet done Trail 8, you must check this one out. It's quiet, well-signed, and 5 miles, making for a delightful way to kill a few hours and work up a sweat.

What a gem this trail turns out to be! Trail 8, nestled in the Phoenix Mountains Preserve, has some pretty tough competition nearby (Trail 100, Piestewa Peak, North Mountain, etc.). But taken in its entirety, you can walk from 40th Street and Shea Boulevard to the Piestewa Peak parking lot, enjoying the ambient and quiet east end of the mountains. With only 700 feet in elevation gain spread over 5 miles, this trail is an ambitious yet attainable goal for a family hike. Bonus: The 40th Street trailhead is tucked away in a neighborhood, so the crowds that bombard other areas (like Piestewa Peak or North Mountain) are easily avoided.

To start the hike, find the Trail 8 trailhead on the west end of the 40th Street

Trail 8 ends with a spectacular view to Piestewa Peak.

© LILIA MENCONI

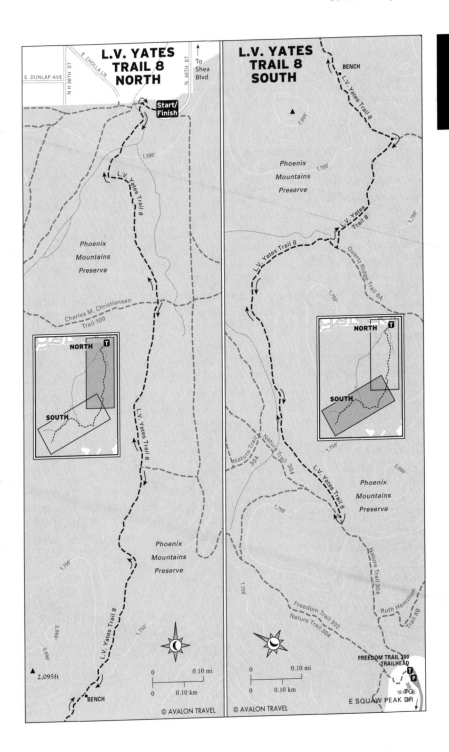

L.V. YATES TRAIL 8 NORTH

E DUNLAP AVE
E CHOLLA LN
N 38TH ST
N 40TH ST
To Shea Blvd
Start/Finish
1,500'
L.V. Yates Trail 8
Phoenix Mountains Preserve
Charles M. Christiansen Trail 100
NORTH
SOUTH
L.V. Yates Trail 8
Phoenix Mountains Preserve
1,750'
2,000'
2,000'
L.V. Yates Trail 8
2,095ft
BENCH

0   0.10 mi
0   0.10 km

© AVALON TRAVEL

L.V. YATES TRAIL 8 SOUTH

BENCH
L.V. Yates Trail 8
2,000'
Phoenix Mountains Preserve
1,750'
1,750'
L.V. Yates Trail 8
L.V. Yates Trail 8
Quartz Ridge Trail 8A
1,750'
NORTH
SOUTH
Nature Trail 304
Nature Trail 304
L.V. Yates Trail 8
2,000'
Phoenix Mountains Preserve
1,750'
1,750'
Nature Trail 304
Ruth Hamilton Trail 8B
Freedom Trail 302
Nature Trail 304
FREEDOM TRAIL 300 TRAILHEAD
E SQUAW PEAK DR

0   0.10 mi
0   0.10 km

© AVALON TRAVEL

trailhead parking lot. Follow the trail west for a few feet, then turn south to cross a small wash. Continue south along Trail 8, taking care to avoid any trailblazed paths along the way. At approximately 0.5 mile, cross over Trail 100 and continue south to follow a steady incline that lasts for the next 0.8 mile and climbs 320 feet. At 1.3 miles, you reach the tallest point of the hike on an unnamed saddle at 1,830 feet. Take a seat on a nearby bench for a break but don't get too comfy; you still have another 1.2 miles to go before you can turn around.

After leaving the saddle, follow Trail 8 for a brief descent. Be sure to turn right at 1.5 miles to follow Trail 8 signs that lead west. Cross a wash at 1.8 miles, then follow the path when it curves at 1.9 miles to head southwest. From here, climb 150 feet over the next 0.6 mile as you veer left to avoid other connecting trails. When the trail reaches another saddle at its junction with Trail 304, you've reached your turnaround spot. This spot also happens to overlook the Piestewa Peak parking lot, with Piestewa Peak visible to the southwest and the city to the south. You couldn't ask for a better way to end the first leg of a hike.

After taking in those sweet views, simply follow Trail 8 back for the remaining 2.5 miles to the 40th Street trailhead parking lot.

Options

For hikers who can't commit to the entire 5 miles, the first unnamed saddle reached along Trail 8 makes for an excellent stopping point. Simply follow Trail 8 for the first 1.3 miles until you reach the saddle, marked by a bench. Turning around here for the return trip totals 2.6 miles. It may be half the hike but it maintains almost all of the trail's appeal.

Directions

From downtown Phoenix, take AZ-51 north for approximately 10 miles. Take exit 9 and turn right onto Shea Boulevard, heading east for 0.8 mile. Turn right onto 40th Street, heading south, and follow it for 1 mile until the road ends at the 40th Street trailhead parking lot (9200 North 40th St.). The L. V. Yates Trail 8 trailhead is located on the west side of the parking lot; gates are open sunrise-sunset.
GPS Coordinates: 33.5679 N, 111.9966 W

Information and Contact

There is no fee. Dogs on leash are allowed. Maps are available online at www.phoenix.gov/parks. For more information, contact City of Phoenix Parks and Recreation Main Office, Phoenix City Hall, 200 West Washington Street, 16th Floor, Phoenix, AZ 85003, 602/262-6862, www.phoenix.gov/parks.

🄐 PIESTEWA NATURE TRAIL 304
Phoenix Mountains Park and Recreation Area,
Phoenix Mountains Preserve

BEST❰ Kid-Friendly Hikes

Level: Easy

Total Distance: 1.3 miles round-trip

Hiking Time: 1 hour

Elevation Gain: 320 feet

Summary: This lovely loop is an interpretive trail that starts with a climb and passes through the beautiful terrain of the Phoenix Mountains Preserve.

This is truly one of the more delightful trails among all the miles in the Phoenix Mountains Preserve. It's interpretive, which means there are educational plaques along the trail with interesting information about local plants and wildlife. Did you know that a hummingbird can fly upside down? Pretty sweet! The educational plaques are far enough away from one another to provide opportunities for substantial goal-setting for kids. Yes, exercise, education, and quality family time are rolled into one hike on the Nature Trail.

Hikers cruise through this intepretive path among the saguaro in the morning sun.

This description reviews the trail from this starting point, which initially shares a path with Trail 8B and travels the loop counterclockwise. You may come across some intersections of unofficial trails throughout, so, when in doubt, look ahead for the turquoise-colored plaques or metal trail markers that are scattered throughout Trail 304.

To start the hike, enter at the Trail 304 trailhead at the far northwest end of Squaw Peak Drive, on the right side of the posted map kiosk. For the first 0.4 mile, expect a pretty steep climb of 190 feet as you travel northeast. The ascent goes fast, and just when you're ready to take a break (or when the kids start to complain), the trail levels out. At the top of the climb, be sure to look to the left to see the first educational plaque of the trail. This one features s few factual tidbits about ocotillo (it's a succulent, not a cactus).

Weave through the flat terrain and enjoy the surrounding hills as the trail travels northwest. Massive saguaro, ocotillo, and teddybear cholla are plentiful, and don't be surprised if you see a few critters, like cactus wrens, along the way. As the loop reaches its northern curve at 0.6 mile, veer left to head west. Be sure to glance at the winding trails of the remainder of the Phoenix Mountains Preserve to the north.

Once the trail curves south at approximately 0.9 mile, it shares the path with the Freedom Trail 302. At 1.3 miles (the trailhead is visible from here) the two trails split. Follow the signs for Trail 304 and veer to the left (southeast).

The finale to this loop is a small gorge, and once you ascend the far side, you pop up in the parking lot.

Now, make sure those kids take some time to stretch. Good habits start early.

Options

For a more challenging trek, travel the loop in reverse, choosing the path to the left (south) of the large map posted at the trailhead. This direction travels the loop clockwise and offers a cumulative elevation climb of 440 feet in a total of 1.3 miles.

Directions

From downtown Phoenix, take AZ-51 north for approximately 6 miles. Take exit 5 for Glendale Avenue toward Lincoln Drive. Turn right onto Glendale Avenue and continue for 0.6 mile as the street turns to Lincoln Drive. Turn left onto Squaw Peak Drive and follow it northeast for 1 mile, through the Phoenix Mountains Park and Recreation Area entrance gate and to the end of the road. The Piestewa Nature Trail 304 trailhead is on the northwest side of the parking lot.

GPS Coordinates: 33.5433 N, 112.0153 W

Information and Contact

There is no fee. Dogs on leash are allowed. Maps are available online at www. phoenix.gov/parks. For more information, contact City of Phoenix Parks and Recreation Main Office, Phoenix City Hall, 200 West Washington Street, 16th Floor, Phoenix, AZ 85003, 602/262-6862, www.phoenix.gov/parks.

🔟 FREEDOM TRAIL 302

Phoenix Mountains Park and Recreation Area,
Phoenix Mountains Preserve

Level: Easy/Moderate

Total Distance: 3.7 miles round-trip

Hiking Time: 2 hours

Elevation Gain: 1,200 feet

Summary: Up, down, and (with this hike) around. Hikers just can't get enough of Piestewa Peak.

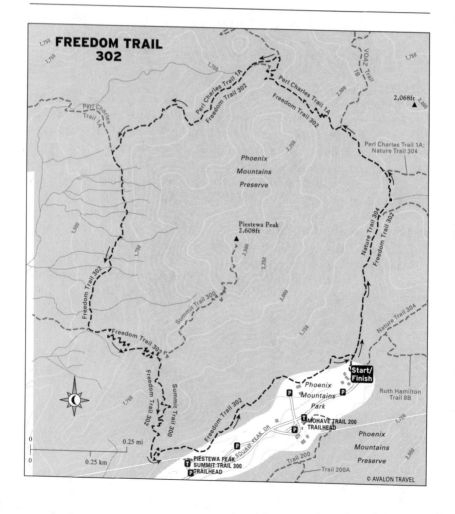

When the Freedom and Summit Trails meet, you see the west end of the Phoenix Mountains.

© LILIA MENCONI

Most people are obsessed with hiking *up* a mountain. But when it comes to this trail, it's easy to develop a taste for walking *around* a mountain. The Freedom Trail 302 in the Phoenix Mountains Park and Recreation Area is often referred to as "The Circumference Trail." No matter what you call it, you can add "dang awesome" to the beginning of its title because this is one fine hike.

Trail 302 circles around the base of Piestewa Peak, but make no mistake—this is no easier than the Summit Trail 300. It still has its fair share of climbing, and at 3.7 miles total, you cover more ground. Especially if you're seeking an escape from the crowds without a long drive outside of the city, this trail is just the ticket. For this review, the loop is traveled counterclockwise and begins at the Nature Trail 304 trailhead. The only trick to this trek is that even though you remain on Trail 302 the entire way, it is often shared with other trails (Trails 304, 1A, and 300, to be specific).

To start the loop, enter the park at the Trail 304 trailhead at the far northwest end of Squaw Peak Drive. Take a left onto Trail 304, heading west, and in less than 0.1 mile, Trail 302 joins the path from the southwest (this is your return route at the hike's end). Continue north and ascend along the now-shared Trail 302/304. After 0.6 mile, the trail turns to the northwest as Trail 304 drops off and Trail 1A joins. Now follow the combined Trail 302/1A heading northwest for a short 0.2 mile.

Ignore any turnoffs to the north and continue following Trail 302/1A as it curves west and traces the northwest face of Piestewa Peak. At 1.8 miles, Trail 302 finally shakes off Trail 1A. Travel Trail 302 for another 0.8 mile as it veers south. Once you start a steep ascent moderated by switchbacks heading southeast, you're closing in on the junction with Trail 300. At 2.6 miles, the climb is over and you reach the junction with Trail 300 (the heavily populated Piestewa Peak Summit Trail). Turn right to head south for a descent along the shared Trail 302/300. Here, you should no doubt see other hikers on their grueling hike to the summit.

At 3.1 miles, as the summit-hikers drop off to the Trail 300 trailhead and parking lot to the south, continue northeast to follow Trail 302 for 0.5 mile along flat terrain. At approximately 3.6 miles, close the loop and return via Trail 304 to your point of origin, the Trail 304 trailhead and parking lot.

Options

To add some serious grr-factor to this hike, combine it with the **Summit Trail 300**. When you encounter Trail 300 at 2.6 miles, simply turn left, heading northeast along Trail 300. After 0.6 mile of some serious climbing, you reach the rocky summit of Piestewa Peak, with incredible views to all mountain ranges in the Phoenix area in every direction (South Mountain Park to the south, McDowell Mountains to the northeast, White Tank Mountains to the west, and so on). Then simply retrace your steps along Trail 300 back to the junction with Trail 302 and continue along Trail 302 to close the loop. The total mileage for this option is 4.9 miles.

Directions

From downtown Phoenix, take AZ-51 north for approximately 6 miles. Take exit 5 for Glendale Avenue toward Lincoln Drive. Turn right onto Glendale Avenue and continue for 0.6 mile as the street turns to Lincoln Drive. Turn left onto Squaw Peak Drive and go northeast for 1 mile, through the Phoenix Mountains Park and Recreation Area entrance gate and to the end of the road. The trailhead is on the northwest side of the parking lot (open 5am-11pm).
GPS Coordinates: 33.5421 N, 112.0186 W

Information and Contact

There is no fee. Dogs on leash are allowed. Maps are available online at www.phoenix.gov/parks. For more information, contact City of Phoenix Parks and Recreation Main Office, Phoenix City Hall, 200 West Washington Street, 16th Floor, Phoenix, AZ 85003, 602/262-6862, www.phoenix.gov/parks.

11 MOHAVE TRAIL 200
Phoenix Mountains Park and Recreation Area,
Phoenix Mountains Preserve

Level: Easy

Total Distance: 1.2 miles round-trip

Hiking Time: 30 minutes

Elevation Gain: 300 feet

Summary: This super-speedy climb is the perfect option when you're short on time and ready to work up a sweat.

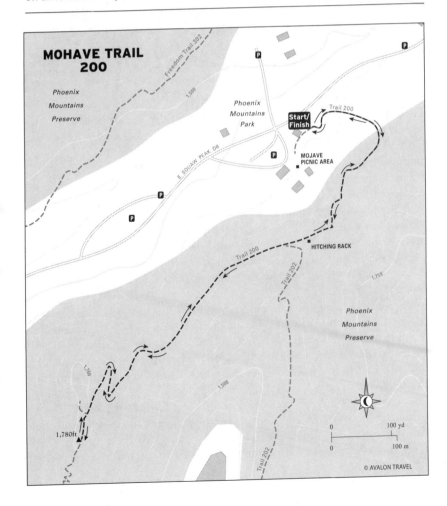

The Mohave Trail is a short and slightly intense hike with a big payoff of views to the south.

The Piestewa summit may dominate the skyline of the Phoenix Mountains Preserve, but many may not know there's another, smaller summit nearby. If you want a climb to a view but don't want to get hung up by the crowds on the Piestewa Summit Trail, Mohave could be your baby.

That said, the hike is quite brief. At only 1.2 miles round-trip, it's finished before you know it. But don't let the low mileage mislead you—this trail is no piece of cake. With a quick elevation climb of 300 feet, the huffing and puffing comes on fast.

The Mohave Trail trailhead sits on the east side of Squaw Peak Drive, just north of the Mohave picnic area, and is easily accessed by a small parking lot on the east side of the street. If you choose to park near the picnic ramadas, look to the north side of the lot for signs that lead you to the Mohave Trail 200, which is just a short walk away.

Once on Trail 200, the path quickly turns south as you march up a gradual incline. Continue past the wood hitching rack to encounter a fork in the trail at 0.2 mile. Veer right to remain on Trail 200 heading southwest. As the trail continues to climb for the next 0.2 mile, be aware of unofficial trails spurring from Trail 200. When in doubt, continue to favor the option to the right, remaining in a southwest direction.

At just over 0.4 mile, follow a couple sharp-turned switchbacks. Here, it's easy to lose sight of the trail. Stop, stand on your tippy-toes or a rock, and you can soon find the path again. Most likely, you probably just hit a sharp turn.

The final 0.2 mile is a short climb that heads southwest until you come upon a large pile of stones surrounding a metal post. This marks the end of your short journey. Catch your breath, wander around the summit area, and take in this generous view, looking south to midtown Phoenix with South Mountain Park in the distance.

The return trip is merely a matter of retracing your steps and descending your way back to the parking lot.

Options

Summiting the Mohave Trail 200 could make a great finish to a longer trek by combining it with **Trail 202**. Start on Trail 200, only this time take a left onto Trail 202 at 0.2 mile, heading south and then east. Follow Trail 202 for 1 mile until it runs into Trail 8A. Turn around here and retrace your steps along Trail 202 for the return mile until you reunite with Trail 200. Now, turn left onto Trail 200 heading southwest. It's just a short 0.4 mile to the summit from here. To return, simply retrace your steps along Trail 200, heading northwest for a return leg of 0.6 mile. This option totals 3.2 miles.

Directions

From downtown Phoenix, take I-10 east toward Tucson for approximately 2 miles. Take exit 147B to merge onto AZ-51. Follow it north for 5.5 miles. Take exit 5 for Glendale Avenue. Turn right, heading east onto Glendale Avenue. Continue as Glendale Avenue becomes Lincoln Drive. Follow Lincoln Drive for 0.3 mile and turn left, heading northeast, onto Squaw Peak Drive for 0.8 mile, through the Phoenix Mountains Park and Recreation Area entrance gate (2701 East Squaw Peak Dr.) and past the Mohave picnic area. The small Mohave Trail 200 parking lot and trailhead is on the right (east).
GPS Coordinates: 33.5412 N, 112.018 W

Information and Contact

There is no fee. Dogs on leash are allowed. Maps are available online at www.phoenix.gov/parks. For more information, contact City of Phoenix Parks and Recreation Main Office, Phoenix City Hall, 200 West Washington Street, 16th Floor, Phoenix, AZ 85003, 602/262-6862, www.phoenix.gov/parks.

12 PIESTEWA PEAK SUMMIT TRAIL 300

Phoenix Mountains Park and Recreation Area,
Phoenix Mountains Preserve

BEST Summit Views

Level: Moderate

Total Distance: 2.4 miles round-trip

Hiking Time: 1.5 hour

Elevation Gain: 1,190 feet

Summary: A steady climb–steep enough to kick up your cardio and make you sweat like a dog–rewards with stunning views.

Be a Phoenician. Scale the Piestewa Peak Summit Trail 300, one of the city's most popular hikes.

Phoenix natives still might mistakenly refer to this towering mountain on the south side of the Phoenix Mountains Preserve as "Squaw Peak"—"squaw" is an outdated and derogatory term. In 2003, the name was officially changed to honor Lori Piestewa, the first female Native American soldier to die on foreign soil.

© LILIA MENCONI

Cactus needles glow in the setting sunlight on the Piestewa Peak Summit Trail, which offers supreme views of The Valley of the Sun.

The 2.4-mileage may seem innocent enough, but this trail makes you work for every inch as you experience an intense cardio workout. It's a steep hike with a rocky terrain. Trail 300 is well traveled and easy to follow, with ample benches scattered throughout to take breaks. Keep sure feet, as many city hikers confidently rush up and down the mountain, paying little or no attention to trail etiquette. As a runner whizzes by, it's in your best interest to be aware of the dramatic drop-offs and dusty rocks that offer potential for slipping. The trail makes a few twists and turns throughout, but generally heads northeast and promises only a few switchbacks to moderate the climb.

From the Piestewa Peak Summit Trail 300 parking lot, you see two trailheads. Both lead to Trail 300 within the first 50 feet, so take your pick and start climbing as the trail heads southwest. The ascent begins immediately, without much opportunity for a proper warm-up.

After approximately 0.2 mile, the trail turns northeast. The path becomes increasingly steep and you're required to take large steps to accommodate craggy boulders. Keep climbing until you reach the 0.6 mile marker. This is the halfway mark for the ascent in distance only—be prepared for slightly more intense climbing on the second half. From here, your heart rate indicates that the real elevation gain has begun. Luckily, the rest of the path to the summit is clear of intersections or off-shoots, so navigation is simple, lending to an uninterrupted grunt all the way up.

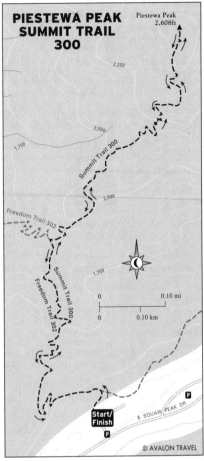

Encounter the final bench at 0.9 mile (it's the one with a plaque for Kim Lambert). Look up at the remainder of your climb and notice the metal handrails. You won't be able to see the actual summit from here, but feel assured that you're almost there. It's only 10-15 minutes more of discomfort as you climb a bunch of jagged rock. The final pass is a steep, exposed trek along the west side of the peak. When you run smack into a pile of giant boulders at 1.2 miles, make a very short scramble up towards the west (left) to join the hikers basking in the glory of the 2,600-foot summit.

Take a break. You made it.

And take a look around. You've got your pick of incredible views to all the mountain ranges in the Phoenix area. Check out South Mountain Park to the south, McDowell Mountains to the northeast, White Tank Mountains to the west, Camelback and the Papago Buttes to the southeast, and, on a super-clear day, the Superstition Mountains waaaaaaaay to the southeast.

Once you've sufficiently enjoyed your reward for all the hard work, scramble off the summit and back onto the trail. Retrace your steps down (way down) to the parking lot below.

Options

For a short warm-up, park your car at the first lot you encounter on the east (right) side of Squaw Peak Parkway, before reaching the park gates. From the gate, enter a small trail that runs along the west (left) side of the street, heading northwest. This takes you to the Piestewa Peak Summit Trail 300 trailhead and gets your blood pumping in preparation for the ascent. It only lasts for 0.1 mile, making a total hike of 2.6 miles.

Directions

From downtown Phoenix, take I-10 east toward Tucson for 2.2 miles. Take exit 147B to merge onto AZ-51, and follow it north for 5.5 miles. Take exit 5 for Glendale Avenue toward Lincoln Drive for 0.3 mile. Turn right onto Glendale Avenue, heading east for 0.3 mile. Continue onto Lincoln Drive and follow it east for 0.3 mile. Turn left onto Squaw Peak Drive and go northeast for 0.6 mile through the Phoenix Mountains Park and Recreation Area entrance gate (2701 East Squaw Peak Dr.). The Piestewa Peak Summit Trail 300 parking lot is on the left (west) side of the road. The Piestewa Peak Summit Trail 300 trailhead is on the west side of the parking lot.

GPS Coordinates: 33.5395 N, 112.0234 W

Information and Contact

There is no fee. Dogs are not allowed. Maps are available online at www.phoenix.gov/parks. For more information, contact City of Phoenix Parks and Recreation Main Office, Phoenix City Hall, 200 West Washington Street, 16th Floor, Phoenix, AZ 85003, 602/262-6862, www.phoenix.gov/parks.

13 QUARTZ RIDGE TRAIL 8A
Phoenix Mountains Preserve

Level: Easy/Moderate

Total Distance: 2.2 miles round-trip

Hiking Time: 1.5 hour

Elevation Gain: 500 feet

Summary: The secret is out: Quartz Ridge Trail kicks serious booty and everyone knows it.

This used to be one of the best-kept secrets of Phoenix Mountains Preserve trails. In the last five years, however, the Quartz Ridge Trail 8A has become a local favorite. It's the perfect fitness hike for friends or families, with about a half mile warm-up over relatively flat terrain, a mid-hike series of small hills, topped off by a final climb to an unnamed saddle. It's a decent sweat session with a rewarding view of the Phoenix Mountains Preserve trails to the north and midtown Phoenix to the south. Nah, you can't really fault Phoenix hikers for spreading the word about this little treasure.

It's a no-brainer as to how the Quartz Ridge Trail got its name. Throughout

© CRAIG SMITH

Ocotillo, saguaro, trail, peak, and city—this is a Phoenix hike.

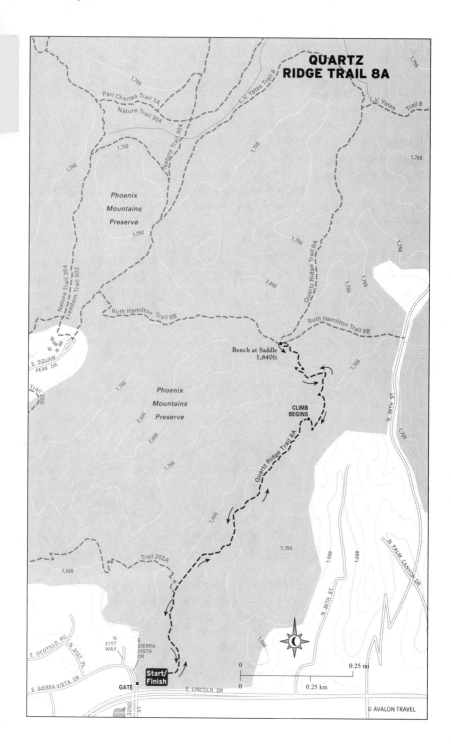

this trek you can't take a step without crunching a few chunks of white quartz that have tumbled their way down the canyon slopes. Keep your eyes to the east to see these slopes speckled with this white rock, which takes on a luminescence during twilight. The final hours of sunlight are the best time to hit this trail in the summer months; there's shade all the way, which lends opportunity for coyotes, great horned owls, bats, and other desert critters to emerge early.

To start, enter Trail 8A on the east side of the 32nd Street trailhead. The wide path quickly turns northeast and enters a shallow canyon that gloriously buffers out the sounds of civilization. At 0.3 mile, ignore a turnoff to Trail 202 from the west and continue northeast along Trail 8A as it traverses a wash and climbs a few small hills.

At 0.8 mile, the trail briefly heads south to climb a wide switchback that marks the beginning of the big ascent. Huff your way up as the trail wiggles its way north then northwest for another 0.5 mile, in which you climb the remaining 300 feet to the Quartz Ridge saddle.

That's all there is to it. Take a seat on the bench and catch your breath as you view the vast Phoenix Mountains Preserve trails to the north and enjoy city sights to the south. When ready, retrace your steps for a 1.3-mile cruise back to your car.

Options

If you're looking to lengthen your hike, consider combining Trail 8A with some neighboring trails to test your navigation skills and to make a 3.7-mile loop. Once you reach the saddle, turn left (west) to follow Trail 8B. After a quick, steep climb and descent that totals 0.5 mile, reach the Trail 304/8 combination trail. Turn left to follow this trail south for a mere 0.1 mile. When you find yourself on a paved road (Squaw Peak Drive), follow it south for 0.2 mile to the Trail 200 trailhead on the east side of the road. Hop on Trail 200 and follow it south for 0.2 mile. Then turn left to follow Trail 202 southeast for 1 mile until it collides with Trail 8A. You've closed the loop here. Take a right to head south for a brief 0.3 mile back to the 32nd Street trailhead.

Directions

From downtown Phoenix, take AZ-51 north for approximately 6 miles. Take exit 5 for Glendale Avenue toward Lincoln Drive. Turn right onto Glendale Avenue and head east for 0.3 mile. Glendale Avenue becomes Lincoln Drive. Continue east on Lincoln Drive for 0.7 mile. Make a slight left to stay on Lincoln Drive for 0.9 mile. Turn left onto 32nd Street heading north for 190 feet. Make an immediate right (east) through the gate and into the 32nd Street trailhead parking lot. The Quartz Ridge Trail 8A trailhead is on the east side of the parking lot.

GPS Coordinates: 33.5324 N, 112.0124 W

Information and Contact

There is no fee. Dogs on leash are allowed. Maps are available online at www.
phoenix.gov/parks. For more information, contact City of Phoenix Parks and
Recreation Main Office, Phoenix City Hall, 200 West Washington Street, 16th
Floor, Phoenix, AZ 85003, 602/262-6862, www.phoenix.gov/parks.

14 ECHO CANYON SUMMIT TRAIL

Camelback Mountain, Echo Canyon Recreation Area

🚻 🐕

BEST(Climbing and Scrambling, Summit Views

Level: Moderate

Total Distance: 2.5 miles round-trip

Hiking Time: 1.5 hours

Elevation Gain: 1,350 feet

Summary: This is one of the most popular trails in The Valley—for very good reason.

Camelback Mountain is easy to identify. When viewed from the south, the iconic mass of granite and layered sandstone creates the unmistakable shape of a resting camel with its head pointing west. When you arrive at the summit of this heart-pumping and challenging trail, you'll feel so accomplished that you'll want to turn to your partner for some celebratory fist-pumping. And if you do this trail a few times a week, you'll quickly find your fittest self.

The Echo Canyon trailhead used to have a bad reputation for being impossibly

© LILIA MENCONI

Gorgeous isn't it? This kind of beauty isn't easy to come by. You're going to have to work for this one!

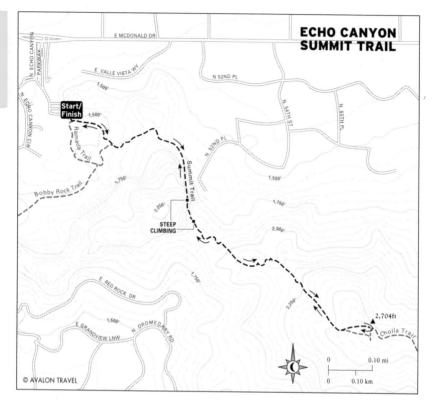

packed with a long queue of waiting cars that sometimes extended way beyond the lot. In 2013, the City of Phoenix began work to expand the lot and make much-needed trail improvements. The work, scheduled to complete in fall 2013, slightly changes the hike experience as it's described here. For trail updates, consult City of Phoenix Parks and Recreation (602/262-6862, www.phoenix.gov/parks).

The Echo Canyon Summit Trail accesses the mountain from its northwest side and offers a very steep, very intense climb. As the highest summit in Phoenix at 2,704 feet, it's well worth the effort. But, steel yourself for a haul. First-timers may find this trail to be quite a brutal experience.

From the Echo Canyon parking lot, find the Summit Trail trailhead at the southwest corner, next to the restrooms and a small seating area. The trail begins with a short descent and then begins its merciless climb. Wood railroad ties are bolted to the ground to create luxurious steps. Soon, the creature comforts subside and you continue up a rocky slope that veers east. At approximately 0.25 mile, the trail takes a turn to the right (south). The rocky walls loom high above on the right, making for a respite from the afternoon or evening sun.

Now, it's party time. The real climb begins as you encounter two bouts of ridiculously steep sandstone. Notice the metal handrails. Use them. Not only is this for your safety, but it also gives you a decent upper-body workout.

After passing the metal handrails, the climb momentarily lets up. Don't get too excited; you've only traveled 0.5 mile and your next challenge is just around the bend. The rest of the trail is a straight shot to the southeast, climbing 550 feet of craggy boulders for another 0.75 mile all the way to the top. Take your time. Drink plenty of water. In summer, consider bringing a pair of gloves to protect yourself from the hot surface of the rocks.

You won't be relieved from the climbing until you reach the summit at 1.25 miles. This is a sight you don't want to miss. You get a true sense of The Valley's vast stretch in every direction. Check out an unobstructed view to Papago Buttes, South Mountain Park, and the Sierra Estrella Mountains to the south. Looking west, the Phoenix Mountains Preserve dominates the valley floor. And to the north, grab some stellar views of the McDowell Mountains. Snap some photos, chug some water, and feel those endorphins course through your body.

Ahhhhh. (Don't forget the celebratory first pumping).

The return leg is a steep descent back to the Echo Canyon parking lot.

Options

To experience Camelback from end to end, combine the Echo Canyon Summit Trail with the **Cholla Trail**, which continues southeast another 1.5 miles from the summit along the ridge. Consider arranging for a pickup ride if you're not in the mood to turn around and trek all the way back to the Echo Canyon trailhead. A one-way trip totals 2.75 miles; out-and-back totals 5.5 miles.

Directions

From downtown Phoenix, take I-10 east for approximately 2 miles. Take exit 147A to merge onto the AZ-202 Loop and then go east for 2.6 miles. Take exit 2 for 40th Street toward 44th Street. Continue straight for 0.8 mile, through 40th Street. Turn left onto 44th Street and go north for 5.1 miles. Follow the street as it veers right and becomes McDonald Drive. Turn right to remain on McDonald Drive for 0.1 mile. Take the first right onto Echo Canyon Parkway for 0.2 mile. The road ends at the Echo Canyon Recreation Area and trailhead parking lot. Find the Echo Canyon Summit Trail trailhead on the southeast corner of the parking lot.
GPS Coordinates: 33.5214 N, 111.9735 W

Information and Contact

There is no fee. Dogs on leash are allowed. Maps are available online at www.phoenix.gov/parks. For more information, contact City of Phoenix Parks and Recreation Main Office, Phoenix City Hall, 200 West Washington Street, 16th Floor, Phoenix, AZ 85003, 602/262-6862, www.phoenix.gov/parks.

15 CHOLLA TRAIL
Camelback Mountain

Level: Moderate

Total Distance: 3.6 miles round-trip

Hiking Time: 2 hours

Elevation Gain: 1,300 feet

Summary: Experience the climb to Camelback Mountain's summit from the east side.

They say that the Cholla Trail is the easier of the two summit hikes on Camelback Mountain (the other hike is the Echo Canyon Summit Trail). In reality, it's about six of one, half dozen of the other. The Cholla Trail begins from the east tip of the mountain. With a stroll on the sidewalk followed by a relaxed elevation climb for the first 1.3 miles, it really socks it to ya at the end, when your scrambling skills are put to the test as you dangle high above the city. Okay, well, "dangle" is probably an exaggeration. But it's surely a rush to be fondling footholds on the sheer rock at elevations of 2,000 feet or more.

© LILIA MENCONI

Camelback's Cholla Trail offers plenty of scrambling.

Your first major challenge happens before you even approach the Cholla Trail trailhead: parking. With the trailhead tucked away on a neighborhood street, there's no proper parking lot. Instead, hikers get a chance to show off their parallel parking skills (for better or worse) into a small strip of a streetside, signed parking area along a busy thoroughfare (Invergordon Road).

Once you've squeezed into a parking space, take the sidewalk on Invergordon Road north for about 0.1 mile then turn left on Cholla Lane. Follow Cholla Lane west for another 0.3 mile until you find the Cholla Trail trailhead to the left. You can't miss it.

The well-signed and beautifully maintained Cholla Trail swings east, then follows the ridgeline west, toward

the summit. As you navigate the gentle climb, you quickly experience sweeping views of the McDowell Mountains to the north, the Superstition Mountains far to the east, and the Papago Buttes to the south. Peer to the southwest to find the tower at Sky Harbor International Airport.

For this first 1.3 miles, expect the trail to become increasingly steep. No switchbacks offer any relief so even the most-fit people find themselves working up a sweat. After you come across a large, circular clearing in the trail along the ridge, the intense climbing begins. Carefully follow the signs and trail markings—which are indicated by blue spray-painted dots on the rock sides. Scramble your way up one boulder after the other for the remainder of the trail (approximately 0.6 mile).

Join other hikers at the top, where the rock flattens out at 2,704 feet. You've earned this 360-degree view of the city for sure.

To return, simply follow your steps and, in this case, your grips the same way you came.

Options

To experience Camelback from end to end, combine the Cholla Trail with the

Echo Canyon Summit Trail that continues another 1.25 mile from the summit and down the canyon heading northwest. Consider arranging for a pick up and ride if you're not in the mood to turn around and trek all the way back to the Cholla Trail parking. A one-way trip totals 3.15 miles; out-and-back totals 6.3 miles (both of these mileages include the walk from the Cholla trailhead to the parking area).

Directions

From downtown Phoenix, take I-10 east toward Tucson for approximately 2 miles. Take exit 147A to merge onto the AZ-202 Loop heading east. Follow it for 2.6 miles. Take exit 2 for 40th Street toward 44th Street. Continue straight (east) for 0.8 mile, through 40th Street. Turn left onto 44th Street, heading north for 5.1 miles. Follow the street as it veers right (east) and becomes McDonald Drive. Turn right to remain on McDonald Drive, and follow it for 1.9 miles east. Turn right onto Invergordon Road and go 0.9 mile south. Pass Cholla Lane and look for the street-side parking strip on the right. Walk north along the sidewalk on Invergordon Road for about 0.1 mile and then turn left on Cholla Lane. Follow Cholla Lane west for another 0.3 mile until you find the Cholla Trail trailhead on the south side of Cholla Lane.
GPS Coordinates: 33.5113 N, 111.9434 W

Information and Contact

There is no fee. Dogs on leash are allowed. Maps are available online at www.phoenix.gov/parks. For more information, contact City of Phoenix Parks and Recreation Main Office, Phoenix City Hall, 200 West Washington Street, 16th Floor, Phoenix, AZ 85003, 602/262-6862, www.phoenix.gov/parks.

16 ARIZONA CANAL LOOP AT ARIZONA FALLS

G. R. Herberger Park

BEST Hikes near Water

Level: Easy

Total Distance: 3.2 miles round-trip

Hiking Time: 1.5 hour

Elevation Gain: 50 feet

Summary: A lovely walk in the heart of Arcadia is just a taste of the massive system of canal trails in The Valley.

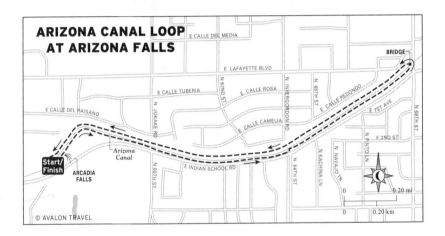

Oh, if only all of Phoenix had the dedication and funding to develop the 131 miles of canals into a chic waterfront. For now, we wait. And we enjoy some of the existing structures that take advantage of this unique feature.

Completed in 1885, the Arizona Canal carried water from the Salt River to the many citrus orchards that populated the valley south of Camelback Mountain. Arizona Falls is a natural 20-foot drop along the canal. In the late 1800s, early Phoenicians often flocked to the site for gatherings and celebrations. By 1902, the falls became the site of the first hydroelectric plant in Phoenix. The plant was revived in June 2003 and now generates up to 750 kilowatts of electricity—enough to power 150 homes.

It also happens to be the start of this easy 3.2-mile stroll that starts at 56th Street,

The Arizona Canal stretches a whopping 38 miles across The Valley, while Camelback Mountain looms to the north.

crosses the water at 68th Street, and returns along the north side of the canal. Enjoy the spectacular view of Camelback Mountain to the north and sneak peeks of downtown Scottsdale in the distance to the east. Ramps and a flat terrain make this hike wheelchair- or stroller-friendly for families with a wide range of ages.

On the north side of the G. R. Herberger Park parking lot, locate the stairs or ramp that leads to the waterfall pavilion at Arizona Falls. Head east as you walk along the south side of the canal, and take notice of the interpretive plaques, which offer a wealth of historic information about the Arizona Canal and the surrounding neighborhood. The packed-dirt canal bank is a wide, flat walkway that seemingly stretches on into oblivion.

After 1.6 miles, notice your first opportunity to cross the canal over a bridge along the west side of 68th Street. Walk north on the bridge to reach the north side of the canal. Turn around to head west along the canal with the neighboring houses to your right. Once you complete the return leg on the north bank, cross the canal once more, heading south along a metal bridge that leads to the Arizona Falls waterfall pavilion. With canal water gushing from various ledges on all sides of the pavilion, nearby traffic noise is completely muffled by the splashing water. Exit the pavilion via the ramps on the south side of the falls. This exploration of the Arizona Falls viewing platform is your reward at the end of this 3.2-mile walk.

Options

The Arizona Canal is one of eight canal systems in The Valley run by **Salt River**

Project. The canals boast an incredible cumulative 131 miles. Each canal system offers miles of waterfront pathways available for walking, jogging, biking, and fishing that stretch end to end across The Valley. Consult www.srpnet.com/water/ canals to find your local canal.

Directions

From downtown Phoenix, take I-10 east for 2.2 miles. Take exit 147A to merge onto the AZ-202 Loop; go east for 2.6 miles. Take exit 2 for 40th Street toward 44th Street. Continue straight (east) for 0.8 mile, through 40th Street. Turn left onto 44th Street, heading north for 2.4 miles. Turn right onto Indian School Road, heading east for 1.8 miles. Pass 56th Street and look for the G. R. Herberger entrance (56th St. and Indian School Rd.) and parking lot (5:30am-10pm daily) on the left. Arizona Falls and the entrance to the canal path are to the northwest of the parking lot.

Public Transportation: The Valley Metro Bus system (www.valleymetro.org/vm) offers service on Route 41—Indian School. Exit at the Indian School Road and 56th Street bus stop.

GPS Coordinates: 33.4898 N, 111.9585 W

Information and Contact

There is no fee. Dogs on leash are allowed. Maps are available online. For more information, contact SRP Land Department, 602/236-3126, www.srpnet.com.

17 HOLE IN THE ROCK TRAIL
Papago Park

BEST Kid-Friendly Hikes

Level: Easy

Total Distance: 0.3 mile round-trip

Hiking Time: 15 minutes

Elevation Gain: 60 feet

Summary: Take a very simple climb and get a huge payoff as you enjoy an unbeatable view to the southwest from this sandstone alcove.

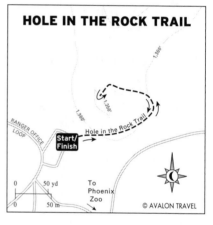

Attention beginners, seniors, and families with small children: This is your hike! Hole in the Rock is often the very first trail completed by little ones who grow up in The Valley. It's a short, simple climb with a big reward of a clear view to South Mountain Park to the south and an aerial peek into the Phoenix Zoo, which sits southeast of this sandstone butte.

Your perch for this view is, literally, a giant hole in a big rock. Centuries of wind and weather erosion on the sandstone butte have carved out this shady cove. Enjoy the company of other hikers here, as it's a popular destination for couples and families with small children.

From the parking lot at the base of the butte, the Hole in the Rock trailhead is clearly marked with a large sign. Follow the trail to the northeast as it curves around the butte. Continue over a small hill and take a sharp left (west). Notice the well-worn incline. The packed dirt is supported by bolted logs and creates a gentle flight of stairs. Climb the few feet of elevation gain until you reach a flat area of the rock. Duck through the rock opening facing south (this is the hole), go down a few steps, and enjoy the cavernous space.

Find a spot in the carved-out sandstone to sit, catch your breath, and take in the view. When you've had your fill, return to the trail and retrace your steps to the parking lot.

© LILIA MENCONI

Centuries of wind eroded this mound of sandstone to create Hole in the Rock, a popular year-round destination for families and folks seeking a quick hike with beautiful scenery.

Options

The Hole in the Rock trailhead and surrounding Papago Park areas have many ramadas and picnic tables, so Hole in the Rock can be a wonderful activity to burn off the picnic meal. Or walk along the **Ranger Office Loop Trail**, a paved road heading south of Hole in the Rock, to find a nearby fishing lagoon (fishing license required).

Directions

From downtown Phoenix, take I-10 east toward Tucson for approximately 2 miles. Take exit 147A to merge onto the AZ-202 Loop and follow it east for about 4 miles. Take exit 4 toward Van Buren Street. After 0.5 mile merge onto 52nd Street and follow it through the AZ-202 Loop/Red Mountain Freeway ramp. Turn left, heading east onto Van Buren Street. Take Van Buren Street for 0.8 mile and turn left, heading north, onto Galvin Parkway. After 0.3 mile turn right at Moreland Street. After 0.1 mile, turn left onto Ranger Office Loop Trail. After 0.2 mile take a slight right to stay on Ranger Office Loop Trail. Pass two parking lots on the left. After about 500 feet, turn right into the first parking lot (open 6am-7pm) to the right at the base of the Hole in the Rock butte.

Public Transportation: On METRO light rail, exit at the 24th Street/Jefferson Light Rail Station. Board the Route 1 - Washington East to Phoenix Zoo bus. From the Phoenix Zoo bus stop at the entrance, walk north for approximately 0.25

mile (or less) to exit the Phoenix Zoo parking lot on its northeast corner. Take a slight right to follow the paved Ranger Office Loop Trail heading northeast. Pass two parking lots on the left. After about 500 feet, turn right into the first parking lot to the right at the base of the Hole in the Rock butte.

GPS Coordinates: 33.4559 N, 111.9457 W

Information and Contact

There is no fee. Dogs on leash are allowed. Maps are available online at www. phoenix.gov/parks. For more information, contact Papago Park, 625 North Galvin Parkway, 602/495-5458, or Phoenix Parks and Recreation Main Office, Phoenix City Hall, 200 West Washington Street, 16th Floor, Phoenix, AZ 85003, 602/262-6862, www.phoenix.gov/parks.

18 ELIOT RAMADA TO DOUBLE BUTTE LOOP

Papago Park

BEST(**Wheelchair-Accessible Trails**

Level: Easy

Total Distance: 1.6 miles round-trip

Hiking Time: 1 hour

Elevation Gain: 100 feet

Summary: This short walk through the desert passes by dramatic sandstone buttes uniquely shaped by years of desert erosion.

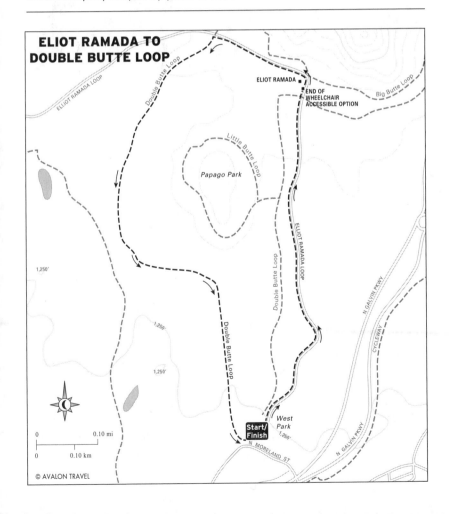

The sandstone buttes in Papago Park are quite a sight.

Papago Park is a funny little area—in a good way. It features museums, the Desert Botanical Gardens, the Phoenix Zoo, fishing lagoons, a golf course, an archery range, and (what else?) hiking trails. The trails here are quite simple to complete with easy navigation and very little elevation gain. Fantastic for family outings, jogging, or biking, this is just one loop among the gorgeous sandstone buttes.

This hike combines the Eliot Ramada Loop and Double Butte Loop Trails in the West Park area of Papago Park. It travels around the north end of the Little Butte, passing between the Eliot Ramada and the Big Butte. While other trails are available in this area to lengthen your Papago Park adventure, this loop is a brief reprieve from the city and stays away from busy roads or flying golf balls from the nearby Phoenix Municipal Golf Course. Plus, you get up-close views of the glittering terra-cotta buttes, which are rounded and softly sculpted by wind and rain.

From the West Park trailhead, take the Eliot Ramada Loop Trail north for a wheelchair-friendly paved portion that lasts 0.6 mile. At 0.6 mile, the trail turns left (northwest) and passes by the Eliot Ramada, an artificial shade structure. After you pass the Eliot Ramada, there are many different trail options. Choose the dirt trail clearly marked with the number 5, which heads west. This 0.1-mile portion of the loop passes along the south side of the Big Butte, offering close-up views of this Mars-like rock.

At 0.7 mile, turn left to follow the Double Butte Loop heading southwest. Cross over a few washes and be sure to follow trail markers for Trail 5 along the way. At

1.2 miles, the trail veers east and then heads south for the remaining 0.4 mile. The Double Butte Loop Trail emerges on the south end of the West Park parking lot.

Options

To increase distance, opt to travel the entirety of the **Double Butte Loop**. At 0.6 mile, turn right (east) to follow the Double Butte Loop as it traces around the Big Butte's north side. At approximately 1.3 miles, the trail curves southwest for the return leg. This option totals 2.3 miles.

Directions

From downtown Phoenix, take I-10 east toward Tucson for approximately 2 miles. Take exit 147A to merge onto the AZ-202 Loop, and follow it east for about 4 miles. Take exit 4 toward Van Buren Street. Merge onto 52nd Street heading south and continue through the AZ-202 Loop/Red Mountain Freeway ramp. Turn left, heading east onto Van Buren Street, and continue for 0.8 mile. Turn left, heading north onto Galvin Parkway. After 0.3 mile take the first left onto north Moreland Street. After about 400 feet veer right to stay on Moreland Drive. The road ends in the Papago West Park parking lot (open 6am-7pm). The Eliot Ramada Loop trailhead is on the northeast corner of the lot.

Public Transportation: On METRO light rail, exit at the 24th Street/Jefferson Light Rail Station. Board the Route 1 - Washington East to Phoenix Zoo bus. From the Phoenix Zoo, walk northwest across the parking lot and onto Moreland Street (toward Galvin Parkway). Cross Galvin Parkway heading northwest to reach the Papago West Park parking lot. The walk from the Phoenix Zoo totals 0.5 mile. **GPS Coordinates:** 33.4554 N, 111.9542 W

Information and Contact

There is no fee. Dogs on leash are allowed. Maps are available online at www.phoenix.gov/parks. For more information, contact Papago Park, 625 North Galvin Parkway, 602/495-5458, or Phoenix Parks and Recreation Main Office, Phoenix City Hall, 200 West Washington Street, 16th Floor, Phoenix, AZ 85003, 602/262-6862, www.phoenix.gov/parks.

19 HAYDEN BUTTE SUMMIT TRAIL
Hayden Butte Preserve Park

Level: Easy

Total Distance: 0.9 mile round-trip

Hiking Time: 30 minutes

Elevation Gain: 400 feet

Summary: Hayden Butte, affectionately known as A Mountain, offers a short climb that's a must-do for Tempe visitors and residents.

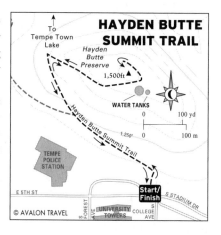

Few Valley dwellers can avoid the climb up Tempe's Hayden Butte. Sooner or later, everyone takes a turn dragging themselves up this popular trail for some stellar views of all of Tempe, including Tempe Town Lake to the north. Sitting in the heart of downtown Tempe, it's a favorite for families and students from nearby Arizona State University. The south side of this well-traveled butte boasts a large concrete letter A (hence its nickname, A Mountain). Typically, the letter is painted white or gold (ASU's school color). Due to heated rivalries with other universities, however, you may discover an entirely different color (reflecting the rival's school colors) during college football season. That is, if the ASU students fail to follow the tradition of guarding the letter from such attempts.

With so much action and urban activity surrounding Hayden Butte (yes, that's a nice way of saying graffiti and litter…sigh), you may miss the historic features. The northwest foot of the butte includes the remains of a sandstone quarry. The smaller water tank on the south side was constructed in 1950. And, from way back in time, you may even spy a few petroglyphs.

To reach the summit from the south side of Hayden Butte near Sun Devil Stadium, access the Leonard Monti Trail (named after the founder of nearby Monti's La Casa Vieja) from the trailhead located on the north side of Veterans Way. Follow the clearly signed trail west as it gently climbs and curves northwest after 0.2 mile.

At approximately 0.3 mile, make a sharp right turn (southeast) to follow a paved

Tempe's Hayden Butte (aka "A" Mountain) offers a stellar view to the old flour mill and Tempe Town Lake.

service road. At a cleared viewing pavilion at 0.4 mile, step off the paved portion and onto the dirt trail heading north to finish the remaining 0.1 mile to the summit. The summit is a small outcrop of craggy rock next to spindling radio towers. You'll have friends up here even on the hottest days of the year, so don't expect to satisfy a need for solitude.

Instead, satisfy your desire to take in striking views of downtown Tempe to the west, the ASU campus to the south, and the towering remains of Tempe's historic flour mill by the glittering surface of the Tempe Town Lake to the north.

Options

The Hayden Butte summit can also be accessed by the access road from the west side of the mountain. Find a small parking lot on the east side of Mill Avenue, just south of the historic flour mill. The paved access road heads east for a straight shot to the aforementioned viewing pavilion. This option makes for a shorter hike totaling approximately 0.6 mile.

Directions

From downtown Phoenix, take I-10 east toward Tucson for approximately 2 miles. Take exit 147A to merge onto the AZ-202 Loop, and follow it east for 7.4 miles. Take exit 7 for Scottsdale Road. Turn right, heading south, onto Scottsdale Road. After 0.5 mile Scottsdale Road becomes Rural Road. Continue on Rural Road for 0.3 mile and then turn right, heading west, onto 6th Street. Take the third right onto Veterans Way and find public parking close to Sun Devil Stadium. The Leonard Monti Trail trailhead is on the north side of Veterans Way, just east of 5th Street, northeast of the light rail stop.

Public Transportation: On Metro light rail, exit at the Veterans Way/College light rail station.

GPS Coordinates: 33.4258 N, 111.9349 W

Information and Contact

No fees are required. Dogs on leash are allowed. For more information, contact the city of Tempe Parks and Recreation at 480/350-5200, www.tempe.gov.

WEST VALLEY

© LILIA MENCONI

Of all the areas in the Valley of the Sun, the West Valley has the fewest hikes. But don't let that sway you. These hikes are all about quality, not quantity. With the incredible White Tank Mountain Regional Park, hiking enthusiasts can experience spectacular day hikes that yield beautiful views of the park's 30,000 acres. This range is also a great place to spy ancient petroglyphs made by the Archaic People. The other hiking hub is Estrella Mountain Regional Park, south of the White Tank Mountain Regional Park. The Sierra Estrella Mountains fulfill a hiker's need with more than 33 miles of easy and moderate trails—great for long, peaceful jaunts. Though these West Valley parks may be a little topographically impaired, you can keep yourself very busy out here.

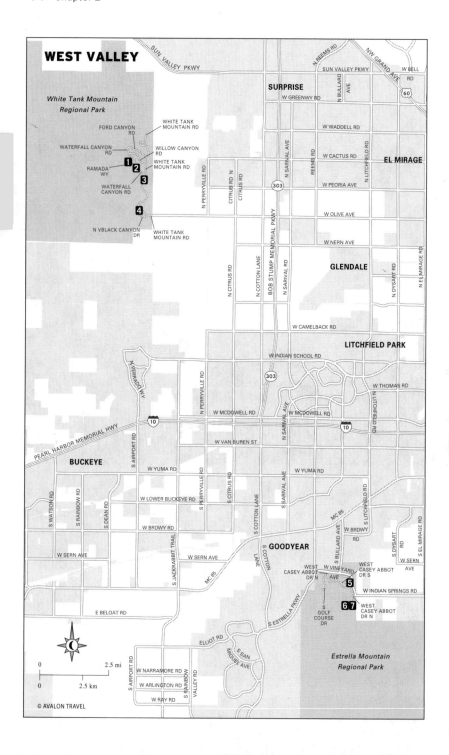

WEST VALLEY

White Tank Mountain
Regional Park

FORD CANYON RD

WHITE TANK MOUNTAIN RD

WATERFALL CANYON RD

WILLOW CANYON RD

WHITE TANK MOUNTAIN RD

RAMADA WY

WATERFALL CANYON RD

N VBLACK CANYON DR

WHITE TANK MOUNTAIN RD

SUN VALLEY PKWY

N REEMS RD

NW GRAND AVE

SUN VALLEY PKWY

W BELL RD

60

SURPRISE

W GREENWY RD

N BULLARD AVE

W WADDELL RD

N SARIVAL AVE

REEMS RD

W CACTUS RD

N LITCHFIELD RD

EL MIRAGE

303

W PEORIA AVE

N PERRYVILLE RD

CITRUS RD N

CITRUS RD

W OLIVE AVE

BOB STUMP MEMORIAL PKWY

W NERN AVE

N EL MIRAGE RD

N CITRUS RD

N COTTON LANE

N SARIVAL RD

GLENDALE

N DYSART RD

W CAMELBACK RD

LITCHFIELD PARK

W INDIAN SCHOOL RD

N VERRADO WY

303

W THOMAS RD

N LITCHFIELD RD

N PERRYVILLE RD

N SARIVAL AVE

W MCDOWELL RD

W MCDOWELL RD

10

10

S AIRPORT RD

W VAN BUREN ST

PEARL HARBOR MEMORIAL HWY

BUCKEYE

W YUMA RD

S SARIVAL AVE

W YUMA RD

S WATSON RD

S RAINBOW RD

S DEAN RD

W LOWER BUCKEYE RD

S PERRYVILLE RD

S CITRUS RD

S COTTON LANE

W BRDWY RD

MC 85

S LITCHFIELD RD

W BRDWY RD

S DYSART RD

S EL MIRAGE RD

S BULLARD AVE

W SERN AVE

S JACKRABBIT TRAIL

W SERN AVE

MC 85

S COTTON LANE

GOODYEAR

WEST CASEY ABBOT DR N

W VINEYARD AVE

WEST CASEY ABBOT DR S

W SERN AVE

W INDIAN SPRINGS RD

E BELOAT RD

S ESTRELLA PKWY

S GOLF COURSE DR

WEST CASEY ABBOT DR N

ELLIOT RD

S SAN MIGUEL AVE

S AIRPORT RD

W NARRAMORE RD

VALLEY RD

S RAINBOW

Estrella Mountain
Regional Park

0   2.5 mi

0   2.5 km

W ARLINGTON RD

W RAY RD

© AVALON TRAVEL

TRAIL NAME	FEATURES	LEVEL	DISTANCE	TIME	ELEVATION	PAGE
1 Ford Canyon Loop BEST⟨		Strenuous	9.4 mi rt	5 hr	1,350 ft	96
2 Waterfall Trail BEST⟨		Easy	1.9 mi rt	1 hr	150 ft	100
3 Black Rock Long Loop		Easy	1.2 mi rt	30 min	100 ft	103
4 Goat Camp Trail		Strenuous	6.4 mi rt	3.5 hr	1,675 ft	106
5 Gila to Baseline Loop BEST⟨		Easy	2.6 mi rt	1 hr	300 ft	109
6 Rainbow Valley to Toothaker Loop		Easy/Moderate	6 mi rt	3 hr	675 ft	112
7 Butterfield to Gadsden Trails		Moderate	6.8 mi rt	3.5 hr	800 ft	115

1 FORD CANYON LOOP

White Tank Mountain Regional Park

BEST(**Solitude**

Level: Strenuous

Total Distance: 9.4 miles round-trip

Hiking Time: 5 hours

Elevation Gain: 1,350 feet

Summary: This all-day loop combines four trails, and you get the works—ridges, washes, canyons, an old dam, and tons of tanks.

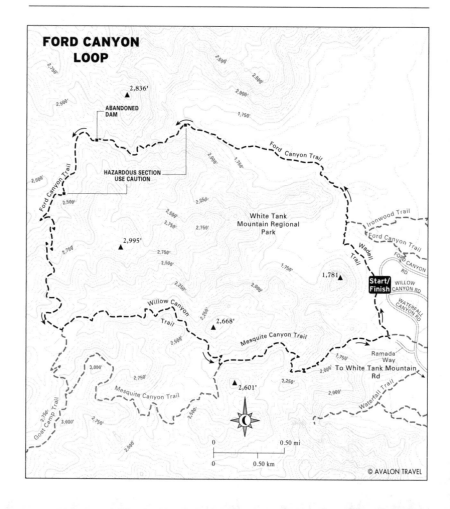

© KRISTINA SMITH

Deep basins scoured into the white rock are filled with water.

Holy geez, this is a good one! Talk about a fantastic way to burn some hours and some calories. At 9.4 miles, this big loop travels counterclockwise up a mountain, through a wash, over a dam, along a hill, and into three canyons. The first few miles of the Waddell Trail to the Ford Canyon Trail pass by the Willow Canyon to the west. After crossing over the canyon wall, you enter the Ford Canyon and travel deep into the park. The trail then follows a wash and passes an abandoned dam to once again climb over canyon walls to enter the Willow and Mesquite Canyons, through which you return to complete the loop. The solitude and scenery on this long hike are unparalleled, and it's unwise to pass it up. This trail never has a moment of dull terrain as it travels deep into the northern region of White Tank Mountain Regional Park.

Oh, and there are tanks, too. Even on a hot day, the deep basins scoured into the rock are filled with water. Sure, the water might look unappealing, but even nasty water is a welcome sight in these parts. Sold yet? Let's get going.

Begin the hike from the Waddell Trail trailhead and follow the trail heading north. After a short 0.5 mile, abandon Waddell Trail and hop onto Ford Canyon Trail, which continues north, then curves west at 0.8 mile. At 2 miles, the trail passes by a posted warning sign for Hazardous Conditions. Things get a little rocky and intense as you climb 400 feet to travel along the south side of Ford Canyon. At 2.6 miles, the trail mellows out as you follow a wide, sandy wash along the quiet floor of Ford Canyon. At 3.1 miles, leave the wash to pass by on the right side of the small abandoned dam.

Ford Canyon Trail turns south at 3.2 miles and begins to travel over the range that constitutes the north wall of Willow Canyon. At 3.9 miles, follow the trail as it finally deserts the wash (be careful not to mistakenly stay in the wash, which heads west). This begins the final leg of major elevation gain—410 feet in 0.8 mile. Once at 4.7 miles total, take a moment to stop and look around—this is the tallest point of the loop at 2,815 feet. You're now on the ridge of the range that separates the Ford Canyon (to the northeast) and Willow Canyon (to the southeast).

From here on out, you descend all the way. At 5.4 miles, be sure to follow signs to connect with the Willow Canyon Trail heading east. Enjoy as you cross over and into Willow Canyon. At 5.7 miles, take a moment to explore the area just south of a small campground to find a very slowly trickling spring. Then continue along Willow Canyon Trail as it heads east and curves southeast at 6.6 miles. Willow Canyon Trail meets Mesquite Canyon Trail at 7.2 miles. Follow Mesquite Canyon Trail east as you walk along Mesquite Canyon (this is the final canyon of the hike). At 8.9 miles, turn onto the Waddell Trail heading north for the last little bit of trail—just another 0.5 mile and you're home free. (And by "home," I mean the Waddell trailhead.)

Options

For a much shorter jaunt, take the trail to the old dam and back for an excellent stopping point at 3.1 mile. Simply follow the Waddell Trail to the Ford Canyon Trail. Once you reach the dam, turn back and retrace your steps to the Waddell trailhead for a total journey of 6.2 miles.

Directions

From downtown Phoenix, take I-10 west toward Los Angeles for about 18 miles. Take exit 125 for Sarival Avenue and turn right, heading north, onto Sarival Avenue. After 0.2 mile, turn left onto McDowell Road. Take McDowell Road west for 2 miles and turn left, heading north, onto Citrus Road. Take Citrus Road for 7 miles and then turn left onto Olive Avenue. Take Olive Avenue west for 3 miles until it turns into White Tank Mountain Road. Pass through the park gate and pay the fee. Take White Tank Mountain Road for 2.1 miles as it curves north. Turn left onto Waterfall Canyon Road, heading northwest, for 1.2 miles. The small parking lot and the Waddell trailhead are located between area 8 and 9 on the west side of the road.

GPS Coordinates: 33.5986 N, 112.5126 W

Information and Contact

There is a fee of $6 per vehicle. An annual pass is available for $75. Dogs on leash are allowed. Maps are available at the park entrance. The park is open daily (6am-8pm

Sun.-Thurs., 6am-10pm Fri.-Sat.). For more information, contact White Tank Mountain Regional Park, 20304 West White Tank Mountain Road, Waddell, AZ 85355, 623/935-2505, www.maricopa.gov/parks/white_tank.

2 WATERFALL TRAIL
White Tank Mountain Regional Park

BEST Hikes near Water, Historical Hikes, Kid-Friendly Hikes,
Wheelchair-Accessible Trails

Level: Easy

Total Distance: 1.9 miles round-trip

Hiking Time: 1 hour

Elevation Gain: 150 feet

Summary: Take this interpretive and wheelchair-accessible trail to discover some of the most incredible petroglyphs in the area.

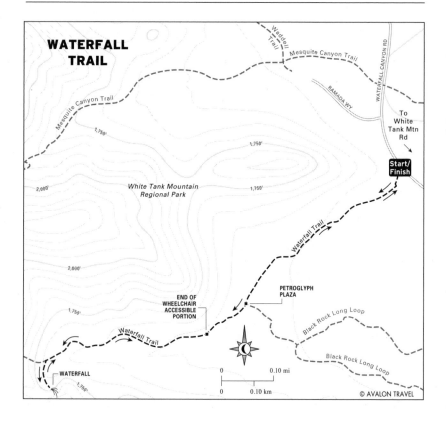

© LILIA MENCONI

The Waterfall Trail offers close-up views of some of the best petroglyphs in town.

The Waterfall Trail is just filled with delights. The graded-dirt portion includes educational plaques with details about surrounding plants, animals (bobcats, ringtails, bats, and hawks), and petroglyphs. Along this trail, you also find a massive collection of some of the best petroglyphs in town. Interpretive plaques explain how native peoples created these incredible rock drawings almost 7,000 years ago. It's truly inspiring to explore this area and nearly impossible to keep your imagination from running wild.

As if that isn't motivation enough, the trail leads to a waterfall. Say what? It's true! Winter and spring offer the greatest chance to see water actually falling (not trickling). And though you may not see a constant torrent of water around here, there's been enough of it over the centuries to erode the park's granite, creating the deep pools or "tanks" that give the area its name. Even in the dead of summer, the Waterfall Trail leads to one of these pools of water—with water still in it. The pools will be green and buzzing with bugs in the hotter months, so this trail is at its best in winter or spring.

Start the hike from the Waterfall Trail trailhead on the southwest side of the parking lot. The entry to the wide path is flanked by cases filled with maps, park information, and signage for mountain lion warnings. The firmly packed dirt makes for a very easy cruise. As the trail heads southwest, it offers ample opportunity for pit stops to read each plaque. Read them. Learn. There's no point in rushing this trail. Benches line the path, so embrace the leisurely vibe and enjoy your experience.

The main site, Petroglyph Plaza, appears on the right side of the trail at 0.4 mile, and it's worth your while to spend a moment here. Contemporary Native Americans consider petroglyph sites sacred. After a few seconds viewing the overlapping mass of spirals and designs etched into the rock, it's easy to understand why.

At 0.5 mile, unfortunately, the wheelchair-accessible portion of the trail comes to an end. If you're not on wheels, feel free to keep moving as the terrain becomes slightly more rugged. Soon, you're walking alongside a rocky creek. If you're lucky, flowing water will be weaving in and among the granite boulders. Notice the dramatic change here as the canyon walls begin to jut high on either side. They will collide at the site of the waterfall, which sits just shy of 1 mile in. After a good rain, you may see anything from a trickle to a rush of water cascading down the vertical drop of rock to splash into a deep tank.

When you're ready, simply turn around and follow the trail back to the parking lot.

Options

For a longer hike, take a little detour from the Waterfall Trail to the **Black Rock Long Loop** via the signed connecting trail at 0.4 mile. Take a left turn (southeast) for a very short jaunt until you meet up with the Black Rock Long Loop. Veer right on the loop and follow it counterclockwise as it boomerangs back to the connecting trail. This detour adds 1.2 miles to the trip with minimal elevation gain.

Directions

From downtown Phoenix, take I-10 west toward Los Angeles for about 18 miles. Take the exit for Sarival Avenue and turn right, heading north, onto Sarival Avenue. After 0.2 mile, turn left onto McDowell Road. Take McDowell Road west for 2 miles and turn right, heading north, onto Citrus Road. Take Citrus Road for 7 miles and then turn left onto Olive Avenue. Take Olive Avenue west for 3 miles until it turns into White Tank Mountain Road. Pass through the park gate and pay the fee. Take White Tank Mountain Road for 2 miles as it curves and heads north. Turn left onto Waterfall Canyon Road heading northwest. After 0.4 mile, turn left into the Waterfall Trail trailhead parking lot. The Waterfall Trail trailhead is on the southwest side of the lot.
GPS Coordinates: 33.5901 N, 112.507 W

Information and Contact

There is a fee of $6 per vehicle. An annual pass is available for $75. Dogs on leash are allowed. Maps are available at the park entrance. The park is open daily (6am-8pm Sun.-Thurs., 6am-10pm Fri.-Sat.). For more information, contact White Tank Mountain Regional Park, 20304 West White Tank Mountain Road, Waddell, AZ 85355, 623/935-2505, www.maricopa.gov/parks/white_tank.

3 BLACK ROCK LONG LOOP
White Tank Mountain Regional Park

Level: Easy

Total Distance: 1.2 miles round-trip

Hiking Time: 30 minutes

Elevation Gain: 100 feet

Summary: This is a flat, easy interpretive trail that loops around a big ol' rock.

The title of this trail almost says it all. There's a black rock. You walk all the way around it. The end.

Just kidding! Of course, there's a little more to this hike. In fact, not only is it an interpretive trail, it's surprisingly scenic. Nestled in the foothills of the White Tank Mountains, the trail travels among a heavily populated forest of saguaro cacti. The place is littered with these desert giants, whose blossom is the official Arizona state flower. All in all, the flat path is easy to follow, so it's ideal for families who are in a "stop and smell the creosote" kind of mood.

Start the hike at the Black Rock trailhead on the west side of White Tank Mountain Road. Since the first portion of the trail is shared with the Black Rock

© LILIA MENCONI

The Black Rock Loop makes for a leisurely stroll around two small hills.

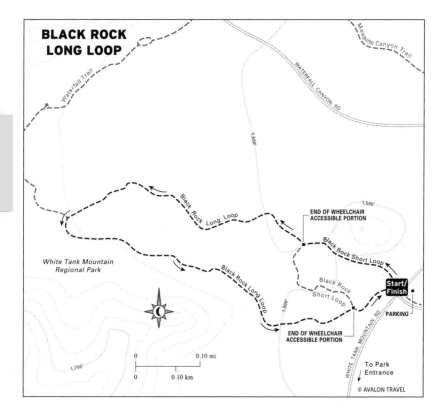

Short Loop, it's wheelchair friendly. Signs indicate that hikers should travel counterclockwise so that you and your party are spared from pesky traffic jams. Begin
the trail on the path to the right and head west.

Follow the packed-dirt path and enjoy the lush landscape filled with paloverde
and mesquite trees. Keep your eyes peeled for jumping cholla cacti that edge the
trail. See those small pedestals topped with hinged boxes? Flip open the lids and
you'll see an illustration paired with tidbits about the surrounding wildlife (you'll
be reminded that a javelina is not a pig). Exciting stuff.

At about 0.2 mile, the trail splits. Continue straight ahead for the remainder of
the Black Rock Long Loop trail. Here, the path becomes sandy and narrow as it
approaches a curve. At its westernmost point (about 0.6 mile) you encounter a signed
connecting path that leads to the neighboring Waterfall Trail. Move past it and continue along the loop as it turns and heads east, toward the Black Rock Trail trailhead.

From here on out, the walk is super easy to follow. Look to the left (north) and
you soon see the other side of the big, black rock you've been circling around. At
just over 1 mile, you hook back up with the shared, wheelchair-accessible Black
Rock Short Loop for the remaining 0.1 mile of the hike.

Options

For a much-shorter hike that remains wheelchair friendly throughout and tops out at a mere 0.5 mile, opt for the **Black Rock Short Loop**. Start the hike at the Black Rock trailhead heading counterclockwise. At 0.2 mile, turn left (south) at the signed split in the trail to follow the Black Rock Short Loop. Continue as the trail whips back around to head east to return to the Black Rock trailhead.

Directions

From downtown Phoenix, take I-10 west toward Los Angeles for about 18 miles. Take the exit for Sarival Avenue and turn right, heading north onto Sarival Avenue. After 0.2 mile, turn left onto McDowell Road. Take McDowell Road west for 2 miles and turn right, heading north onto Citrus Road. Take Citrus Road for 7 miles and then turn left onto Olive Avenue. Take Olive Avenue west for 3 miles until it turns into White Tank Mountain Road. Pass through the park gate and pay the fee. Take White Tank Mountain Road for 2 miles, then turn right onto Wildlife Way, heading east into the large parking lot. The Black Rock trailhead is across the street from the parking lot, on the west side of White Tank Mountain Road. **GPS Coordinates:** 33.5839 N, 112.502 W

Information and Contact

There is a fee of $6 per vehicle. An annual pass is available for $75. Dogs on leash are allowed. Maps are available at the park entrance. The park is open daily (6am-8pm Sun.-Thurs., 6am-10pm Fri.-Sat.). For more information, contact White Tank Mountain Regional Park, 20304 West White Tank Mountain Road, Waddell, AZ 85355, 623/935-2505, www.maricopa.gov/parks/white_tank.

4 GOAT CAMP TRAIL
White Tank Mountain Regional Park

Level: Strenuous

Total Distance: 6.4 miles round-trip

Hiking Time: 3.5 hours

Elevation Gain: 1,675 feet

Summary: More than six miles of beautiful scenery in and over Goat Canyon. Why aren't there more people on this trail?

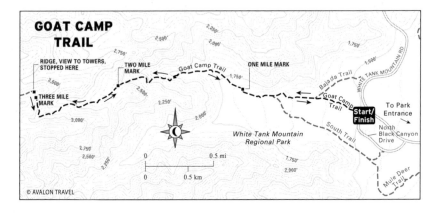

This is the perfect not-too-long, not-too-short trail. While the Goat Canyon Trail extends a lengthy 6.5 miles (one way) into the park along its southern boundary, this summary only covers the first 3.2 miles and stops at the ridge between Goat and Yellow Bull Canyons. The views to metal radio towers and the remaining White Tank Mountains to the north are the treat before you make the return trip.

As an up-and-back hike, the trip totals 6.4 miles. And you should take the "up" part of that very literally. Even though the first mile lulls you into a false sense of ease, the remaining distance to the ridge climbs almost 1,500 feet in a little over 2 miles. And without the aid of switchbacks—yeah, you'll be feeling that.

Start from the Goat Camp Trail trailhead and follow the trail heading west. Plan to maintain a general westerly direction for the entirety of this hike. At 0.7 mile, pass by the signed South Trail to your left (south). Keep moving west along the Goat Camp Trail, which has convenient green trail markers at each mile. Pass mile 1 with ease as you wiggle through flat terrain, a wash, and plenty of breathtaking views of the surrounding slopes that create Goat Canyon.

This hike feels as good as it looks.

Immediately after the first mile, you begin the hardy ascent that's not going to let up until you reach the distant saddle. Push, push, and push as you climb along the canyon's southern wall. At approximately 1.8 miles (after a particularly grueling portion), you reach a sandy clearing. Just a few more steps up and you reach the east end of Goat Canyon. Here, you have passed over the towering canyon walls. Enjoy as the terrain briefly mellows for a short quarter mile or so as you pass the mile 2 marker. Then the ascent picks up again, and at 2.8 miles, things get particularly steep as the trail suddenly turns right (north).

Pass the 3-mile marker and ascend the final 0.2 mile to the top of the ridge. From here, you can enjoy your hard-earned view of Yellow Bull Canyon to the north (as well as the remaining canyons and ridges throughout the White Tank Mountains), radio towers perched on the ridgelines to the west, and Goat Canyon to the east. You can easily see the remainder of the Goat Camp Trail as it cuts along the land to continue northwest.

Nice, right?

As tempting as the rest of the trail may be, this is a great place to turn around and enjoy a breezy descent back to the trailhead in the shade of Goat Canyon. It's all yours!

Options

If you're in the mood to go real big on this one, try for the entire **Goat Canyon Trail**. Instructions for this are pretty simple. When you get to the ridge between

Goat and Yellow Bull Canyons (at 3.2 miles), just keep following the Goat Camp Trail to the northwest and northeast. At approximately 6.3 miles, you encounter the junction with the Ford Canyon and Mesquite Canyon Trails. Turn around here and retrace your many, many steps back to the Goat Camp trailhead. Your total mileage for this hike is 12.6 miles. You went big!

Directions

From downtown Phoenix, take I-10 west toward Los Angeles for about 18 miles. Take the exit for Sarival Avenue and turn right, heading north, onto Sarival Avenue. After 0.2 mile, turn left onto McDowell Road. Take McDowell Road west for 2 miles and turn right, heading north, onto Citrus Road. Take Citrus Road for 7 miles and then turn left onto Olive Avenue. Take Olive Avenue west for 3 miles until it turns into White Tank Mountain Road. Pass through the park gate and pay the fee. Take White Tank Mountain Road for 0.6 mile. Turn left onto Black Canyon Drive and follow it for about 400 feet until the road curves north. The Goat Camp Trail trailhead and parking lot are on the left (west) side of Black Canyon Drive.

GPS Coordinates: 33.5688 N, 112.5055 W

Information and Contact

There is a fee of $6 per vehicle. An annual pass is available for $75. Dogs on leash are allowed. Maps are available at the park entrance. The park is open daily (6am-8pm Sun.-Thurs., 6am-10pm Fri.-Sat.). For more information, contact White Tank Mountain Regional Park, 20304 West White Tank Mountain Road, Waddell, AZ 85355, 623/935-2505, www.maricopa.gov/parks/white_tank.

5 GILA TO BASELINE LOOP

Estrella Mountain Regional Park

BEST Wheelchair-Accessible Trails

Level: Easy

Total Distance: 2.6 miles round-trip

Hiking Time: 1 hour

Elevation Gain: 300 feet

Summary: Have any opinions about the 1854 Gadsden Purchase? You might after this hike.

Why walk on the hard sidewalk when you can take a walk through the desert on a trail like this? Mostly flat and easy to follow, this little stroll wraps itself in and among the foothills of the Estrella mountain range. For this hike's fun fact, check out the flat rock at the Gila Trail trailhead, which marks the 1854 Gadsden Purchase Boundary Line. Without this purchase, the Sierra Estrella and the rest of southern Arizona would still belong to Mexico. That means no Wyatt Earp in Tombstone, no copper mines in Bisbee, and no Tucson. No thanks.

This hike was made possible by the Gadsden Purchase, which claimed the Sierra Estrella (and southern Arizona) from Mexico.

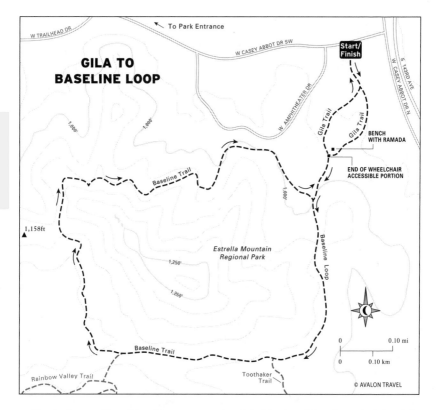

From the small parking lot, start on the Gila Trail and head south. The Gila Trail is a small, wheelchair-accessible, interpretive loop. You'll travel both sides of this loop by the end of this hike but, for now, veer left when you come to the fork in the path. After a scant 0.2 mile, you reach a small shaded bench at the south end of the Gila Trail loop. Follow the trail marker labeled "BA" and turn left (south) onto the Baseline Trail.

Continue south along the Baseline Trail for another few hundred feet. Notice that the Baseline Trail forks to the right (this will be your return route). Ignore the fork for now and continue south. The trail is easy to follow as it curves west with dramatic views of the Sierra Estrellas to the east. Notice a junction with the Toothaker Trail on the south side of the hill. Again, ignore this turnoff and continue on the Baseline Trail.

As the Baseline Trail curves north at 1.1 miles, expect an easy ascent of 100 feet. At 1.4 miles, the trail heads east. Notice that many other trails lead farther north. Continue along the Baseline Trail as it levels out and heads east. At 2 miles, you pass through a gentle dip in the landscape and close the loop. Make a sharp left turn (north) to follow the Baseline Trail. After just 0.1 mile, you once again reach the shaded bench on the Gila Trail. Take the Gila Trail branch on the left to experience the other side of this small loop. After 0.3 mile, you're back at the Gila Trail trailhead.

Two loops, one hike. Thank you, Gadsden Purchase.

Options
If you've got small children or a wheelchair in tow, opt for the shorter **Gila Trail**. The Gila Trail loop is a mere 0.5 mile round-trip with a wide, dirt-packed trail. It's also interpretive, so it's filled with educational information posted on pedestaled plaques.

Directions
From downtown Phoenix, take I-10 west toward Los Angeles for approximately 18 miles. Take exit 126 for Estrella Parkway/Pebble Creek Parkway. Turn left, heading south, onto Estrella Parkway for approximately 5 miles. Turn left, heading east, onto Vineyard Road. After 0.6 mile take the second right onto Casey Abbot Drive. Pass through the gate and pay the fee. Continue on Casey Abbot Drive for 0.8 mile as the road turns north, then heads east. Follow the road south as it becomes 143rd Drive. After 0.2 mile, take a right turn onto West Casey Abbot Road heading west. After approximately 400 feet, turn left (south) into the Gila Trail trailhead and parking area.
GPS Coordinates: 33.3816 N, 112.3703 W

Information and Contact
There is a fee of $6 per vehicle. An annual pass is available for $75. Dogs on leash are allowed. Maps are available at the park entrance. The park is open daily (6am-8pm Sun.-Thurs., 6am-10pm Fri.-Sat.). For more information, contact Estrella Mountain Regional Park, 14805 West Vineyard Avenue, Goodyear, AZ 85338, 623/932-3811, www.maricopa.gov/parks/estrella.

6 RAINBOW VALLEY TO TOOTHAKER LOOP

Estrella Mountain Regional Park

Level: Easy/Moderate

Total Distance: 6 miles round-trip

Hiking Time: 3 hours

Elevation Gain: 675 feet

Summary: What can be said about this hike? It's nice, it's pretty; not too hard, not too easy. It's like the baby bear's porridge to Goldilocks.

This loop begins with the Rainbow Valley Trail and eventually hooks into the Toothaker Trail. The loop walks over gentle slopes, briefly enters a canyon, traverses washes, and generally provides all the things a desert-lover is looking for.

To begin the hike, enter the Rainbow Valley and Toothaker Trails trailhead from the small ramada on the west side of the parking lot. Within a few feet, the trail splits between the Rainbow Valley and Toothaker Trails. Veer right to follow the Rainbow Valley Trail, which heads northwest. Note that this is where you'll eventually close the loop in about 6 miles.

The Rainbow Valley Trail is well signed and easy to follow. Within the first mile, you pass by a couple of intersections with the Baseline and Quail Trails. Just follow the Rainbow Valley Trail as you climb up and over a series of small foothills. At 1.75 mile, the trail takes a sharp turn south to travel away from the hills and over flat land. See the shady canyon to the southwest? You'll get there at mile 3 of this hike.

Once in the canyon you experience the main climb, approximately 375 feet over 1.4 miles. The trail is narrow along this stretch, and, for the first time, the civilization that's been lurking in the background finally melts away. At 3.75 miles, you emerge from the canyon and find the intersection with Toothaker Trail.

Take the Toothaker Trail northeast for the return leg to the trailhead. It's an easy descent that stretches along a mere two miles.

Options

For a shorter hike, take the **Dysart Trail** to cut the loop. Follow the Rainbow Valley Trail for approximately 2.75 miles and then take the Dysart Trail southeast for 0.6 mile until it intersects with the Toothaker Trail. Turn left to follow the Toothaker Trail northeast for 1 mile until you return to the trailhead. This hike amounts to 3.25 miles.

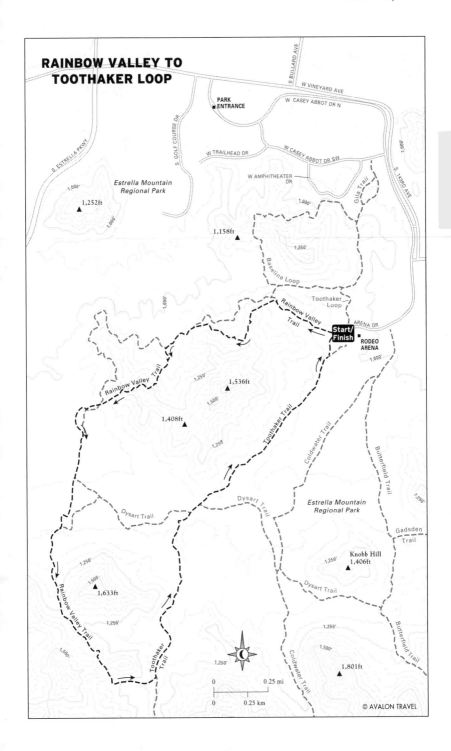

RAINBOW VALLEY TO
TOOTHAKER LOOP

PARK
ENTRANCE

W VINEYARD AVE
W CASEY ABBOT DR N

S BULLARD AVE
S GOLF COURSE DR
S ESTRELLA PKWY

W TRAILHEAD DR
W CASEY ABBOT DR SW

W AMPHITHEATER
DR

S 143RD AVE

Gila Trail

Estrella Mountain
Regional Park

1,000'

1,252ft

1,000'

1,000'

1,158ft

1,250'

Baseline Loop

1,000'

Toothaker
Loop

Rainbow Valley
Trail

ARENA DR

Start/
Finish

RODEO
ARENA

1,000'

Rainbow Valley Trail

1,250'

1,536ft

1,500'

1,408ft

Toothaker Trail

Coldwater Trail

1,250'

Butterfield Trail

1,250'

Dysart Trail

Dysart Trail

Estrella Mountain
Regional Park

Gadsden
Trail

1,250'

Knobb Hill
1,406ft

1,250'

1,250'

Dysart Trail

Rainbow Valley Trail

1,500'

1,633ft

1,250'

1,250'

Butterfield Trail

1,500'

Toothaker Trail

1,250'

Coldwater Trail

1,500'

1,801ft

0   0.25 mi

0   0.25 km

© AVALON TRAVEL

Follow the path into the canyon on the Rainbow Valley Trail.

Directions

From downtown Phoenix, take I-10 west toward Los Angeles for approximately 18 miles. Take exit 126 for Estrella Parkway/Pebble Creek Parkway. Turn left, heading south, onto Estrella Parkway and follow it for approximately 5 miles. Turn left, heading east, onto Vineyard Road. After 0.6 mile take the second right onto Casey Abbot Drive. Pass through the gate and pay the fee. Continue on Casey Abbot Drive for 0.8 mile as the road turns north, then heads east. Follow the road south as it becomes 143rd Drive. After 1 mile, take a slight right onto Arena Drive. The road ends in a large parking lot and Rodeo Arena staging area. The Rainbow Valley Trail trailhead is on the west side of the lot.
GPS Coordinates: 33.3705 N, 112.3727 W

Information and Contact

There is a fee of $6 per vehicle. An annual pass is available for $75. Dogs on leash are allowed. Maps are available at the park entrance. The park is open daily (6am-8pm Sun.-Thurs., 6am-10pm Fri.-Sat.). For more information, contact Estrella Mountain Regional Park, 14805 West Vineyard Avenue, Goodyear, AZ 85338, 623/932-3811, www.maricopa.gov/parks/estrella.

7 BUTTERFIELD TO GADSDEN TRAILS
Estrella Mountain Regional Park

Level: Moderate

Total Distance: 6.8 miles round-trip

Hiking Time: 3.5 hours

Elevation Gain: 800 feet

Summary: Estrella Mountain Regional Park brings it again with another lengthy loop.

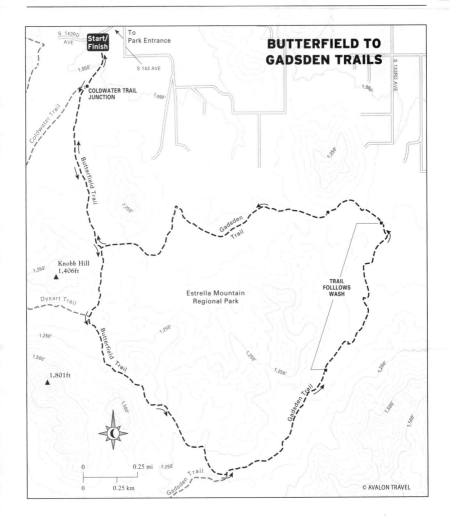

On a rainy day, this hiker rocked the poncho on the Butterfield and Gadsden Trails.

Man, there's just no shortage of long-winded loops in this park. This combination of trails explores the east side of the Estrella Mountain Regional Park and butts right up to the massive Sierra Estrella Mountains to the east. After a gentle ascent on the Butterfield Trail of 400 feet over the first 2 miles, you hop onto the Gadsden Trail to follow a large wash. Once out of the wash, the Gadsden Trail heads back toward the Butterfield Trail to create this lasso-shaped loop. It's yet another desert stroll available to hikers interested in mileage rather than elevation gain.

Start the hike at the Coldwater Trail trailhead on the south side of the parking area. Head southwest on Coldwater Trail, a wide dirt road, for just 0.1 mile. Look to the left (east) side of the road for the Butterfield Trail sign. Hop on the Butterfield Trail and follow it south as you begin the gentle ascent. The trail wiggles its way southeast as it climbs the terrain. Take note of the turnoff at 1.1 miles to Gadsden Trail; this will be your point of return after creating the "lasso" of this hike. For now, continue southeast on the Butterfield Trail.

At 1.5 miles, the trail enters an area speckled with quartz rock, making for some pretty trailside scenes. At 2 miles, the trail reaches its high point at 1,370 feet. Here's your best view of the Sierra Estrella Mountains to the east. At 2.4 miles, veer left to join the Gadsden Trail heading east. Continue along Gadsden Trail as it curves to the northeast and enters a large wash at 3 miles. The trail bounces in and out of the wash once or twice, then remains along the sandy bottom. With the wash's tall walls surrounding you, the rest of the world is blocked out until mile 4, when you finally emerge onto higher land.

From here, the Gadsden Trail heads west as you stroll up and down some rolling hills. At 5.7 miles, the Gadsden Trail runs into the Butterfield Trail. Turn right to follow the Butterfield Trail north as you retrace your steps for 1 mile. When you collide with the Coldwater Trail, take a right to follow it north for just 0.1 mile back to the trailhead and parking lot.

Options

For a shorter walk through this side of the park, opt for a tiny loop by combining the Butterfield Trail with the Dysart and Coldwater Trails. For this, follow the Butterfield Trail south for only 1.3 miles. Take a right onto Dysart Trail, heading west for 0.5 mile. Turn right (north) onto Coldwater Trail and follow it for the 1.1 miles back to the Coldwater trailhead. This option totals 3.1 miles.

Directions

From downtown Phoenix, take I-10 west toward Los Angeles for approximately 18 miles. Take exit 126 for Estrella Parkway/Pebble Creek Parkway. Turn left, heading south, onto Estrella Parkway and follow it for approximately 5 miles. Turn left, heading east, onto Vineyard Road. After 0.6 mile take the second right onto Casey Abbot Drive. Pass through the gate and pay the fee. Continue on Casey Abbot Drive for 0.8 mile as the road turns north, then heads east. Follow the road south as it becomes 143rd Drive. After 1 mile, take a slight right onto Arena Drive and then immediately veer left into the parking lot, located east of the arena. The Butterfield Trail trailhead is on the southeast end of the lot.

GPS Coordinates: 33.3703 N, 112.3686 W

Information and Contact

There is a fee of $6 per vehicle. An annual pass is available for $75. Dogs on leash are allowed. Maps are available at the park entrance. The park is open daily (6am-8pm Sun.-Thurs., 6am-10pm Fri.-Sat.). For more information, contact Estrella Mountain Regional Park, 14805 West Vineyard Avenue, Goodyear, AZ 85338, 623/932-3811, www.maricopa.gov/parks/estrella.

SOUTH VALLEY

© LILIA MENCONI

The blinking red lights atop the metal towers on
South Mountain's ridgelines are a familiar sight to Valley residents. Those
symbols of industry are perched among more than 16,000 acres of desert
preserve, where hikers can explore endless combinations of ridgeline passes,
wash walkways, and paved roads in this 51-mile spider web of trails. Petroglyphs
are scattered throughout the Ma Ha Tauk, Gila, and Guadalupe ranges in South
Mountain Park, which also boast a wealth of small lookout structures built by the
Civilian Conservation Corps. Hikers know Picacho Peak, southeast of Phoenix,
as an adrenaline-junkie's dream, while San Tan Mountain Regional Park awaits
with 10,000 acres filled with creosote and saguaro forests and a mass of intersecting trails. Take your pick—you really can't go wrong with the South Valley.

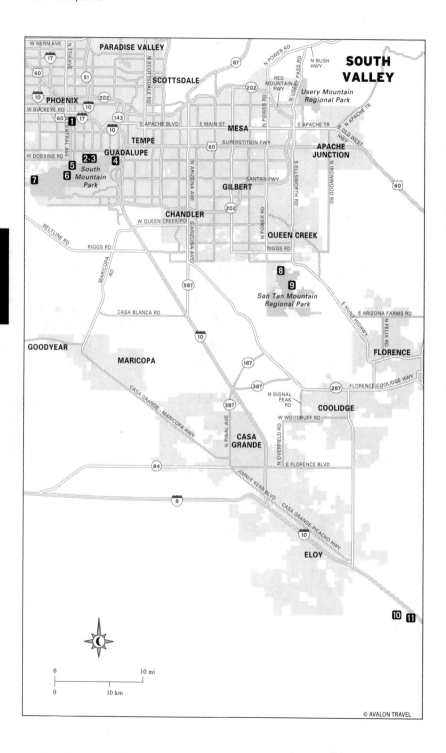

TRAIL NAME	FEATURES	LEVEL	DISTANCE	TIME	ELEVATION	PAGE
1 North Overbank and North Terrace Loop		Easy	3.5 mi rt	1.5 hr	150 ft	122
2 Mormon Trail to Hidden Valley Loop		Easy/Moderate	3.6 mi rt	2 hr	1,000 ft	125
3 Geronimo Trail		Moderate	5 mi rt	2.5 hr	1,200 ft	128
4 Pima Wash Trail		Easy	2.9 mi rt	1.5 hr	250 ft	131
5 Holbert Trail		Easy/Moderate	3.6 mi rt	2 hr	950 ft	134
6 Kiwanis Trail to Telegraph Pass Lookout		Easy/Moderate	2.7 mi rt	1 hr	700 ft	137
7 National Trail BEST		Butt-kicker	14.7 mi one-way	8.5 hr	2,400 ft	140
8 Goldmine and Dynamite Loop		Easy/Moderate	4.7 mi rt	2 hr	650 ft	145
9 San Tan Loop BEST		Moderate	7.4 mi rt	3.5 hr	800 ft	148
10 Sunset Vista Trail BEST		Moderate	4.7 mi rt	2.5 hr	1,100 ft	152
11 Hunter Trail BEST		Butt-kicker	3 mi rt	4.1 hr	1,900 ft	155

1 NORTH OVERBANK AND NORTH TERRACE LOOP

Rio Salado Habitat Restoration Area

Level: Easy

Total Distance: 3.5 miles round-trip

Hiking Time: 1.5 hours

Elevation Gain: 150 feet

Summary: Take this opportunity to explore a rare Sonoran wetland.

No bones about it, this hike puts the "urban" in urban hiking. Located in south-central Phoenix (running along the south side of the I-10), this trail walks on a tiny strip of riparian preserve land surrounded by industrial businesses. Just a heads-up; you're more likely to see a few folks from the street rather than nature-hungry hikers along this trek.

The Rio Salado Habitat opened in 2005 and initiated an effort to recreate some of the natural habitat that characterized the area before the Salt River was dammed. Today the Rio Salado Habitat Restoration Area offers 16 miles of trails that stretch on the north and south sides of the Salt River riverbed, from 19th Avenue to 24th Street. While most of the riverbed remains rocky and dry, some areas are bombarded with lush cottonwood and willow trees that drink from the remaining pools of water. Local wildlife such as herons, owls, and egrets can be seen along the way. For this hike, the trip begins at the duck pond on the east side

This hike begins under the bridge downtown.

of Central Avenue, follows a paved path overlooking the riverbed, and then returns along its rocky "shores." Best done midday with a group or as a family, this hike is flat all the way and perfect for a chat-filled walk.

To begin the hike, head for the pond at the south side of the Northeast Central Avenue trailhead parking lot. Head to the east along the paved sidewalk and continue as it turns to asphalt. It's well-marked all the way; just follow signs for the North Overbank Trail. A few alternative routes explore the nooks and crannies of this area, but keep veering east and you'll soon find yourself on a lone, straight path that is the North Overbank Trail.

A paved asphalt walkway continues for 1.5 miles. The riverbed is to your right with industrial sites on your left (here's the urban part). Enjoy the view below of this unique area—by the way, your return leg walks you right through it.

By approximately 1.5 miles you've passed under a few bridges to finally reach the overpass for 16th Street. Veer right as the path descends to the riverbed. Then make a U-turn onto the North Terrace Trail to walk west along the riverbed. Did you see anything you liked during the first leg? Now you can get a closer look. This return trip walks along a Sonoran wetland—a rare place today since 90 percent of Sonoran wetlands have disappeared or been destroyed in the last few hundred years.

At approximately 3.1 miles, you'll pass over a water drainage that has been fashioned into a small, peaceful waterfall. Then, after about 3.3 miles total, take the turnoff to your right and ascend up from the "waterfront." Within 0.2 mile, pass through the signed Monarch Waystation, where you might see a flurry of fluttering orange and black wings surround you (especially during September).

After passing the Monarch Waystation, you're close to the parking lot. You're also revisiting the multiple trails that weave around this area. Remember, the Northeast Central Avenue trailhead parking lot is to the north (if you pass under Central Avenue heading west, you've gone too far).

Options

To add another leg to this journey, consider exploring the portion of the North Overbank Trail that runs west from Central Avenue to 19th Avenue. When you complete the North Overbank and North Terrace Loop, pass by the Northeast Central Avenue parking lot heading west to reconnect with the North Overbank Trail. Continue west to see more of the Salt River's riverbed and riparian areas. After 1.2 miles, the pavement turns to a soft dirt trail. Follow this for another 0.5 mile and turn around to head east when it comes to an end at 19th Avenue. Once you pass Central Avenue, find the Northeast Central Avenue trailhead parking lot to the north. Adding this portion of the trail makes for a total of 7 miles.

Directions

From downtown Phoenix, head west on Washington Street and turn left, heading south, onto 4th Avenue. Take the first left onto Jefferson Street heading east for 0.2 mile. Turn right onto 1st Avenue and follow it south. Stay left at the fork and continue onto Central Avenue. After about 1 mile turn left, heading east into the Northeast Central Avenue trailhead parking lot (2439 S. Central Ave., open sunrise-sunset). The North Overbank trailhead is on the east side of the parking lot and duck pond.

GPS Coordinates: 33.4239 N, 112.0923 W

Information and Contact

There is no fee. Dogs on leash are allowed on the paved trails only. Maps are available online at www.phoenix.gov/parks. For more information, contact City of Phoenix Parks and Recreation Main Office, Phoenix City Hall, 200 West Washington Street, 16th Floor, Phoenix, AZ 85003, 602/262-6863, www.phoenix.gov/parks.

2 MORMON TRAIL TO HIDDEN VALLEY LOOP

South Mountain Park

Level: Easy/Moderate

Total Distance: 3.6 miles round-trip

Hiking Time: 2 hours

Elevation Gain: 1,000 feet

Summary: Whatever you do, don't neglect this incredible trail to a natural rock tunnel, Fat Man's Pass, and the Hidden Valley.

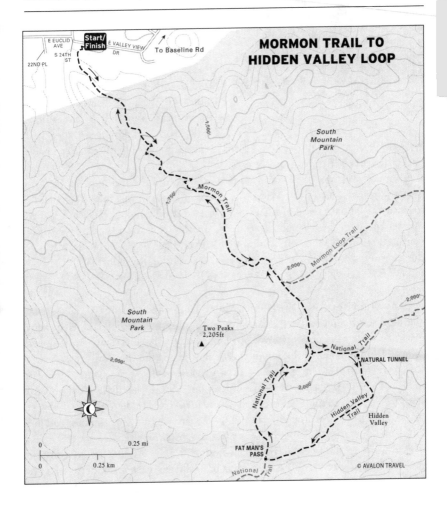

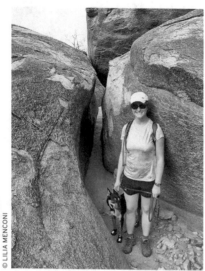

Squeezing through Fat Man's Pass proves to be little challenge to this pair of hikers.

Woo-hoo! This trail is awesome!

That's what you'll feel like saying after you trek 3.6 miles and up 1,000 feet to experience one of the best natural hide-outs in the city, the Hidden Valley of South Mountain Park. Hidden Valley is a curious basin of flat terrain that sits on top of the Guadalupe Range. The mini-valley is filled with bushy desert vegetation (like paloverde and creosote), towering saguaros, and two naturally occurring rock passes—the Natural Tunnel and Fat Man's Pass—on either end of the Hidden Valley trail. The Mormon Trail leads you to this wonderful place and, conveniently, provides a heart-pumping climb with beautiful views of the city to the north. Kids will dig the curious rock passes and parents will get their desired workout. And if that's not enough to keep the kids interested, keep an eye out for possible petroglyphs in the area.

From the Mormon Trail trailhead parking lot, find the trailhead on the lot's west end. Haul yourself up a steady climb of 800 feet in just one mile heading southeast. Right after you hit that first mile (at 1.2 miles), notice a clearly signed intersection with the Mormon *Loop* Trail, which juts in from the east (not to be confused with the Mormon Trail, on which you have traveled thus far). Ignore the Mormon *Loop* Trail and continue southeast on the Mormon Trail for a short 0.2 mile. Here, take a left turn (east) to briefly hook up with the National Trail for a mere 0.2 mile.

Hang a right turn onto the Hidden Valley Trail at the next signed intersection and head south. Soon after the turn, you encounter the Natural Tunnel, a shady mass of boulders under which you can comfortably walk. The rock here is rubbed smooth from the many hikers' hands that have traced the cool walls.

Soon the trail gets a little funny—it's easy to lose track of where you're supposed to be. When the proper path seems to peter out, pick a friendly boulder on your right (west) and scramble over it. Boom. You're in The Hidden Valley.

It's tough to decipher the official trail in this sandy basin. Do your best and just follow the direction of the land. Rocky borders tower on either side of the valley, so it's intuitive to follow the trail's southwest direction. After 0.5 mile, you find the well-known Fat Man's Pass, which is basically a narrow crack between a few boulders that you can squeeze through (though you may need to remove your pack to make it). Or you can bypass the squeeze with a trail to the right.

Once you've made it through Fat Man's Pass, notice signs for the National Trail. Turn right (north) at the signed juncture and follow the National Trail for 0.4 mile until it hooks back up with the Mormon Trail. Turn left (north) and retrace your steps for 1.4 miles down the mountain and back to your car.

And then say, "Woo-hoo! This trail is awesome!"

Options

For a longer hike, combine these trails with the **Mormon Loop Trail**. Follow the Mormon Trail for 1.2 miles. This time, turn left, heading northeast, on the Mormon Loop Trail for 1.1 miles. Make a right turn heading south for 0.2 mile (on a short connecting trail), then turn right onto the National Trail. Follow the National Trail heading southwest for 1.4 miles. Take a left at the sign for Hidden Valley Trail to scramble over the boulders into the Hidden Valley. Follow the Hidden Valley Trail for 0.5 mile southwest through the Natural Tunnel and Fat Man's Pass. Turn right to take the National Trail north for 0.4 mile and then turn left to reconnect with the Mormon Trail. Take the Mormon Trail northwest for 1.4 miles back to the Mormon Trail parking lot. This option totals 6.2 miles.

Directions

From downtown Phoenix, take 7th Avenue south for approximately 5 miles. Turn left, heading east onto Baseline Road. Take Baseline Road for 3 miles, then turn right onto 24th Street. Take 24th Street south for 0.8 mile and continue on as it curves east and becomes Valley View Drive. Follow Valley View Drive for 250 feet. Turn right into the Mormon Trail trailhead parking lot (8610 S. 24th St., open 5am-7pm). The trailhead is on the west side of the lot.
GPS Coordinates: 33.3664 N, 112.0306 W

Information and Contact

There is no fee. Dogs on leash are allowed. Maps are available online at www.phoenix.gov/parks. For more information, contact City of Phoenix Parks and Recreation Main Office, Phoenix City Hall, 200 West Washington Street, 16th Floor, Phoenix, AZ 85003, 602/262-6862, www.phoenix.gov/parks.

3 GERONIMO TRAIL

South Mountain Park

Level: Moderate

Total Distance: 5 miles round-trip

Hiking Time: 2.5 hours

Elevation Gain: 1,200 feet

Summary: This little-known trail with its teeny-tiny trailhead turned out to be a favorite of South Mountain Park.

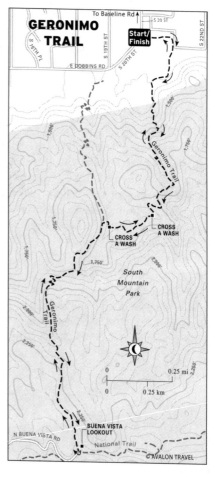

Have you ever had one of those days when you're writing a hiking book and the trail you're supposed to hike that day doesn't have an accessible trailhead? And so you scramble to find a replacement trail and then end up hiking the most amazing (and totally off the radar) trail in the city? No?

Hmmm. Okay, so maybe you're a regular person who hikes for leisure, not for a living. No matter what your inspiration for hiking might be, you'll discover even more inspiration on the Geronimo Trail. With its blink-and-you-miss-it trailhead nestled deep in a south Phoenix neighborhood, this relatively unknown trail is a true diamond in the rough. Follow it to discover a quiet, unnamed canyon in the Guadalupe Range, then climb up to the fantastic Buena Vista Lookout at 2,360 feet.

Start the hike from the Geronimo trailhead to the south of the small dirt clearing (hardly worthy of the label "parking lot"). The first 0.5 mile passes by private residences heading east, then turns south to pass a Boy Scouts

The Geronimo Trail guarantees stellar views of downtown Phoenix.

of America park and reaches the north side of the Guadalupe Range in South Mountain Park.

At 0.5 mile, begin to climb a healthy 400 feet over the next half mile. After 1 mile, you reach a small saddle and (whoa!) can look down to a secluded canyon. Don't forget to glance north to see a smashing view of the downtown Phoenix skyline. Make a short descent into the canyon, cross a dry wash, and enjoy the flat terrain for the next 0.2 mile heading southwest. Cross another wash, then begin to climb out of the canyon. At 1.5 miles, ignore an unmarked turnoff to the north and continue along the Geronimo Trail south.

Be prepared to keep climbing, because this elevation gain takes you all the way to the top. Ignore any connecting trails to the northwest. When you see a bench and the parking lot of the Buena Vista Lookout beyond, you've reached your stopping point at 2.5 miles. You can see the south side of the Guadalupe Range from here and absolutely superb views of Camelback and Phoenix Mountains to the north.

From Buena Vista Lookout, simply turn around to follow the Geronimo Trail northeast, back to your car.

Options

The Buena Vista Lookout is great and all, but this trail promises beautiful views for most of the hike. For a shorter jaunt with a sweaty climb and rewarding views, simply take the Geronimo Trail to that first saddle a mere 1 mile into the park. From there, you're guaranteed a satisfying view of the downtown Phoenix skyline to the north and that spectacular little canyon to the south. Return to the parking area from there for a hike that totals 2 miles.

Directions

From downtown Phoenix, take 7th Avenue south for 4.9 miles. Turn left, heading east onto Baseline Road. After 2.4 miles turn right, heading south, onto 20th Street. After 0.9 mile veer left to stay on 20th Street (the main road veers to the right and becomes Dobbins Road). Turn right into a very small dirt clearing and park. The trailhead is on the south side of the parking area.
GPS Coordinates: 33.3651N, 112.0401W

Information and Contact

There is no fee. Dogs on leash are allowed. Maps are available online at www.phoenix.gov/parks. For more information, contact City of Phoenix Parks and Recreation Main Office, Phoenix City Hall, 200 West Washington Street, 16th Floor, Phoenix, AZ 85003, 602/262-6862, www.phoenix.gov/parks.

4 PIMA WASH TRAIL
South Mountain Park

Level: Easy

Total Distance: 2.9 miles round-trip

Hiking Time: 1.5 hours

Elevation Gain: 250 feet

Summary: Saunter along the sandy trail in a wash that cuts through the east end of South Mountain Park.

Hikes in and along a wash always offer a relaxed, serene approach to hiking...if the wash is not filled with a torrential gush of rainwater, that is. But you know you're never to hike in a wash if there's a storm anywhere near the area.

On clear days, the flat, sandy terrain makes you feel like you're walking on the sandy shores of a beach (minus the ocean, of course). The Pima Wash Trail makes a dramatic gash through the packed dirt and rock in the foothills south of the Guadalupe Range in South Mountain Park. As you follow this easy trail, you feel cut off from the rest of the park with the tall, dusty walls on either side of you. As a waterway, the wash boasts an abundance of leafy mesquite and paloverde

Follow this sandy wash for an easy stroll through South Mountain Park.

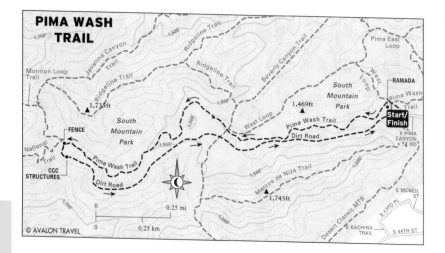

trees. You're not the only one who can enjoy this riparian landscape. As you stroll along, you may come across a chuckwalla lizard (yes, this happened in real life). A chuckwalla may be quick to scurry away, but you can't miss this crazy lizard—those suckers can grow up to 16 inches in length.

From the Pima Canyon trailhead parking lot, look for the Pima Wash Trail trailhead on the east side of the ramada. The signpost is labeled "West Pima Trail." After descending a small ravine, look to the left for your next trail marker, which reads "Pima Wash." Beyond it, you can easily follow the sandy wash as it winds its way west. The trail is well-marked and won't often put your navigation skills to the test. It will, however, lead you out of the wash from time to time but always returns to the wash after a few feet.

That's really all there is to it. You know you've reached the end of the wash when, at 1.6 miles, you run smack into a fence. Take a left turn and follow the trail as it climbs southwest. Soon, you see trail signs for the National Trail (its east end-point is here). Look to the southeast to see two Civilian Conservation Corps structures.

Here, you have your choice of returning to the trailhead via the Pima Wash Trail or, for new scenery, following the wide dirt road that takes you east and back to the Pima Canyon trailhead parking lot to complete a 2.9-mile loop.

Options

For a longer and more strenuous trek, add a loop by combining the Beverly Canyon and Javelina Canyon Trails with the **Ridgeline Trail**. For this 5.3-mile journey, take the Pima Wash Trail for approximately 0.8 mile west, then take a right turn onto the Beverly Canyon Trail to the northeast. After 0.9 mile, veer left to head northwest as the trail runs into the 46th Street trailhead and becomes the Javelina Canyon Trail. Follow the Javelina Canyon Trail for 1.8 miles southwest and climb approximately 420 feet. Once you've reached the ridge, turn left onto the Ridgeline Trail, which follows a ridge for 1 mile and descends to close the loop at your starting point, back at Beverly Canyon Trail. Take Beverly Canyon Trail south for approximately 0.1 mile. Turn left onto Pima Wash Trail and head east for 0.8 mile back to the Pima Wash trailhead.

Directions

From downtown Phoenix, take I-10 toward Tucson for about 10 miles. Take exit 155 for Baseline Road (toward Guadalupe) for 1 mile. Turn right, headed west, onto Baseline Road. After 0.6 mile turn left, heading south onto 48th Street for 0.6 mile. At the traffic circle, take the second exit onto Pointe Parkway. Follow the curvy Pointe Parkway for 0.9 mile and make a sharp right turn onto 48th Street. After 275 feet, make an immediate turn left, heading west onto Pima Canyon Road. Pass through the entrance gate. After 0.6 mile, the road ends at the Pima Canyon trailhead parking lot (open 5am-7pm). The Pima Wash trailhead is on the northeast side of the lot, east of the large ramada.

GPS Coordinates: 33.3629 N, 111.9856 W

Information and Contact

There is no fee. Dogs on leash are allowed. Maps are available online at www.phoenix.gov/parks. For more information, contact City of Phoenix Parks and Recreation Main Office, Phoenix City Hall, 200 West Washington Street, 16th Floor, Phoenix, AZ 85003, 602/262-6862, www.phoenix.gov/parks.

5 HOLBERT TRAIL
South Mountain Park

Level: Easy/Moderate

Total Distance: 3.6 miles round-trip

Hiking Time: 2 hours

Elevation Gain: 950 feet

Summary: Trace the west side of Piedmont Canyon all the way up to Dobbins Lookout, the highest accessible point of South Mountain Park.

At 2,330 feet, Dobbins Lookout is as high as you can get in South Mountain Park. And because everyone should enjoy such a wonderful spot, most people just drive there. But not you. You're going to hike. And then feel really awesome about it because, for a hiker, driving to a lookout just *feels* wrong.

There's no question that the Holbert Trail is the hiker's preferred way to reach Dobbin's Lookout. Following a single trail all the way, this is a no-brainer for route finding. And with 950 feet of climbing, you may not have the energy for brain activity anyhow. But, try to remember as your cardio workout gets moving that you're in petroglyph country and you'll miss some fine examples if you're not looking.

© KRISTINA SMITH

Portions of the Holbert Trail hit the pavement, but there's still plenty of dirt and desert rocks.

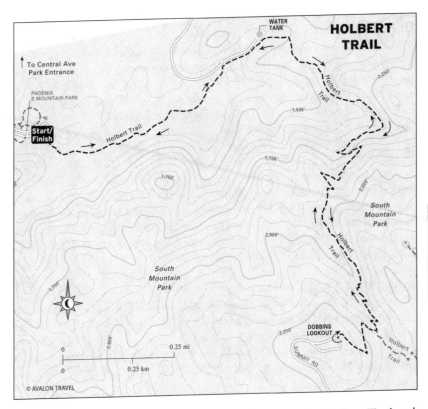

From the east end of the large parking lot, hop onto the Holbert Trail and head east, along a flat dirt path. At 0.6 mile, veer right to follow the paved road for 0.2 mile. At 0.8 mile, pass by the water tank to the north and continue on the Holbert Trail as it heads east and then curves south at 0.9 mile. This is where the real climbing begins. In just 1 mile, you climb approximately 750 feet along the west wall of Piedmont Canyon. Only a couple of switchbacks ease the journey. At 1.8 miles, veer right to follow a small spur heading west to Dobbins Lookout. Again, follow the switchbacks for the additional 150 feet gained in just 0.2 mile.

After the climb, you suddenly pop out of the canyon and onto the paved Summit Road. Dobbins Lookout is on the north side of the road and is recognizable by the CCC-built structure. Others will be there, choking the air with their car exhaust. But that's okay, you can still enjoy the amazing view to the north of Phoenix Mountains, McDowell Mountains, and (on a clear day) Four Peaks. That's what 2,330 feet will give you.

Once satisfied, leave Dobbins Lookout and retrace your steps along Holbert Trail for a 1.8-mile descent to the trailhead.

Options

Why not make a go at the entire Holbert Trail while you're at it? It's pretty easy. After returning to Holbert Trail from Dobbins Lookout, take a sharp right to continue along the remaining 0.7 mile of the trail heading south. After 0.3 mile, cross Buena Vista Road then start a 0.4-mile ascent of 300 feet that ends when Holbert Trail smacks into the National Trail. Turn around here and return the way you came, following Holbert Trail north all the way for a total of 5 miles.

Directions

From downtown Phoenix, take Central Avenue south for about 6 miles. Follow the road as it curves southwest. Approximately 0.3 mile from the curve, just past the park main entrance (10409 S. Central Ave.), turn left and head east for approximately 0.4 mile. Pass the South Mountain Environmental Education Center and park at the far eastern end of the large parking lot to find the Holbert trailhead. **GPS Coordinates:** 33.3518 N, 112.0701 W

Information and Contact

There is no fee. Dogs on leash are allowed. Maps are available at the **South Mountain Environmental Education Center** (10409 S. Central Ave., 602/753-6047) or online at www.phoenix.gov/parks. For more information, contact City of Phoenix Parks and Recreation Main Office, Phoenix City Hall, 200 West Washington Street, 16th Floor, Phoenix, AZ 85003, 602/262-6862 or 602/262-7393, www.phoenix.gov/parks.

6 KIWANIS TRAIL TO TELEGRAPH PASS LOOKOUT

South Mountain Park

Level: Easy/Moderate

Total Distance: 2.7 miles round-trip

Hiking Time: 1 hour

Elevation Gain: 700 feet

Summary: One of the best weeknight hikes in The Valley, this hike travels through a small canyon and climbs to Telegraph Pass Lookout.

Throw away that gym membership. If you can complete this hike multiple times per week, you won't need a treadmill or a stair machine. Not to mention, the scenery is undoubtedly better. The Kiwanis Trail leads hikers through a boulder-speckled canyon, over sandy washes, and among ancient petroglyphs. You can see two rock-wall dams built by the Civilian Conservation Corps in the 1930s and plenty of wildlife dashing (or slithering) between paloverde trees. After ending the Kiwanis Trail at a road on the opposite side of the canyon, you hop on the National Trail for a quick 0.3 mile to Telegraph Pass Lookout, complete with a

© LILIA MENCONI

Kick back at the Telegraph Pass Lookout structure built by the CCC.

stone structure built by (you guessed it) the CCC.

From the trailhead, follow the well-traveled Kiwanis Trail south. Enjoy the shade as you enter this canyon and continue along the Kiwanis Trail, which, in spite of a few wiggles, remains heading southward. Even though the walls on either side get steeper, you're ascending at a steady rate. There shouldn't be any problems navigating your way, so don't forget to keep on the lookout for petroglyphs carved into the neighboring rocks.

At just about 1 mile in, notice cars cruising on Summit Road, which curls around the south end of the canyon. After passing by the rock dam, a short climb leads to the pavement. Follow the sign to the National Trail, which requires you to head south, across the street. Pick up the trail on the other side of the road and continue south on the National Trail, which climbs through a few somewhat-strenuous switchbacks. After 0.3 mile, arrive at the stone structure on top of the ridge, marking Telegraph Pass Lookout.

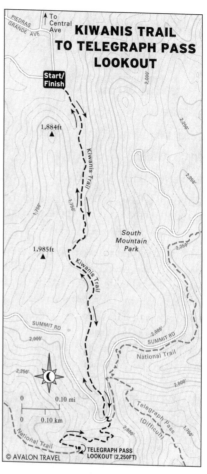

Have a seat, take in the views, and decipher the graffiti scrawled in the CCC structure. Hey, at least it's on a man-made structure rather than the surrounding boulders, right?

Once you've had your fill, retrace your steps and enjoy the 1.3-mile descent during the return trip to the Kiwanis Trail trailhead.

Options

For a longer hike, consider adding the **Telegraph Pass Trail**. After taking in the views at Telegraph Pass Lookout, retrace your steps along the National Trail, back to the road. Instead of crossing onto the Kiwanis Trail, continue east on the National Trail for a short 0.1 mile until you find the Telegraph Pass Trail to the right (south). Turn right onto the Telegraph Pass Trail to descend approximately 600 feet. After 0.9 mile, you come to a fork. Veer right (west) to avoid the eastbound

Desert Classic Trail and remain on the Telegraph Pass Trail for another 0.5 mile. The trail ends on the trailhead on the south side of the park. Turn back to ascend the mountain and try to retrace your steps along the Telegraph Pass Trail to the National Trail to the Kiwanis Trail. This option creates an out-and-back adventure that totals approximately 6 miles.

Directions

From downtown Phoenix, take Central Avenue south for approximately 6 miles until it curves southwest and into the main entrance for South Mountain Park. Follow the road southwest to pass the South Mountain Park Main Entrance and restrooms. After approximately 0.5 mile from the curve, follow the sign for Kiwanis Trail and turn left, heading southeast on Las Lomitas Trail. In less than 0.5 mile, take a left turn, heading east to follow the sign for Kiwanis Trail. In approximately 100 feet, turn right into the Kiwanis trailhead parking lot. The Kiwanis Trail trailhead is on the southeast corner of the lot.

GPS Coordinates: 33.3407N, 112.0762W

Information and Contact

There is no fee. Dogs on leash are allowed. Maps are available online at www.phoenix.gov/parks. For more information, contact City of Phoenix Parks and Recreation Main Office, Phoenix City Hall, 200 West Washington Street, 16th Floor, Phoenix, AZ 85003, 602/262-6862, www.phoenix.gov/parks.

7 NATIONAL TRAIL
South Mountain Park

BEST Butt-Kickers

Level: Butt-kicker

Total Distance: 14.7 miles one-way

Hiking Time: 8.5 hours

Elevation Gain: 2,400 feet

Summary: This is the longest and most glorious hike in the area, and it's a huge accomplishment for any hiker.

"I almost want to say that hike was spiritual," a Phoenix hiker remarked after completing the daunting and incredible National Trail. Well put.

At 14.7 miles, this all-day hike hauls from end to end of South Mountain Park. And it's no cake-walk, kids. With a cumulative elevation gain of 2,400 feet, you have to grunt your way up relentless inclines for miles on end. It's brutal—and it's absolutely incredible. All that work pays off with ah-*mazing* views in every direction, passing by abandoned mineshafts, various CCC-built lookout structures, rock formations, and junctions with almost every other trail in the entire park. Bring a trusted friend on this trail and you'll forge a lasting bond unique to the experience of conquering an intimidating challenge together.

Okay, enough of the squishy stuff. Here's what you need to know: Start early.

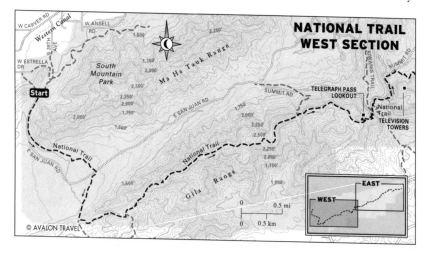

Bring enough water for an entire day of hiking. Bring plenty of food and snacks. Take along an extra pair of socks to make a mid-hike switch-out. Pack some moleskin for the inevitable blister. Arrange for a ride or a pre-parked car at the Pima Canyon trailhead on the far east end of South Mountain Park (this review covers the trail from west to east). Check online (www.phoenix.gov/parks) to validate that the west end trailhead is accessible, because its hours can vary. Oh, and print yourself a map. Though the trail is frequently labeled and easy to follow, this trail starts in the Ma Ha Tauk Range, passes through the Gila Range, then follows the Guadalupe Range. Yes, covering this kind of mileage requires you to know where you are at all times.

Let's get started. From the National Trail trailhead on the west end of the park (across the parking lot from the San Juan Lookout), follow the National Trail heading south as it traces the paved San Juan Road. At just 0.5 mile, the trail veers southeast and momentarily leaves the road, only to cross over it at 1.5 miles, officially leaving the Ma Ha Tauk Mountain Range. After crossing, veer right (southwest) to follow the clearly marked National Trail.

At approximately 2.2 miles, you're treated to the first dramatic view of the Sierra Estrella Mountains, which completely dominate the horizon to the west. It's here also that you begin to climb, heading east/northeast, which is the general direction for the remainder of the hike. So far, the trail has been flat and easy. This is about to change big-time. Drag yourself up 1,200 feet in 2.7 miles only to continue climbing up and down the ridgeline of the Gila Mountain Range. This stretch also passes by abandoned mineshafts, which are easily recognized (they are the really big, really deep holes). Don't go in them.

At 4.9 miles, you reach the highest point of the hike at 2,507 feet. No signs or lookouts mark this spot, but when you can first see the metal television towers

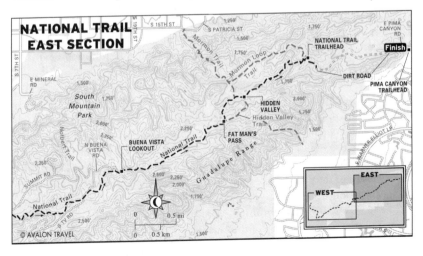

© LILIA MENCONI

Some might say this challenging 14.7-mile hike is downright spiritual.

in the distance, you know you've reached the high point (and you've successfully completed approximately one-third of the hike).

At 6.3 miles, near an unsuspecting trail marker, you can look below to the Telegraph Pass Lookout to the east, built by the Civilian Conservation Corps. In fact, you can look below to just about everything in town, with vast views of the Phoenix Sky Harbor Airport and the Phoenix Mountains Preserve to the northeast and the San Tan Mountains to the southeast.

After passing by the Telegraph Pass Lookout structure at 6.8 miles, follow a few switchbacks heading north, toward the paved Summit Road. Take a sharp right to follow the signed National Trail (now a narrow dirt path along the east side of the road) as it wiggles north. At 7.9 miles, you may groan as you climb approximately 400 feet over the next mile.

Things soon mellow out, and aside from the occasional brief walk up an incline, your major climbing is finished for the day (whew!). At 9.4 miles, you encounter another paved road. Look to the east, across the street, for a sign to continue following the National Trail east. At 10.1 miles, follow another paved road as you pass the Buena Vista Lookout and parking lot. The trail follows the south side of Buena Vista Road with a large trail sign to the east of the parking lot. Thankfully, that's the last of the paved roads and you've now cleared approximately two-thirds of the entire journey.

The next few miles travel through some of the most beautiful terrain of the park. This flat area sits on top of the Guadalupe Range, and while it's not quite a mesa, the dramatic rock formations, sandy washes, and abundance of paloverde trees make you feel like you're in a valley. It's fitting, because at 11.8 miles, you encounter Fat Man's Pass, a tight squeeze between two enormous boulders that act as the west entrance to the Hidden Valley. The National Trail merely passes by Fat Man's Pass and the Hidden Valley. Be aware, because in this area there are many trail junctions. Just keep your eyes open for National Trail signs, follow them, and you'll be fine.

After passing by the east end of the Hidden Valley Trail at 12.3 miles, you can officially consider yourself on the home stretch with a mere 2.4 miles to go! At 12.4 miles, however, there's a tear-inducing climb of 130 feet over a mere 0.4 mile. Ouch, ouch, ouch, ouch, ouch! But here's the silver lining: Once you clear that final ascent, you can see a dirt road in the distance. That's the last bit of trail before you end the hike. *Yes!*

It's a breezy descent for the next 0.5 mile or so. At 13.3 miles, look alive, because the National Trail gets a little tricky here for the first time. Veer right to pick up the trail heading south after some very tiny switchbacks. Within just a few feet of this weird little wiggle in the trail, you encounter the large trailhead for the National Trail. You did it! You completed the National Trail!

But, unfortunately, the National Trail does not end at a parking lot. Instead, you must hike your way out of the park. Take the wide dirt road to the south of the National Trail trailhead. The road lasts a short, flat, 1.3 miles heading east. After clearing this distance, you reach the large Pima Canyon trailhead and the end of your 14.7-mile, bucket-list, holy-crap-I-am-so-awesome hike.

Make some whooping noises, hug it out with your friends, and snap some group photos of this big moment. You kick butt!!

Options

The National Trail is so humungous, a hiker could slice and dice the thing in any which way. But this option still allows for the completion of this epic hike. Rather than following the National Trail, which bypasses the Hidden Valley, opt for following the **Hidden Valley Trail**, which explores this curious flatland created by a wash that runs along the top of Guadalupe Range. At 11.8 miles, take a sharp right turn to squeeze through Fat Man's Pass. Then follow the Hidden Valley Trail through the sandy Hidden Valley for 0.5 mile heading northeast. At 12.3 miles, pass under the Natural Tunnel (yet another amazing rock formation) and then scramble over a few boulders, heading north to intersect with the National Trail. Follow the National Trail northeast for the remainder of the hike. This option shaves just 0.1 mile off the total mileage, amounting to 14.6 miles.

Directions

From downtown Phoenix, take Central Avenue south for approximately 6 miles until it curves southwest and into the main entrance for South Mountain Park. Follow the road southwest to pass the South Mountain Park Main Entrance and restrooms. Continue heading southwest along the main road (it turns from Central Avenue to Stephen Mather Drive and then back to Central Avenue). After 1.2 miles take a slight right onto San Juan Road, passing through a gate. Follow San Juan Road southwest, then northwest for about 4 miles. The road ends at the San Juan Lookout parking lot. The National trailhead is on the northeast side of the lot.

Note: As of press time, the San Juan Road is open to vehicles only on the first full weekend of every month. Check www.phoenix.gov/parks for updated schedules.

GPS Coordinates: 33.3305 N, 112.1442 W

Information and Contact

There is no fee. Dogs on leash are allowed. Maps are available online at www.phoenix.gov/parks. For more information, contact City of Phoenix Parks and Recreation Main Office, Phoenix City Hall, 200 West Washington Street, 16th Floor, Phoenix, AZ 85003, 602/262-6862, www.phoenix.gov/parks.

8 GOLDMINE AND DYNAMITE LOOP

San Tan Mountain Regional Park

Level: Easy/Moderate

Total Distance: 4.7 miles round-trip

Hiking Time: 2 hours

Elevation Gain: 650 feet

Summary: Trek up, over, and around Goldmine Mountain to enjoy views of The Valley to the north and San Tan Park to the south.

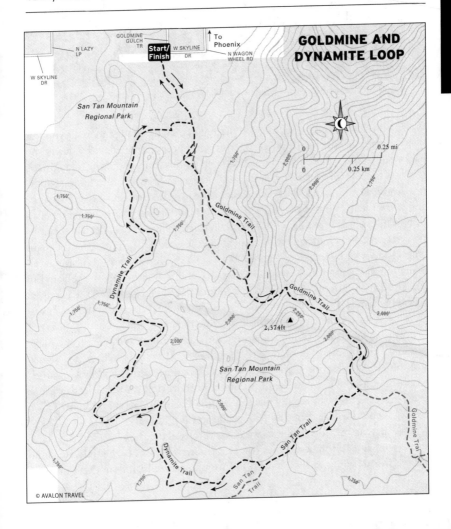

This loop is best experienced with a good friend in tow.

Well, this is just a mighty fine loop. At 4.7 miles, it's long enough to make you feel like you made a worthwhile physical effort without spending an entire day in the backwoods. And, with only a couple scattered climbs throughout the hike, there's plenty of breathing room to engage in a nice, long conversation with a hiking buddy. For families looking to kill a few hours outside, this hike offers a decent distance and a few intense climbs that ensure bonding (especially for surly teenagers).

This hike starts on the San Tan Mountain Regional Park's north end and climbs the western tip of Goldmine Mountain along the Goldmine Trail. After the main climb is over, you overlook the entire San Tan Park, with miles of trail stretching along the flat land to the south. You then descend to briefly hop on the San Tan Trail (the main "artery" of the San Tan Mountain Regional Park) and then connect to the Dynamite Trail, which offers views of downtown Phoenix to the northwest as you travel over a few small foothills to close the loop.

From the Goldmine trailhead parking lot, pass through the gate on the south side and follow the lone, unmarked trail south. After 0.2 mile, you come to a signed fork for the intersection of Goldmine and Dynamite Trails. Follow Goldmine Trail south and, within 50 feet or so, notice a short trail spur that leads west to some graves. This is the resting place of Mansel Carter and Marion Kennedy, two friends who mined the San Tan Mountains in the 1940s and '50s.

After paying respects to these two adventurous dudes, hop back on the Goldmine Trail and continue south as you pass through a wash. It's a moderate climb all the way as you pass by a handful of unmarked trails. Ignore them and just keep heading south. At 1 mile, the trail begins to curve east as you climb the most treacherous portion of this trail. The path may be wide, but your shoes desperately grip at the loose dirt and rock underfoot. In only 0.2 mile, you climb 270 feet on this steep and slippery terrain.

You emerge at a tiny saddle where you can catch your breath at the highest point of this hike at 2,160 feet. From there, begin a descent along the Goldmine Trail, which veers southeast. At 1.7 miles, turn right to follow the San Tan Trail southwest for a very short 0.4 mile. At 2.1 miles, turn right once more to follow the Dynamite Trail west. The Dynamite Trail then turns north as it zigzags through the foothills on the west end of Goldmine Mountain. At 3.2 miles, begin a subtle descent as you approach the original intersection of Goldmine and Dynamite Trails (where you started this loop). Once you encounter the intersection at 4.5 miles, take a left to head north for a mere 0.2 mile back to the Goldmine trailhead and parking lot.

Options

A popular way to shorten this hike is to create an up-and-back route to the saddle. From the Goldmine trailhead follow the Goldmine Trail south for 1.2 miles, during which you ascend a total of 550 feet. After the treacherous portion on the steep slippery slope, you reach a small saddle at 1.2 miles. This is your stopping point. Turn around here and descend carefully for a heart-pumping hike of 2.4 miles total.

Directions

From downtown Phoenix, take I-10 east for approximately 5 miles. Take a slight right onto US-60 and go east for 18.8 miles. Take exit 190B for southbound AZ-202. Merge onto AZ-202, heading south for 1.9 miles. Take exit 33 for Elliot Road. Turn left on Elliot Road and continue east for 0.5 mile. Turn right onto Ellsworth Road, heading south for 10.2 miles. Turn right onto Empire Boulevard, heading west for 1.2 miles. Turn left onto Wagon Wheel Road and follow it south for 1 mile. Wagon Wheel Road turns right (west) and becomes Skyline Drive. Follow it for 0.2 mile until the road ends at the Goldmine trailhead parking lot. Pay the fee at the park gate, which is on the south side of the lot.
GPS Coordinates: 33.1904 N, 111.6583 W

Information and Contact

There is a fee of $6 per vehicle. Dogs on leash are allowed. Maps are available at the park entrance. The park is open daily (6am-8pm Sun.-Thurs., 6am-10pm Fri.-Sat.). For more information, contact San Tan Mountain Regional Park, 6533 West Phillips Road, Queen Creek, AZ 85242, 480/655-5554, www.maricopa.gov/parks/santan.

9 SAN TAN LOOP

San Tan Mountain Regional Park

BEST Solitude

Level: Moderate

Total Distance: 7.4 miles round-trip

Hiking Time: 3.5 hours

Elevation Gain: 800 feet

Summary: If you love a flat terrain walk that lasts forever, the San Tan Loop is your baby.

Okay all you introverts seeking serious solitude, this is your hike. The San Tan Trail is virtually deserted (save for a few horseback riders and the occasional mountain biker). Sure, you may be able to see the surrounding neighborhoods, but you most likely won't see too many other hikers as you trek through this lengthy loop.

Unlike for other low-population hikes, however, getting to this trail in the San Tan Mountain Regional Park doesn't require you to drive a high-clearance vehicle on some backcountry dirt road. Sitting on the outskirts of San Tan Valley (southeast

Wander your way through the desert on the San Tan Loop.

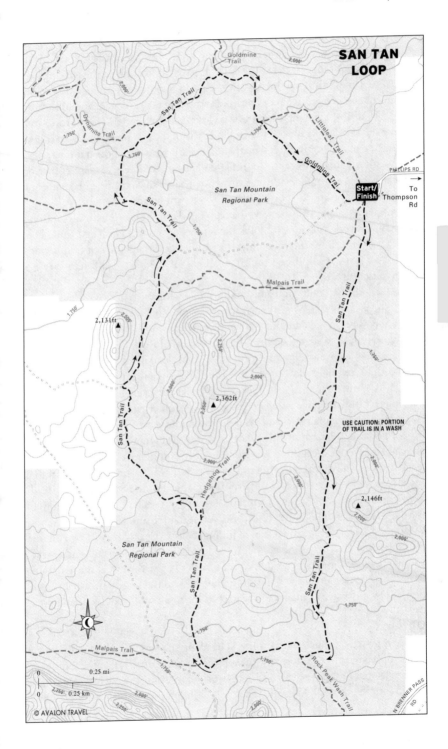

SAN TAN
LOOP

Goldmine
Trail

San Tan Trail

Dynamite Trail

Littleleaf Trail

Goldmine Trail

PHILLIPS RD

Start/
Finish

To
Thompson
Rd

San Tan Mountain
Regional Park

San Tan Trail

Malpais Trail

San Tan Trail

2,131ft

2,362ft

USE CAUTION: PORTION
OF TRAIL IS IN A WASH

Hedgehog Trail

2,146ft

San Tan Trail

San Tan Mountain
Regional Park

San Tan Trail

San Tan Trail

Malpais Trail

Rock Peak Wash Trail

N BRENNER PASS RD

0.25 mi

0.25 km

© AVALON TRAVEL

of Queen Creek, which is southeast of Higley, which is southeast of Gilbert…you get the idea), your quiet escape to the desert is paved all the way to the parking lot.

The San Tan Trail is the longest in the park, maxing out at 6.4 miles. The trail's north end peters out about one mile away from the trailhead, and hikers are required to utilize a neighboring trail to close the loop. For this adventure, you combine the San Tan Trail with the Goldmine Trail for a loop that totals 7.4 miles.

To start, enter the trail system via the main trailhead west of the nature center. Walk west for a mere 50 feet or so until you encounter a massive convergence of four trails. Turn south to see the clearly marked San Tan Trail. Then take note of the Goldmine Trail to the north—this is where you return.

Conveniently signed all the way, the San Tan Trail is easy to follow. Continue south along a wide path until it joins the sandy bottom of a wash at 1 mile. Follow the wash south for 0.5 mile until the trail leads you up and out of the sand. There. You just accomplished the first "climb" of the hike—280 feet over 1.5 miles (you hardly feel it).

Travel another 0.7 mile south and continue following the trail as it makes a sharp turn west. Just a few steps farther, you pass by the Rock Peak Wash Trail to the south. Stay west on the San Tan Trail and enjoy views of the sheer-faced Malpais Hills. Look south to see the thumb-like protrusion of Rock Peak in the distance.

At 2.8 miles, you encounter the junction with Malpais Trail. Make a sharp right turn north to continue following the San Tan Trail for another 0.7 mile until it veers west for 0.3 mile (bypassing the Hedgehog Trail to the east). Then return north once more (this time, bypassing your second encounter with the Malpais Trail). North/northwest remains your general direction for the next 2.7 miles as you pass Moonlight and Dynamite Trails. In other words, just ignore all turnoffs and stay on San Tan Trail—everything is very well signed throughout. You climb up 200 feet, then descend 200 feet during this stretch, but, again, you barely feel a thing.

Once past the Dynamite Trail turnoff at 5.9 miles, the San Tan Trail leads northeast toward Goldmine Mountain. Here's your second elevation climb of the day—180 feet in 0.4 mile. This time, you feel it for sure and it's not the most awesome thing after almost 6 miles of hiking. Muscle through until you run into the Goldmine Trail at 6.3 miles. Follow the Goldmine/San Tan Trail southeast for another 0.4 mile. Ignore the turnoff to the Littleleaf Trail, then walk the remaining 0.6 mile southeast along the Goldmine Trail back to the large four-way intersection. A few more steps east and you're back at the main trailhead. Done and done!

Options

To opt for a much, much shorter hike, start along the San Tan Trail and follow it south for 0.6 mile until you see the turnoff for the Stargazer Trail to the southwest. Turn onto the Stargazer Trail and follow as it curves northwest in just 0.8 mile to run into the Moonlight Trail. Take the Moonlight Trail northeast for 0.7 mile until you return to the four-way trail intersection. Head east to the main trailhead just a few steps away. This loop totals a mere 2.1 miles.

Directions

From downtown Phoenix, take I-10 east for approximately 5 miles. Take a slight right onto eastbound US-60 and go 18.8 miles. Take exit 190B for the southbound AZ-202 Loop and follow the exit ramp for 0.5 mile. Merge onto the AZ-202 Loop and follow it south for 1.9 miles. Take exit 33 for Elliot Road and turn left onto Elliot Road for 0.5 mile. Turn right onto Ellsworth Road and go south for 10.2 miles as the road turns east and becomes Hunt Highway. Follow Hunt Highway east for 1.1 miles. Turn right onto Thompson Road, heading south for 2.1 miles. Turn right (west) onto Phillips Road for 1.1 miles. Pass the San Tan Mountain Regional Park entrance and pay the fee. The road ends at the entrance area parking lot. The main trailhead (which leads to the San Tan Trail) is on the west side of the lot.
GPS Coordinates: 33.1677 N, 111.636 W

Information and Contact

There is a fee of $6 per vehicle. Dogs on leash are allowed. Maps are available at the park entrance. The park is open daily (6am-8pm Sun.-Thurs., 6am-10pm Fri.-Sat.). For more information, contact San Tan Mountain Regional Park, 6533 West Phillips Road, Queen Creek, AZ 85242, 480/655-5554, www.maricopa.gov/parks/santan.

10 SUNSET VISTA TRAIL

Picacho Peak State Park

BEST Wildflowers

Level: Moderate

Total Distance: 4.7 miles round-trip

Hiking Time: 2.5 hours

Elevation Gain: 1,100 feet

Summary: This is the easy side of Picacho Peak, with a lovely walk through desert land on the peak's southwest side.

The Picacho Peak Hunter Trail to the summit, with its historic name (it was named after the Confederate captain who led a Civil War battle in the area in 1862), gets all the glory. The other trails hardly get any attention. Boo-hoo.

Truth is, the Sunset Vista Trail makes for a lovely stroll through the scenic desert along the gentle slopes that trace the west and south sides of Picacho Peak. This review covers the 2.35-mile trail (one-way) that stops short of the intense climbing necessary to reach the summit (technically, the Sunset Vista Trail shares the Hunter Trail to summit the mountain). The first mile is very easy but the second mile is topped off by a 535-foot climb in just 0.35 mile. All along, you gain an

This hiker enjoys a breezy walk with Picacho Peak looming to the east.

appreciation for the uniquely shaped peak as you watch the brave climbers make their way up the south face to the summit. For this hike, quittin' time is called when you run into a steep climb aided by steel cables, leaving the scary climbing for braver souls. Keep in mind also that the big reward for this trail is the vast landscape of wildflowers, such as primrose and desert lupine, exploding in the patch of desert wilderness southwest of the mountain. If you have mixed fitness levels in your family, this is the better option in Picacho Peak State Park.

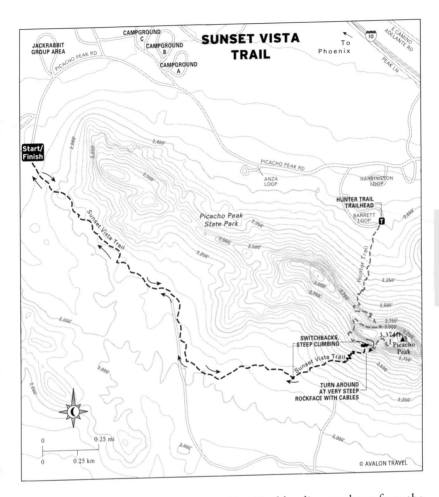

To begin the hike, follow the Sunset Vista Trail heading southeast from the trailhead located on the southwest end of the Sunset Vista parking lot. Continue southeast for 1.1 miles as this lone trail wriggles its way up and over the gentle foothills surrounding Picacho Peak. At 1.1 miles, the trail turns south, then curves east at 1.4 miles. The summit looms to the northeast, and after 2 miles, the trail begins to ascend its south face.

The switchbacks are narrow, with loose rock underfoot as you climb 535 feet in just 0.35 mile. At 2.35 miles, you're suddenly staring up a very steep rock face. Even though the route is passable via footholds and steel cables bolted into the rock, this makes for a great spot to turn around (in fact, this is where the Sunset Vista Trail collides with the Hunter Trail). At 2,654 feet in elevation, this small perch offers some killer views of the desert floor below, with Tucson Mountain Park visible to the far southeast.

From this point on, it's an easy walk back, retracing your steps for the 2.35 miles back to the Sunset Vista trailhead and parking lot.

Options

Can't resist the summit? Totally understandable. And, lucky for you, it's totally doable from the Sunset Vista Trail. At 2.35 miles, go ahead and climb up the rock to join the Hunter Trail heading east (veer right). From here, you encounter more *via ferrata* (the steep climbs aided by steel cables anchored in the rock) as you travel an additional 0.75 mile east to the summit. Once at the top, just turn back and retrace your steps. Don't forget to turn off from the Hunter Trail at approximately 3.9 miles to head south along the Sunset Vista Trail. Then complete the descent and return to the Sunset Vista trailhead and parking lot. This option totals approximately 6.2 miles.

Directions

From downtown Phoenix, take eastbound I-10 toward Tucson for approximately 70 miles. Take exit 219 for Picacho Peak Road and turn right onto Picacho Peak Road, heading west. Pass the entrance gate and pay the fee. After 2.5 miles on Picacho Peak Road, the road curves south and ends at the Sunset Vista parking lot. The Sunset Vista Trail trailhead is on the south end of the lot.
GPS Coordinates: 32.6476 N, 111.4291 W

Information and Contact

There is a fee of $7 per vehicle. Dogs on leash are allowed, but are not recommended on the Hunter Trail. Maps are at the main entrance. For more information, contact Picacho Peak State Park, Eloy, AZ 85131, 520/466-3183, www.azstateparks.com/Parks/PIPE. Picacho Peak is closed during the summer season (usually May-Sept.); check online for specific dates. When open, park hours are 5am-9pm.

11 HUNTER TRAIL
Picacho Peak State Park

BEST Butt-Kickers, Climbing and Scrambling

Level: Butt-kicker

Total Distance: 3 miles round-trip

Hiking Time: 4.1 hours

Elevation Gain: 1,900 feet

Summary: Thrill-seekers and daredevils, this is the hike for you.

The Hunter Trail to the summit of Picacho Peak is the most thrilling hike in this book. Depending on your personality, it is thrilling in a "this hike makes me feel alive!" kind of way or thrilling in a "this hike makes me feel very close to death!" kind of way. Either way, it's a hike you'll never forget. The trail (only 1.5 miles each way) is steep. So steep, in fact, that you're treated to a *via ferrata* route. *Via ferrata* is Italian for "iron road" and is the term used to describe climbing routes aided by steel cables affixed to rock. On Picacho Peak, most hikers grasp the cables to hoist their way over craggy rock faces and aggressive inclines on their way to the summit. It's not a hike for the timid. If you're up for it, be prepared for a slow,

Things get pretty hairy on the Hunter Trail to the summit of Picacho Peak.

careful hike, and bring a pair of gloves (especially if it's a warm day).

The other special aspect to Picacho Peak is that it's the site of a Civil War battle. Re-enactment events happen annually. In fact, the Hunter Trail is named after a Confederate captain, Sherod Hunter.

To start the hike, head south on the Hunter Trail (trailhead is on the southeast side of Barrett Loop). The first 0.9 mile climbs approximately 925 feet up the north side to the saddle with the aid of a few scattered switchbacks. It's a grunt of a 0.9 mile but it's also the "easy" part because once you pass the saddle the *via ferrata* begins. Make use of the steel cables as you follow Hunter Trail south to descend a steep 200 feet in just 0.1 mile.

Once the descent is over, veer left (southeast) to continue toward the summit. The trail is not clearly defined, but keep an eye out for the *via ferrata* and you'll find the proper path. For the next 0.5 mile, the trail is peppered with narrow passes and many more *via ferrata* scrambles; the most challenging occurs very close to the summit. It's steep. Like 20 feet of steep. This intense *via ferrata* climb is followed by a tricky pass along a narrow wood footbridge that hugs the sheer rock. Clear these precarious few steps and then turn right to follow switchbacks that lead to an open clearing on the summit at 3,445 feet.

Catch your breath, shake off those nerves, and have a snack as you take in the tremendous view of the surrounding landscape, which includes the Tortolita Mountain Park, Mount Lemmon, and the city of Tucson to the southeast.

When ready, begin your descent along the *via ferrata* trail. Hopefully, you've got some stamina on reserve for the careful negotiations of the rock as you make the return trip along the Hunter Trail.

Options

If you're not feeling up to the trip to the summit, the saddle makes for a perfectly fine stopping point. Follow the Hunter Trail up the north side of Picacho Peak for 0.9 mile to the saddle at 2,920 feet. This perch offers sweeping views of the south side of the mountain and the untouched desert floor below. Hit it in the spring to see a blast of colors due to wildflowers like primrose and desert lupine blooming in the sun. Return the way you came for a total hike of 1.8 miles and 925 feet of elevation gain.

Directions

From downtown Phoenix, take eastbound I-10 toward Tucson for approximately 70 miles. Take exit 219 for Picacho Peak Road and turn right onto Picacho Peak Road heading west. Pass the entrance gate and pay the fee. After 0.7 mile on Picacho Peak Road, turn left onto Barrett Loop, heading north for 0.4 mile until the road curves east. The Hunter Trail parking lot and trailhead are on the southeast end of Barrett Loop.

GPS Coordinates: 32.6424 N, 111.4025 W

Information and Contact

There is a fee of $7 per vehicle. Dogs on leash are allowed but not recommended on the Hunter Trail. Maps are at the main entrance. For more information, contact Picacho Peak State Park, Eloy, AZ 85131, 520/466-3183, www.azstateparks.com/Parks/PIPE. Picacho Peak is closed during the summer season (usually May-Sept.); check online for specific dates. When open, park hours are 5am-9pm.

EAST VALLEY

© LILIA MENCONI

Some of the most beloved trails await in the East Valley. The Superstition Wilderness Area boasts otherworldly igneous rock formations and a vast network of challenging and awe-inspiring hikes. A must for any hiker's list is reaching The Flatiron, a massive piece of mountain that juts out into space with a large, flat landing at 4,861 feet. Northwest of the Superstition Mountains is Usery Mountain Regional Park. Usery offers a dense thicket of desert vegetation that fills with incredible color during wildflower season in the spring. Family friendly Boyce Thompson Arboretum has 3,200 desert plant species within its grounds. You can learn about each one with the help of winding interpretive trails throughout the arboretum. Sounds incredible, right? Now, pick your hike and head east. The trails are waiting!

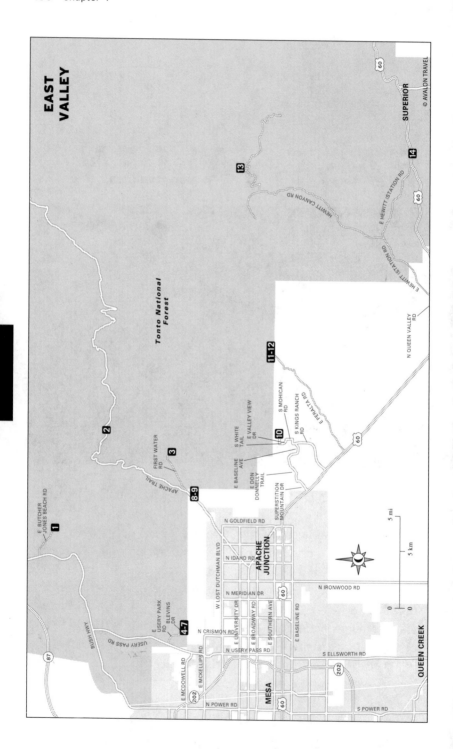

TRAIL NAME	FEATURES	LEVEL	DISTANCE	TIME	ELEVATION	PAGE
1 Butcher Jones Trail BEST		Easy/Moderate	4.7 mi rt	2 hr	600 ft	162
2 Boulder Canyon Trail		Strenuous	8 mi rt	4.5 hr	1,600 ft	165
3 Black Mesa Loop BEST		Strenuous	9.1 mi rt	5 hr	1,100 ft	169
4 Pass Mountain Trail		Moderate	7.2 mi rt	3 hr	850 ft	172
5 Wind Cave Trail		Easy/Moderate	2.8 mi rt	1.5 hr	900 ft	175
6 Merkle Memorial Loop Trail BEST		Easy	1 mi rt	30 min	25 ft	178
7 Blevins to Cat Peaks Loop		Easy	3 mi rt	1.5 hr	300 ft	181
8 Treasure Loop Trail		Easy	2.4 mi rt	1 hr	550 ft	185
9 Siphon Draw Trail to The Flatiron BEST		Butt-kicker	5.8 mi rt	6 hr	2,750 ft	188
10 Hieroglyphic Trail BEST		Easy/Moderate	3 mi rt	1.5 hr	700 ft	192
11 Peralta Trail to Fremont Saddle BEST		Strenuous	4.5 mi rt	2.5 hr	1,400 ft	195
12 Dutchman's and Bluff Spring Loop		Strenuous	9 mi rt	5 hr	1,500 ft	198
13 Rogers Canyon Trail BEST		Strenuous	8 mi rt	5 hr	1,200 ft	201
14 Main Trail BEST		Easy	1.7 mi rt	1 hr	250 ft	205

1 BUTCHER JONES TRAIL

Tonto National Forest

BEST Hikes near Water

Level: Easy/Moderate

Total Distance: 4.7 miles round-trip

Hiking Time: 2 hours

Elevation Gain: 600 feet

Summary: This hike is a lovely stroll next to the glittering waters of Saguaro Lake. Heaven!

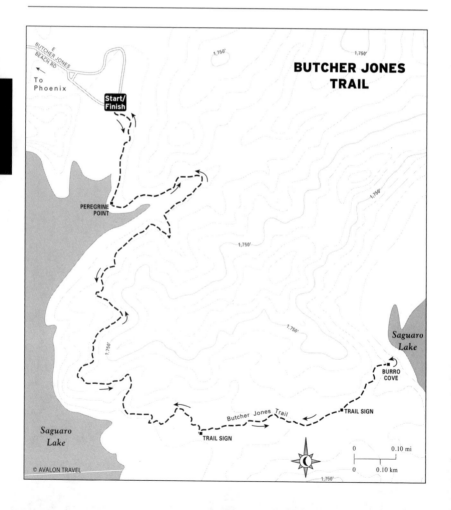

© LILIA MENCONI

The serene Saguaro Lake is tucked within the beautiful desert.

If there's one thing that will make us dirt-sniffing desert-dwellers swoon, it's water. And when there's a whole bunch of it pooled in one place (these are called "lakes" and other climates have lots of them), we just can't stay away.

Saguaro Lake is one such collection of water that keeps calling to swimmers, boaters, and fishers. For hikers, the Butcher Jones Trail offers a delightful out-and-back walk near the waterline, through the desert, onto a stunning viewpoint on Burro Cove, then back. All this happens in a little under 5 miles. The Butcher Jones Trail starts from the Butcher Jones Recreation Site on the northwest side of Saguaro Lake and crosses a wide peninsula that protrudes from the north.

The trailhead is on the east side of the main beach at Butcher Jones Recreation Site and is clearly marked with a large brown sign imprinted with the "hiker guy" icon. For the first 0.2 mile, follow the sandy, shady trail covered by low-lying trees. Pass some handrails and continue along the path as it curves south. Cruise by another set of handrails along a paved portion lined with educational plaques that describe the local fish and riparian wildlife (like bass, bald eagles, great blue herons, and ringtail cats). Pass the dilapidated docks on the right until you reach the signed Peregrine Point at 0.4 mile. Here you experience the first glorious view of crystal-blue Saguaro Lake.

Continue along the trail as it narrowly traces the shoreline heading northeast. At 0.5 mile, the trail enters an overgrown riparian area and then spits you back out into the desert after a mere 0.2 mile. Climb a brief ascent (only about 100 feet) as the trail turns south and offers even more spectacular views of Saguaro Lake below.

At approximately mile 2, find the Butcher Jones Trail sign, which indicates that Burro Cove is to the northeast. Follow the sign and veer left as you walk away from the water and into the thick of the desert. You are now crossing the peninsula. Be sure to glance up to see a spectacular view of the Four Peaks to the north at 2.2 miles, where you also stumble into another sign indicating that Burro Cove is also to the north. Burro Cove is your destination, so follow the trail as it veers left. At approximately 2.3 miles, the trail peters out onto a small clearing that overlooks the spindly arm of Saguaro Lake.

No joke—the view is pretty spectacular. With the Four Peaks looming in the distance and a few boats below, you feel like you've found an oasis in the desert.

When ready, simply retrace your steps back to the trailhead at the Butcher Jones Recreation Site.

Options

For a much shorter jaunt (especially perfect if you have small children in tow), **Peregrine Point** makes for an excellent stopping point. Simply follow the trail from the Butcher Jones Recreation Site trailhead through the shady area, onto the paved portion, and along the water's edge. This portion of the Butcher Jones Trail is interpretive and offers color illustrations of nearby animal and plant life (like willow, ash, and cottonwood trees). Once your crew reaches Peregrine Point at 0.3 mile, turn around and make your way back to the trailhead (which conveniently spills out onto the beach) for a total 0.6-mile hike.

Directions

From downtown Phoenix, take the AZ-202 Loop approximately 13 miles east and exit on Country Club Drive. Turn left and continue for 2.7 miles, heading north until Country Club Drive becomes AZ-87. Follow AZ-87 approximately 22 miles north. Take exit 199 for Bush Highway and turn right onto Bush Highway, heading south for 2.9 miles. Turn left onto Butcher Jones Beach Road and follow it southeast for 1.8 miles. Make a slight right to remain on Butcher Jones Beach Road and continue southeast for 0.2 mile. The Butcher Jones Trail trailhead is on the south side of the lot, northeast of the beach.

GPS Coordinates: 33.5758 N, 111.5144 W

Information and Contact

A Tonto National Forest Recreation Pass is required. A daily pass costs $6 per vehicle and is available for purchase online or at nearby retail outlets (look for signs at gas stations and convenient stores). Dogs on leash are allowed. Maps are available for purchase at the Tonto National Forest Supervisor's Office. For more information, contact the Tonto National Forest Supervisor's Office, 2324 East McDowell Road, Phoenix, AZ 85006, 602/225-5200, www.fs.usda.gov/main/tonto.

2 BOULDER CANYON TRAIL
Superstition Wilderness

Level: Strenuous

Total Distance: 8 miles round-trip

Hiking Time: 4.5 hours

Elevation Gain: 1,600 feet

Summary: Oh, baby, this canyon hike is 8 miles of beautiful terrain (and some sweet, sweet pain).

Seriously, just when you think you've had enough of the Superstition Wilderness, you try a new trail and fall in love all over again. The Boulder Canyon Trail could certainly woo a weary hiker or two with its challenging, relentless inclines leading to unbelievable views of a cutting canyon forged by La Barge Creek and its tributaries. The trail climbs down and into this quiet canyon floor and satisfies a hiker's need for solitude.

The Boulder Canyon Trail begins with a hefty 640-foot climb, then continues to march up and down as it traces Boulder Canyon's edge. Finally, a steady descent takes you to the rocky bottom of a small tributary of La Barge Creek, after which you cross the canyon floor. The trail could be shorter or longer if you choose to tailor it to your liking. For this review, the goal is to reach Boulder Canyon Trail's intersection with Second Water Trail, creating an 8-mile out-and-back hike.

To get started, locate the Boulder Canyon Trail trailhead on the south side of Highway 88, across the road from the Canyon Lake Marina parking lot. There's only one trail to follow throughout this entire journey, so start with this incline of 640 feet in 1.2 miles of loose rock on a wide path heading south. For this portion, you'll surely see a few other folks taking in the scenery. At 1.2 miles, you reach the tallest accessible point of the Boulder Canyon wall at 2,375 feet. Notice the stunning view of Canyon Lake and the Mormon Flat Dam to the northwest.

Follow a ridgeline for the next 0.5 mile as it wiggles east and south. Weaver's Needle to the southeast should come in and out of view along this stretch. After a series of brief ascents, the trail begins a lengthy descent at 2.3 miles. After 0.6 mile of climbing down, the terrain levels as you begin to cut across the floor of Boulder Canyon. At 3.1 miles, cross the rocky bed of La Barge Creek's tributary by following the cairns that lead to the trail on the other side. At 3.2 miles, pass a small fire pit as the trail squeezes its way by Geronimo Head (east) and Battleship Mountain (southeast). The iron-rich dirt turns bright red during this portion, and

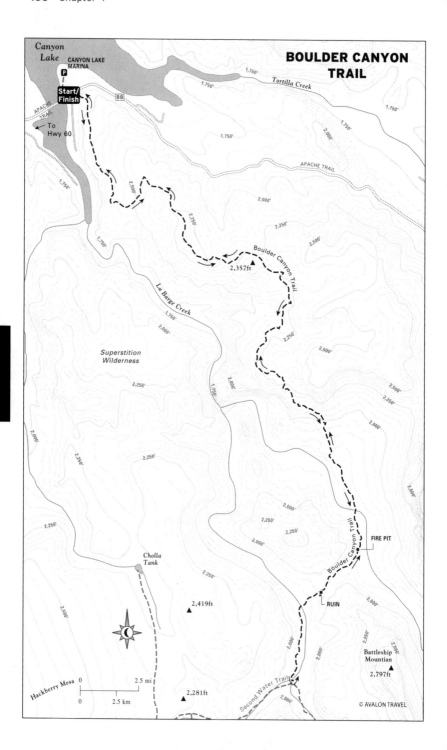

Canyon Lake

CANYON LAKE MARINA

Start/Finish

To Hwy 60

APACHE TRAIL

88

Tortilla Creek

1,750'

1,750'

1,750'

1,750'

1,750'

APACHE TRAIL

2,000'

BOULDER CANYON TRAIL

2,000'

2,000'

2,250'

2,250'

2,250'

2,500'

Boulder Canyon Trail

2,357ft

La Barge Creek

1,750'

2,000'

2,250'

Superstition Wilderness

2,250'

2,250'

2,250'

1,750'

2,000'

2,250'

2,500'

2,500'

2,500'

2,000'

2,250'

2,500'

2,000'

2,000'

2,000'

2,000'

2,250'

2,250'

2,250'

2,250'

Boulder Canyon Trail

FIRE PIT

RUIN

2,500'

2,500'

Cholla Tank

2,419ft

2,000'

2,000'

Battleship Mountain

2,797ft

2,000'

2,250'

2,500'

Hackberry Mesa

0   2.5 mi

0   2.5 km

2,281ft

Second Water Trail

2,000'

© AVALON TRAVEL

Get ready: you are going to walk down into this.

at 3.4 miles, you encounter the brick wall "ruins" of a small hut. The trail is west of the decrepit dwelling and continues southwest.

At 3.8 miles, you cross the rock bed of La Barge Creek, following cairns once more. When you reach the far side of the creek bed, it's only 0.3 mile to the junction with Second Water Trail. The well-signed trail intersection is surrounded by a peaceful clearing. It's a great place to admire the canyon walls. This spot is at 4 miles even and a convenient end-point.

During the return trip, enjoy the flat canyon floor while you can, because the easy terrain won't last forever. It's only 1.2 miles of bliss until you're in for a grueling 460-foot climb out of Boulder Canyon, which is topped off with a reprise of the ridgeline's ups and downs.

Oof. It'll hurt. But remember that 1.2-mile ascent at the very beginning? On the way back, it's all downhill back to Highway 88 and the Canyon Lake Marina parking lot.

After a challenging and beautiful hike like that, you'll be feeling the love for the "Supes" all over again.

Options

Not in the mood for an 8-miler? No worries. You can still get a great hike by cutting the trail short. Try taking the trail just 2.4 miles. This way, you get the main climb with a few more ascents as you enjoy incredible views of the endless layers of cracked land to the south. Turn around at 2.4 miles when you see the trail make a dramatic descent south, toward the canyon floor. Retrace your steps back to the Boulder Canyon Trail trailhead for a total of 4.8 miles.

Directions

From downtown Phoenix, take I-10 east for approximately 5 miles. Take a slight right onto eastbound US-60 and follow it for 24.7 miles. Take exit 196 for Idaho Road (eastbound AZ-88) and follow it for 0.4 mile. Turn left onto Idaho Road and go north for 2.3 miles. Make a slight right onto Apache Trail (AZ-88) and follow it northeast for 14.4 miles. Park in the designated spaces reserved for hikers on the south side of the Canyon Lake Marina parking lot. The Boulder Canyon Trail trailhead is across the road, on the south side of AZ-88.

GPS Coordinates: 33.5341 N, 111.4229 W

Information and Contact

There is no fee as long as you park in the parking spaces designated for hikers in the Canyon Lake Marina parking lot. Dogs on leash are allowed. Maps are available for purchase at the Tonto National Forest Supervisor's Office. For more information, contact the Tonto National Forest Supervisor's Office, 2324 East McDowell Road, Phoenix, AZ 85006, 602/225-5200, www.fs.usda.gov/main/tonto.

3 BLACK MESA LOOP
Superstition Wilderness

BEST Solitude

Level: Strenuous

Total Distance: 9.1 miles round-trip

Hiking Time: 5 hours

Elevation Gain: 1,100 feet

Summary: Ever been to a cholla forest? You can see what it's all about on this incredible loop.

You're going get another hard sell for a hike in the Superstition Wilderness. But, honestly, every hike is soooo worth the effort, and this loop is no exception. Well-maintained and easy to follow, this hike takes place on the west end of the Superstition Wilderness, northeast of Lost Dutchman State Park. Though the trailhead is easily accessible, this lengthy trek offers plenty of solitude as you cross First Water Creek twice (with actual running water if you do this in the cooler months), climb to the top of a mesa dominated by a glowing cholla forest, descend with killer views to Weaver's Needle, and finish by meandering through a rocky basin. Sold!

Weaver's Needle never looked so gorgeous.

To start the loop, find the main trailhead on the southeast corner of the First Water trailhead parking lot. Follow the main trail, traveling southeast 0.3 mile until you encounter a fork. Take a left turn to join the Second Water Trail, which now veers northeast (take note of the sign for the Dutchman's Trail, because this is where you close the loop). Shortly after, hop on a few rocks to cross over First Water Creek. At approximately 1 mile, the trail turns north and, at 1.3 miles, begins to climb 512 feet (this elevation gain is mercifully stretched over the next 2 miles). At 1.8 miles, ignore the unmarked trail that continues north. Instead, turn right to follow the Black Mesa Trail heading

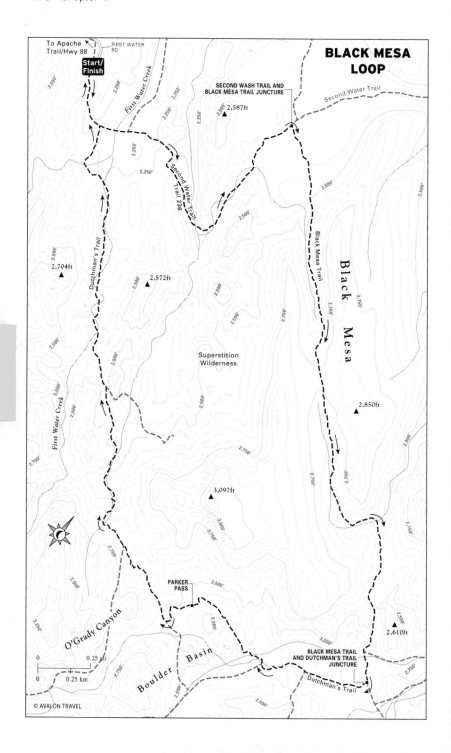

To Apache Trail/Hwy 88
FIRST WATER RD
Start/Finish

BLACK MESA LOOP

SECOND WASH TRAIL AND
BLACK MESA TRAIL JUNCTURE

2,587ft

Second Water Trail

First Water Creek

Second Water Trail 236

Dutchman's Trail

Black Mesa Trail

2,704ft

2,572ft

Black Mesa

Superstition
Wilderness

2,850ft

First Water Creek

3,097ft

2,610ft

PARKER PASS

O'Grady Canyon

Boulder Basin

BLACK MESA TRAIL
AND DUTCHMAN'S TRAIL
JUNCTURE

Dutchman's Trail

0   0.25 mi
0   0.25 km

© AVALON TRAVEL

southeast. At mile 3, you reach the top of Black Mesa, marked by a small, dirt clearing. By now, you're neck-deep in the cholla forest with its incredible thicket of spines covering the mesa. Look southeast to instantly recognize the towering rock spire called Weavers Needle.

Descend into Boulder Basin by following the Black Mesa Trail southeast for the next 1.8 miles. At 4.8 miles, after crossing over a tributary stream, you encounter a small clearing with signs for the Dutchman's Trail. Turn right to follow the Dutchman's Trail west. You make a climb once more, but the mere 420 feet of elevation gain is stretched so thin across the next 1.7 miles, it's barely noticeable. At 6.7 miles, the trail begins a slight descent as it veers northwest. At 8.5 miles your rock-hopping skills are put to the test once more as you cross First Water Creek for the second and final time, indicating that you've almost closed the loop. At 8.8 miles, pass by the Second Water Trail to the east (where this loop began) and continue northwest along the Dutchman's Trail. At 9.1 miles, the trail spills back out into the First Water trailhead parking lot.

So worth it.

Options

Cutting this trail short would be a crime, but if you really, really have to, simply turn around at mile 3. In 3 miles, you travel the Second Water Trail and 1.5 miles (out of 3) of the Black Mesa Trail. This allows you to see the cholla forest, including the incredible views of Weaver's Needle peeking out from the vast Superstition Mountains. The up-and-back trail totals 6 miles.

Directions

From downtown Phoenix, take I-10 east for approximately 5 miles. Take a slight right onto eastbound US-60 and follow it for 24.7 miles. Take exit 196 for Idaho Road (eastbound AZ-88) for 0.4 mile. Turn left onto Idaho Road and go north for 2.3 miles. Make a slight right onto Apache Trail (eastbound AZ-88) and go northeast for 5.2 miles. Turn onto First Water Road and follow the dirt road northeast for 2.6 miles, veering right to reach the First Water trailhead parking lot. The main trail entrance (which quickly leads to the fork for Dutchman's and Second Water Trails) is on the south side of the lot.

GPS Coordinates: 33.4802 N, 111.4430 W

Information and Contact

There is no fee. Dogs on leash are allowed. Maps are available for purchase at the Tonto National Forest Supervisor's Office. For more information, contact the Tonto National Forest Supervisor's Office, 2324 East McDowell Road, Phoenix, AZ 85006, 602/225-5200, www.fs.usda.gov/main/tonto.

4 PASS MOUNTAIN TRAIL
Usery Mountain Regional Park

Level: Moderate

Total Distance: 7.2 miles round-trip

Hiking Time: 3 hours

Elevation Gain: 850 feet

Summary: Spend some serious time getting to know "Scarface" as you hike the 7.2 miles around Pass Mountain.

You looked at Scarface (the nickname for Pass Mountain) from the Cat Peaks and Merkle Trails. You hiked up Scarface on the Wind Cave Trail. And now, friends, it's time to hike all the way around Scarface just so you can say you did. Oh, and so you can experience the best hike in Usery Mountain Regional Park.

Scarface is easily recognizable because of a single, pale-rock layer of ancient volcanic debris that cuts across the mountain's west face. You see plenty of that scar as you make your 360-degree loop on the Pass Mountain Trail.

From the Wind Cave trailhead and parking lot, follow the trail north. Immediately pass the turnoff for Wind Cave Trail to the east. Continue north on

The sprawling east valley hugs Pass Mountain and the Goldfield Mountains.

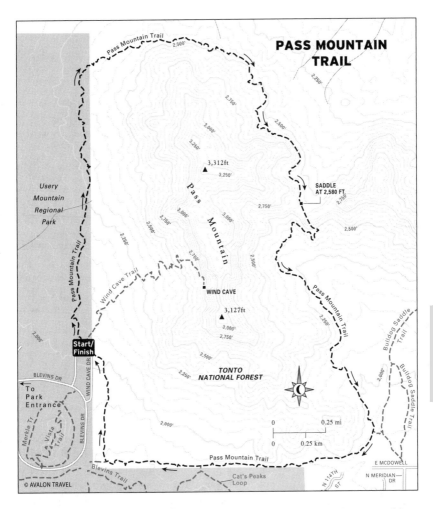

PASS MOUNTAIN TRAIL

Pass Mountain Trail for a very gentle ascent as you near the northern tip of Pass Mountain. At 1.5 miles, the trail turns east. By now, you've climbed approximately 200 feet and can enjoy views of the Superstition Mountains (look east to see this).

Continue along Pass Mountain Trail as a gentle incline continues and the trail heads east, then south. This is the most scenic part of the hike now that the city to the west is out of view. At 3.6 miles, you reach the saddle (2,605 feet) between Pass Mountain and the Goldfield Mountains to the east.

The tough part is over. Descend along Pass Mountain Trail heading south until the trail turns west at 5.3 miles. The trail is flat and easy for the rest of the hike. Ignore any turnoffs that lead south and remain on the Pass Mountain Trail until it makes a final right turn to the north at 6.6 miles. It's just another 0.6 mile north (Usery Park Road is visible to the west) towards the original trail junction with Wind Cave Trail. At the junction, turn left (south) and step into the Wind Cave parking lot.

Options

For a shorter hike that still gives a good workout, consider making a viewpoint at the north end of Pass Mountain your turnaround spot. Reach the viewpoint by taking the Pass Mountain Trail north from the Wind Cave trailhead for 2 miles. The viewpoint sits at 2,340 feet and offers sweeping views of The Valley to the west and the Superstition Wilderness to the east. Turn around here to make a total hike of 4 miles.

Directions

From downtown Phoenix, take I-10 east toward Tucson for approximately 2 miles. Take exit 147A to merge onto the eastbound AZ-202 Loop. Continue east for 22.7 miles. Take exit 23A for Power Road for 0.6 mile. Turn right onto Power Road and go south for 0.6 mile. Turn left onto McDowell Road, heading east for 3.1 miles. Turn left onto Ellsworth Road, which becomes Usery Pass Road, and follow it northeast for 1.5 miles. Turn right onto Usery Park Road and head southeast for 1 mile. Pay the fee at the park entrance. Continue onto Blevins Drive, heading east for 0.3 mile. Turn left onto Wind Cave Drive and head north for 0.2 mile. The Wind Cave parking lot is on the north side of Wind Cave Drive. The Wind Cave Trail trailhead is north of the lot.
GPS Coordinates: 33.4741 N, 111.6074 W

Information and Contact

There is a fee of $6 per vehicle. An annual pass is available for $75. Dogs on leash are allowed. Maps are available at the Usery Mountain Regional Park Nature Center (8am-4pm daily). The park is open daily (6am-8pm Sun.-Thurs., 6am-10pm Fri.-Sat.). For more information, contact Usery Mountain Regional Park Nature Center, 3939 North Usery Pass Road, Mesa, AZ 85207, 480/984-0032, www.maricopa.gov/parks/usery.

5 WIND CAVE TRAIL
Usery Mountain Regional Park

🏕 🐕 👪

Level: Easy/Moderate

Total Distance: 2.8 miles round-trip

Hiking Time: 1.5 hours

Elevation Gain: 900 feet

Summary: This quick climb ends at a wind-eroded "cave," which provides welcome shade for weary hikers.

© LILIA MENCONI

Wind erosion has created some much-needed shade.

The Wind Cave Trail is, by far, the most popular hike in Usery Mountain Regional Park. In just 1.4 miles up 900 feet to a shady, scenic viewpoint, you'll no doubt come across a friend (or five) as you make your way up this well-established and easy-to-follow path up the west side of Pass Mountain.

This trail may be popular, but if you happen to hit it on a warm day, it can be hot, hot, hot. What seems to be a bearable temperature in the parking lot quickly turns brutal on the trail. With the exception of a few hours in the early morning, the west side of Pass Mountain is sizzling in full sun—and you'll sizzle right along with it if your timing is off. That said, with good timing, this popular trail makes for a quick climb to a scenic point.

From the Wind Cave trailhead parking lot, look north to find signs for the Wind Cave Trail. Once on the wide, flat trail, you immediately pass an intersection with Pass Mountain Trail. Ignore it and veer right (northeast) to continue following the Wind Cave Trail as you begin to experience a slight incline.

This gentle slope lasts for the first 0.6 mile, in which you ascend approximately 200 feet. It's the perfect warm-up for the rest of the hike, which really kicks things up with a gain of almost 600 feet in less than a mile. Lucky you, the climb is eased with switchbacks throughout. Once you reach the pale rock of Pass Mountain's

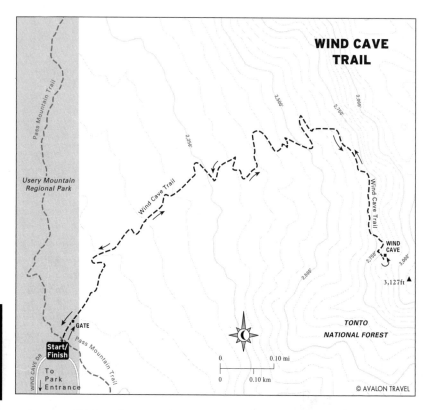

volcanic tuff (a low-density rock composed of volcanic particles), you're just a few steps away from the cave.

At 1.3 miles, take a sharp left turn to reach the large overhang of rock (this is the cave) to your left. Take a seat in the shade and enjoy the view. Depending on the time of year, the walls may be alive with buzzing bees that have made homes in the rock's cracks. In spite of your winged neighbors, there's plenty of room to stretch out and enjoy the view to the west, which stretches across almost the entire metropolitan area. See if you can identify the Phoenix Mountains and South Mountain Park in the distance.

That's it! Simply turn back and follow the Wind Cave Trail for an easy 1.4 miles back to your car.

Options

For an all-day trek to experience Pass Mountain in all its glory, combine Wind Cave Trail with **Pass Mountain Trail** for a total of 10 miles. Immediately after entering the trail, veer left onto Pass Mountain Trail heading north. The Pass Mountain Trail loops around Pass Mountain and climbs to a saddle between

Pass Mountain and Goldfield Mountains at approximately 2,600 feet. As the lower end of the loop (now along the south side of Pass Mountain) turns west, ignore all turnoffs to neighboring trails. After 7.2 miles along the Pass Mountain Trail, you run smack into the Wind Cave Trail. This time, veer right to follow the Wind Cave Trail northeast. Treat it as a lengthy spur to the cave and back for the ultimate Pass Mountain hike.

Directions

From downtown Phoenix, take I-10 east toward Tucson for approximately 2 miles. Take exit 147A to merge onto the eastbound AZ-202 Loop. Continue east for 22.7 miles. Take exit 23A for Power Road for 0.6 mile. Turn right onto Power Road and go south for 0.6 mile. Turn left onto McDowell Road, heading east for 3.1 miles. Turn left onto Ellsworth Road, which becomes Usery Pass Road, and follow it northeast for 1.5 miles. Turn right onto Usery Park Road and head southeast for 1 mile. Pay the fee at the park entrance. Continue onto Blevins Drive and head east for 0.3 mile. Turn left onto Wind Cave Drive, heading north for 0.2 mile. The Wind Cave parking lot is on the north side of Wind Cave Drive. The Wind Cave Trail trailhead is north of the lot.

GPS Coordinates: 33.4740 N, 111.6073 W

Information and Contact

There is a fee of $6 per vehicle. An annual pass is available for $75. Dogs on leash are allowed. Maps are available at the Usery Mountain Regional Park Nature Center (8am-4pm daily). The park is open daily (6am-8pm Sun.-Thurs., 6am-10pm Fri.-Sat.). For more information, contact Usery Mountain Regional Park Nature Center, 3939 North Usery Pass Road, Mesa, AZ 85207, 480/984-0032, www.maricopa.gov/parks/usery.

6 MERKLE MEMORIAL LOOP TRAIL
Usery Mountain Regional Park

BEST **Wheelchair-Accessible Trails**

Level: Easy

Total Distance: 1 mile round-trip

Hiking Time: 30 minutes

Elevation Gain: 25 feet

Summary: Enjoy a very easy loop that circles a small mountain in the desert's natural garden, which is filled with saguaros, barrel cacti, and wildflowers galore in spring.

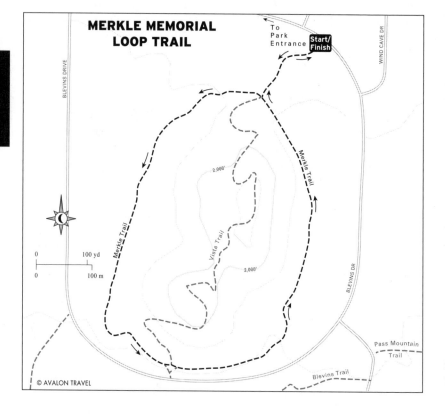

© LILIA MENCONI

Take in the view of Pass Mountain on the east side of this short loop.

Twenty-five million years ago, in what we now call the East Valley, masses of ash and debris settled in three areas after some violent volcanic activity. Today, we call these incredible conglomerates of rock the Superstition Mountains, the Goldfield Mountains, and the Usery Mountains. The Usery Mountains are easily identified by the light-colored stripe on Pass Mountain. Pass Mountain is also known as "Scarface," and its distinctive stripe of rock is composed of quartz particles that take on a sparkling sheen in the setting sunlight.

Pretty interesting stuff, right? All this information and more can be found on the Merkle Trail. It's an interpretive trail (this means it's littered with educational plaques) and is a smooth, flat path—perfect for a family outing. The loop is surrounded by almost every desert plant one desires to see and makes for a fantastic spectacle of color during wildflower season.

From the small parking lot, find signs for the Vista Trail. Follow the Vista Trail south as it quickly runs into the Merkle Trail. The Merkle Trail is a loop, so feel free to choose a left or right turn.

Either way you choose, the smooth trail curves all the way around a small peak that boasts a backdrop of cracked boulders. The trail features benches every few hundred feet. Be sure to check out the educational plaques along the way. They have interesting content about the park's plants (like barrel cactus and ocotillo) and geology.

The best views are on the east side of the loop. View the dramatic outcrop of the Superstition Mountains in the far distance to the east and take a look at the aforementioned quartz-filled "scar," which runs along the face of Pass Mountain to the northeast.

Just after 1 mile is reached, the parking lot and your starting point are visible. Return to your car via the Vista Trail.

Options

To ramp up this hike, take the **Vista Trail**, which runs over the mountain from north to south. The trail quickly ascends approximately 150 feet, follows the ridge, and descends to intersect at the opposite side of the Merkle Trail.

Directions

From downtown Phoenix, take I-10 east toward Tucson for approximately 2 miles. Take exit 147A to merge onto the eastbound AZ-202 Loop. Continue east for 22.7 miles. Take exit 23A for Power Road for 0.6 mile. Turn right onto Power Road and go south for 0.6 mile. Turn left onto McDowell Road, heading east for 3.1 miles. Turn left onto Ellsworth Road, which becomes Usery Pass Road, and follow it northeast for 1.5 miles. Turn right onto Usery Park Road and head southeast for 1 mile. Pay the fee at the park entrance. Continue onto Blevins Drive, heading east for 0.3 mile. The Vista Trail parking lot is on the southwest side of Blevins Drive. The Vista Trail trailhead is southwest of the lot.
GPS Coordinates: 33.4712 N, 111.6080 W

Information and Contact

There is a fee of $6 per vehicle. An annual pass is available for $75. Dogs on leash are allowed. Maps are available at the Usery Mountain Regional Park Nature Center (8am-4pm daily). The park is open daily (6am-8pm Sun.-Thurs., 6am-10pm Fri.-Sat.). For more information, contact Usery Mountain Regional Park Nature Center, 3939 North Usery Pass Road, Mesa, AZ 85207, 480/984-0032, www.maricopa.gov/parks/usery.

7 BLEVINS TO CAT PEAKS LOOP
Usery Mountain Regional Park

Level: Easy

Total Distance: 3 miles round-trip

Hiking Time: 1.5 hours

Elevation Gain: 300 feet

Summary: A low-impact stroll treks around two small peaks and offers stupendous views of Pass Mountain and the Superstition Mountains.

© LILIA MENCONI

Pass Mountain in all its splendor

Usery Mountain Regional Park is well known around town for having one of the most lush desert landscapes. With an abundance of towering saguaro and bursts of needle-rich cholla ("jumping" cacti), the park provides many desert-lovers with delicious eye candy. The Blevins Trail is named after an Old West criminal named Henry Blevins, who, along with King Usery, stole $2,000 worth of silver bullion from the Globe-Florence stage in 1891.

Taking the Blevins Trail to the Cat Peaks Trail is the perfect jaunt through some incredibly beautiful scenery. With Pass Mountain looming to the north and the sheer cliffs of the Superstition Mountains to the east, it's tough to keep your eyes on the trail.

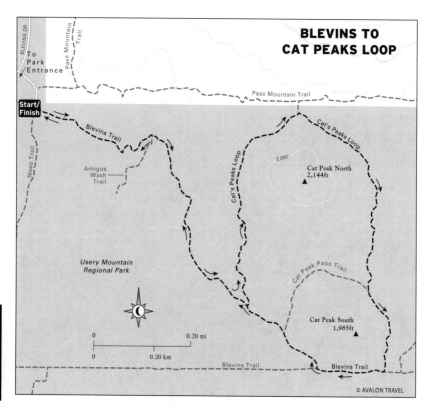

It's in your best interest to keep at least one eye on the dirt in front of you, however, because this path is chock-full of sneaky surprises. Yes, with so many chollas in your midst, the trail is littered with the plant's dropped stems. Each stem has hundreds of needles that jut in every direction—you only need to barely brush by this cactus to find a spiky stem has hitched a ride (this is why they have the reputation of "jumping").

For this balloon-shaped trail, you combine the Blevins and Cat Peaks Trails. Looking east from the trailhead staging area, the two Cat Peaks are clearly visible, as they are two small peaks poking up from the flat desert floor.

Park your vehicle at the Blevins trailhead staging area just off the southeast corner of Blevins Drive. The area is a large dirt lot with a few trash bins and a couple of portable toilets. Here, you have your pick of four trailheads. From the Blevins trailhead on the east side of the horse staging area, head southeast along the flat terrain. Just past 0.3 mile, you come across the Amigos Wash Trail. Just keep moving along the Blevins Trail as it leads south for the next half mile.

At 0.8 mile sits the clearly marked juncture of the Blevins and Cat Peaks Trails.

Take the Cat Peaks Trail north to walk along the west side of the Cat Peaks. Soon the trail takes on a rocky terrain and begins a slight ascent of 100 feet. The north tip of the loop features a small connecting path to the Pass Mountain Trail. Remain on Cat Peaks Trail heading east and follow as it turns to the south. Be sure to take a peek east to see the incredible Superstition Mountains dominating the horizon.

At just under 2 miles, the Cat Peaks Trail ends and connects to the Blevins Trail. Take Blevins Trail west but stay alert; the next turn is a mere 0.2 mile away. This is where things get a little tricky, because Blevins splits into two trails with the same name. Take the Blevins Trail that turns to the northwest. In the next 0.2 mile you pass by both the Cat Peaks Pass Trail and Cat Peaks Trail. Stay on Blevins Trail heading northwest to retrace your steps for the 0.7 mile back to the Blevins trailhead staging area and parking lot.

Options

To make for a bit of a cardio challenge, take advantage of the **Cat Peaks Pass Trail**, which bisects the Cat Peaks Trail. To make things easier, let's refer to them as CPPT (Cat Peaks Pass Trail) and CPT (Cat Peaks Trail). Take Blevins Trail past the turnoff for CPT for 0.9 mile. Turn left to follow the CPPT for 0.3 mile. Climb up and over the Cat Peaks and connect with the CPT on the other side. Turn south onto CPT for 0.2 mile until you reach Blevins Trail. Turn right, heading west on Blevins Trail for 0.2 mile. Turn right and head northwest along Blevins Trail for the 0.7 mile back to the Blevins trailhead. This option totals 2.3 miles.

Directions

From downtown Phoenix, take I-10 east toward Tucson for approximately 2 miles. Take exit 147A to merge onto the eastbound AZ-202 Loop. Continue east for 22.7 miles. Take exit 23A for Power Road for 0.6 mile. Turn right onto Power Road and go south for 0.6 mile. Turn left onto McDowell Road, heading east for 3.1 miles. Turn left onto Ellsworth Road, which becomes Usery Pass Road, and follow it northeast for 1.5 miles. Turn right onto Usery Park Road and head southeast for 1 mile. Pay the fee at the park entrance. Turn right to stay on Usery Park Road, and continue east for 0.7 mile as the road becomes Blevins Drive and then curves south. The Blevins Trail trailhead parking lot and staging area is on the east side of the road. The Blevins Trail trailhead is on the east side of the lot.
GPS Coordinates: 33.4658 N, 111.6070 W

Information and Contact

There is a fee of $6 per vehicle. An annual pass is available for $75. Dogs on leash are allowed. Maps are available at the Usery Mountain Regional Park Nature

Center (8am-4pm daily). The park is open daily (6am-8pm Sun.-Thurs., 6am-10pm Fri.-Sat.). For more information, contact Usery Mountain Regional Park Nature Center, 3939 North Usery Pass Road, Mesa, AZ 85207, 480/984-0032, www.maricopa.gov/parks/usery.

8 TREASURE LOOP TRAIL

Lost Dutchman State Park, Superstition Wilderness

Level: Easy

Total Distance: 2.4 miles round-trip

Hiking Time: 1 hour

Elevation Gain: 550 feet

Summary: This easy jaunt offers a sneak peek into the vast wonderland that is the Superstition Wilderness.

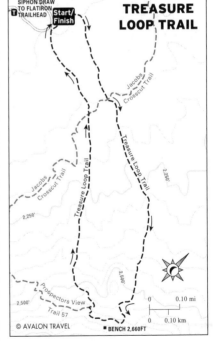

The Superstition Wilderness is well-known for intense, multi-day hikes that require serious gear and a sure-footed scramble to the tippy-tops of stunning viewpoints.

But, if you'd rather admire the sheer beauty of this area from afar, this easy trail is just the thing for you. The Treasure Loop Trail is a simple 2.4 miles with wide paths, a gentle incline, and knockout views of the range's westernmost edge that will no doubt draw you to the curious power these vast mountains hold.

This short loop starts in the Lost Dutchman State Park and leads you out of the park boundary, toward the dominating rock outcrop in the distance. Looking southeast, notice the iconic Flatiron, which tops out at 4,851 feet.

Begin your hike heading northeast (taking a clockwise loop) from the Cholla Day Use Area parking lot. You can easily spot the signed Treasure Loop trailhead. Pass by a few ramadas and through the park boundary fence. Then pass by a handful of intersecting trails as you follow the signs for Treasure Loop Trail. The trail leads you straight toward the sheer rock cliffs. Enjoy this leisurely stroll along this very (very!) gentle incline.

The ground beneath you continues to climb gradually to complete the 550-foot

A hiker enjoys the view from the highest elevation point on this easy trail.

elevation gain. At 1.3 miles, you're at the highest elevation point of the loop at 2,670 feet. Just a few steps farther to the southwest and you encounter a bench that sits in front of those dramatic cliffs and offers a close-up peek at the Green Boulder. Take it all in.

From the bench, remain on the Treasure Loop Trail, which turns northwest (toward the parking lot). A somewhat-craggy descent doesn't last for long and you spill onto a wide, dirt-packed trail within 0.3 mile. That leads northwest, back to your point of origin.

Just within range of the parking lot at about 2.3 miles, your trail-reading skills may be challenged. The proper trail disintegrates into a series of un-signed and trailblazed paths that surround the Cholla Day Use Area. Veer right (north) when you can or just keep heading along the main path until you find the paved road. No matter where you emerge, your car is only a few steps away.

Options

This trail can be bisected for an easier trek that skips all climbing and reduces the total mileage to a scant 0.8 mile. Follow the Treasure Loop Trail 0.3 mile. At that point, hop on **Jacob's Crosscut Trail**, heading south (this trail slices the loop in half, from north to south). Take the Jacob's Crosscut Trail south for approximately 0.2 mile until it reconnects with the Treasure Loop. Turn right to head west on the Treasure Loop Trail for the 0.3 mile back to the Cholla Day Use Area parking lot.

Directions

From downtown Phoenix, take I-10 east for approximately 5 miles. Take a slight right onto eastbound US-60 and go east for 24.7 miles. Take exit 196 for Idaho Road (eastbound AZ-88) and follow the exit ramp for 0.4 mile. Turn left onto Idaho Road and go north for 2.3 miles. Make a slight right onto Apache Trail (still AZ-88) and head northeast for approximately 5 miles. Turn right at the sign for the Lost Dutchman State Park. Pay the fee at the park entrance and continue for 0.5 mile, following signs for Cholla Day Use Area. Take the second left into the Cholla Day Use Area parking lot. The Treasure Loop Trail trailhead is on the northeast side of the lot.

GPS Coordinates: 33.3664 N, 112.0306 W

Information and Contact

There is a fee of $7 per vehicle. An annual pass is available for $75. Dogs on leash are allowed. Maps are available at the park gate; there is a visitors center (8am-4pm daily) and a gift shop. For more information, contact the Lost Dutchman State Park, 6109 North Apache Trail, Apache Junction, AZ 85119, 480/982-4485, www.azstateparks.com/parks/LODU.

9 SIPHON DRAW TRAIL TO THE FLATIRON

Lost Dutchman State Park, Superstition Wilderness

BEST Butt-Kickers, Climbing and Scrambling, Summit Views, Wildflowers

Level: Butt-kicker

Total Distance: 5.8 miles round-trip

Hiking Time: 6 hours

Elevation Gain: 2,750 feet

Summary: Crawl your way up to The Flatiron and complete one of the best hikes in The Valley, as well as one of the best hikes of your life.

So whenever you hang around the west side of the Superstition Wilderness and see that absolutely amazing mass of cliff faces jutting from the floor, you're looking at The Flatiron. (Specifically, The Flatiron is the cliff that boasts a practically 90-degree angle.) While the official Siphon Draw Trail may not take you all the way up to the 4,861-foot high point of The Flatiron, hikers have forged a popular scrambling path to this vantage point that offers unbeatable views of The Valley to the west and equally mind-boggling views of the entire Superstition Wilderness to the east.

© KRISTINA SMITH

See the flat rock on the left? That's your final destination. It's called the Flatiron and it will blow your mind.

For the first 2 miles, the popular Siphon Draw Trail is a wide path with a subtle gain in elevation. It offers stunning views to an endless field of wildflowers as you march toward the dramatic cliff-like mountains. The Siphon Draw Trail ends at the mouth of a smooth rock basin in the Siphon Draw Canyon, but this spot is really just the start of the real hiking. The rest of the trail to The Flatiron is hard-fought and recommended only for experienced hikers in good shape. It's almost a solid mile of scrambling on all fours as you inch your way up steep piles of rock and boulder. No switchbacks. No cleared trail. No flippin' mercy. You must follow the spray-painted arrows that guide you through a virtually vertical gouge in the mountain—a natural drainage choked with prickly vegetation. Bring gloves and your courage, and start early because this one's gonna take a while.

The hike has an innocent beginning as you enter the trail at the Siphon Draw trailhead (on the southwest end of the parking lot) and follow a small portion of the Discovery Interpretive Trail heading south. At 0.2 mile, turn left (east) to follow signs leading to Siphon Draw Trail. At 0.5 mile, pass a large kiosk with the park map and veer southeast to follow the official start of the Siphon Draw Trail. From here, make a subtle elevation gain of 1,100 feet spread over the next 1.5 miles.

By mile 2, you've reached the base of the mountain and are greeted by a smooth rock basin carved by rain drainage. This beautiful, shaded basin marks the beginning of the Siphon

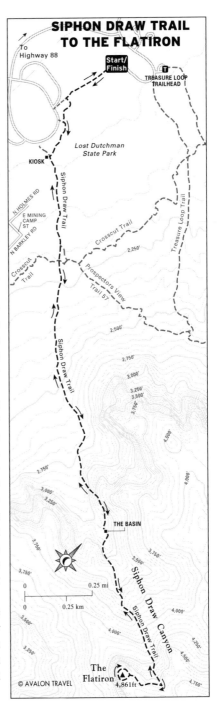

Draw Canyon and the start of possibly the most rewarding hike of your life. Put on your gloves because you'll need them as you start pawing at the rough rocks for the next 0.7 mile, during which you ascend 1,650 feet. Ouch. This consumes so much energy, it feels like 5 miles even to the fittest hiker.

The trail is not maintained for this stretch and follows a shallow drainage path straight up the side of the mountain. Be sure to make calculated moves as you follow spray-painted arrows and dots that mark the way. Remember to lean into the rock as you climb and take your time. There are a few tricky spots that most experienced hikers have no trouble clearing. But just before you reach the final stretch to The Flatiron at 2.6 miles, you run smack into a 12-foot rock face. There's only one way to clear this: Go up. Move slowly, using the cracks in the rock to anchor and wedge your feet. There's also a very handy (and sturdy) tree on the left side that makes for a much-needed grip. Once this rock face is cleared, there's just a few more feet of not-scary-at-all-by-comparison scrambling before the trail suddenly enters a serene clearing at 2.7 miles. You can finally stand upright to follow this easy bit of trail for the next 0.2 mile as it traces the edge of the mountain and leads west to the top of The Flatiron.

The top of The Flatiron is a wide clearing littered by low-lying agave, prickly pear, and buckhorn cholla. It. Is. Breathtaking. Lose your mind as you walk all over the flat top of rock and gaze at the impossibly miniature city to the west. To the east, you're equally blown away by this high-perched view of the rocky peaks and ridges that stretch as far as the eye can see into the Superstition Mountains. It's nuts. It's just totally nuts.

Once you've regained your composure, scarfed a snack, and snapped some photos of your journey to the top of the world, turn back and retrace your steps. Get down on your butt and use your hands to lower yourself during the scrambling descent. Once you return to the smooth rock basin, it's a mere 2-mile walk back to the trailhead.

There you have it. You just completed the best hike of your life.

Options

The Siphon Draw Trail ends at 2 miles and makes for a perfect stopping place (perfect, that is, if you're not in the mood for the best hike of your life). Simply stop at the smooth rock basin. This version makes for a shorter total of 4 miles and skips the scrambling to the top of The Flatiron. Still, the hike climbs up approximately 1,100 feet and makes for a worthy experience as you stop at the gorgeous base of the mountains and the dramatic rock basin.

Directions

From downtown Phoenix, take I-10 east for approximately 5 miles. Take a slight right onto eastbound US-60 and go east for 24.7 miles. Take exit 196 for Idaho

Road (eastbound AZ-88) and follow the exit ramp for 0.4 mile. Turn left onto Idaho Road and go north for 2.3 miles. Make a slight right onto Apache Trail (still AZ-88) and go northeast for approximately 5 miles. Turn right at the sign for the Lost Dutchman State Park. Pay the fee at the park entrance and continue for 0.7 mile, following the signs for Siphon Draw trailhead as the road curls south, then west. Park in the westernmost parking lot and find the Siphon Draw trailhead on the southwest corner of the lot.

GPS Coordinates: 33.4594 N, 111.4797 W

Information and Contact

There is a fee of $7 per vehicle. An annual pass is available for $75. Dogs on leash are allowed. Maps are available at the park gate; there is a visitors center (8am-4pm daily) and a gift shop. For more information, contact the Lost Dutchman State Park, 6109 North Apache Trail, Apache Junction, AZ 85119, 480/982-4485, www.azstateparks.com/parks/LODU.

10 HIEROGLYPHIC TRAIL
Superstition Wilderness

🦌 🏊 ⚙️ 🐴 👫

BEST Historical Hikes

Level: Easy/Moderate

Total Distance: 3 miles round-trip

Hiking Time: 1.5 hours

Elevation Gain: 700 feet

Summary: Just a small effort yields big rewards of a canyon filled with petroglyphs.

You've no doubt come across a few petroglyphs during your travels along the Phoenix-area trails, but this one takes the cake. The Hieroglyphic Trail is inaccurately named—clearly, these are not the hieroglyphics of ancient Egypt. Instead, they are the petroglyphs of ancient America, believed to have been carved into the rock by the Hohokam people, as many as 2,000 years ago. This short jaunt of 1.5 miles leads you on a gentle climb that ends in a rocky canyon carved by the Hieroglyphic Spring. Water may not be flowing all year, but the area has its fair share of large tanks filled with standing water, even in the dead of summer. Literally everywhere you look in the canyon, you see a petroglyph. A great mass exists on the west wall that features shapes of horned animals, spirals, and other stylized symbols.

These petroglyphs are just a small tease for the impressive cache you'll discover.

Start the hike from the Lost Goldmine trailhead and go north for 0.2 mile. Here, the trail splits and is clearly signed with the Lost Goldmine Trail to the right. Stick with the Hieroglyphic Trail heading north and then pass through the gate into the Superstition Wilderness.

The scenery for the rest of the trek is truly unbeatable. The Superstition mountain range rocks the horizon to the north, and The Flatiron is clearly visible to the northwest. The desert floor is scattered with saguaro, cholla, prickly pear, paloverde, and hedgehog cactus.

Continue north as the trail leads into the shady Hieroglyphic Canyon. When the trail collides into the rock, you know you're at the end. Look at, but don't touch, the petroglyphs covering the rocky walls that surround you. Unfortunately, the canyon also features carved images by modern-day hooligans. Sigh.

The best you can do is admire the real stuff from afar and try to resist the temptation to explore the canyon. Seriously, those petroglyphs are everywhere, and you won't be able to avoid stepping on at least one. Or you might stomp one of the teeny-tiny desert toads that scatter underfoot during the summer monsoon season.

Once you've seen all you want, simply turn around and retrace your steps for 1.5 miles of an easy descent back to the parking lot.

Options

For a longer hike that totals 11.4 miles round-trip, take a right turn at the fork at 0.2 mile to follow the **Lost Goldmine Trail** east. The Lost Goldmine Trail follows the southern edge of the Superstition Wilderness and ends at the easternmost Lost Goldmine trailhead, where you turn around for your return trip.

Directions

From downtown Phoenix, take I-10 east for approximately 5 miles. Take a slight right onto eastbound US-60 and head

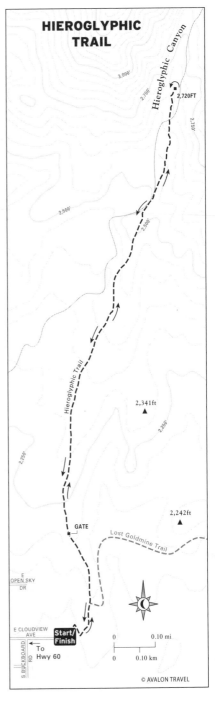

HIEROGLYPHIC TRAIL

© AVALON TRAVEL

east for 31.1 miles. Turn left onto Kings Ranch Road, heading north. Take Kings Ranch Road for 2.9 miles and then turn right onto Baseline Avenue. Take Baseline Avenue east for 0.2 mile and turn left, heading north onto Mohican Road. After 0.4 mile take the third left, heading northwest onto Valley View Drive. Continue as Valley View Drive becomes White Tail. After 0.3 mile turn right, heading east onto Cloud View Avenue. After 0.5 mile, the road ends at the Lost Goldmine Trail parking lot. The Lost Goldmine Trail trailhead is on the north side of the lot. **GPS Coordinates:** 33.3897 N, 111.4245 W

Information and Contact

There is no fee. Dogs on leash are allowed. Maps are available for purchase at the Tonto National Forest Supervisor's Office. For more information, contact the Tonto National Forest Supervisor's Office, 2324 East McDowell Road, Phoenix, AZ 85006, 602/225-5200, www.fs.usda.gov/main/tonto.

11 PERALTA TRAIL TO FREMONT SADDLE

Superstition Wilderness

BEST(Summit Views

Level: Strenuous

Total Distance: 4.5 miles round-trip

Hiking Time: 2.5 hours

Elevation Gain: 1,400 feet

Summary: Hiking the Peralta Trail will make you fall in love with the desert all over again.

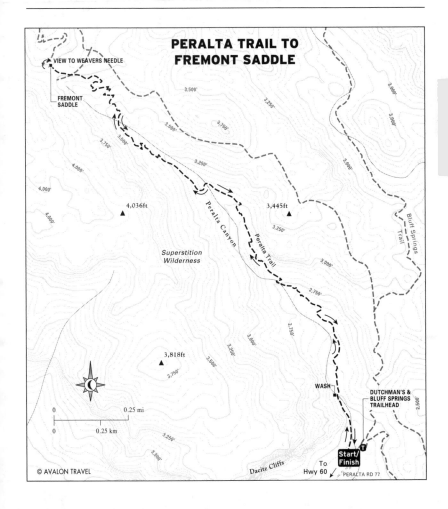

up close and personal with the Weaver's Needle

Want to know why everyone totally freaks out about the Superstition Wilderness? Peralta Trail has the answer, and it goes something like this: because it's way-super awesome.

Seriously, when you need a reminder of why you chose to live in this water-stripped land, hike the Peralta Trail. In just 2.25 miles that take you into the Peralta Canyon, you traverse thick, riparian vegetation and then climb along canyon walls surrounded by jagged fingers of igneous rock reaching upwards to the clear desert sky. As the elevation increases, views to the east of the endless layers of saguaro-filled ridgelines, canyons, and peaks of the Superstition Mountains will knock your socks off. And when you reach Fremont Saddle, you may have to restrain yourself from exclaiming your excitement (any "Oh my God!" or "Holy Cow!" echoes here) when the astonishing rock spire called Weaver's Needle is suddenly revealed. While the hike may be strenuous, the incredible payoff and easy trail navigation makes it a popular pick for families with energetic kids. In case you haven't yet figured it out, this hike completely rules!

To start, enter the Superstition Wilderness from the Peralta trailhead. You have your choice of three trails here. Opt for the Peralta Trail and veer left, heading to the northwest. The trail is well-defined and popular. The only tricky spot is when you cross over a sandy wash at 0.3 mile; the key word is "cross"—don't be lured by the wash's sandy path. Simply cross over and pick up the trail on the north side (veer right).

After you pass the wash, the trail begins to gain elevation and rarely lets up. Take your time, and whatever you do, don't forget to look behind you, because the view to the east is stupendous! The trail is slightly rocky, with a few steep areas, but no scrambling is required. It maintains a northwest course all the way. It climbs 1,400 feet in just 2.25 miles, so, yeah, it's a haul.

You know you're getting close to the end when, during the final quarter mile before the saddle, you reach a series of switchbacks along a desolate, smooth rock face. And with your very last steps to the Fremont Saddle, the rocky canyon walls suddenly give way and then, POW!, the gigantic Weaver's Needle dominates the horizon to the northwest. What a treat. Speaking of treats, the Fremont Saddle is the perfect place to chow down on some delicious snacks. Enjoy the view and explore the area for some righteous photo opportunities.

You probably won't want to leave, but when you do, simply follow the same trail, heading southeast for the 2.25-mile descent back to the Peralta trailhead. Then go home and tell your friends, because everyone should experience this trail!

Options
If you just can't get enough of the Weaver's Needle and you're in the mood for a longer haul, make a very long loop around Weaver's Needle with this combination of trails: From the Fremont Saddle, continue northwest on the Peralta Trail past the saddle as it enters Boulder Canyon and passes along the west side of the needle. After 3.9 miles, connect with the Dutchman's Trail, heading east for 1 mile. Turn right on Terrapin Trail and head southeast for 2.8 miles. Take the turnoff for Bluff Springs Trail for the final 2 miles southeast, back to the Peralta trailhead. This option is really only for extremely fit individuals because it adds up to 11.9 miles.

Directions
From downtown Phoenix, take I-10 east for approximately 5 miles. Take a slight right onto eastbound US-60 and go east for 32.6 miles. Turn left onto Peralta Road, heading northeast for 7.5 miles as the street turns to a well-graded dirt road and ends at the Peralta Trail parking lot. The Peralta Trail trailhead is on the north end of the lot.
GPS Coordinates: 33.3967 N, 111.3479 W

Information and Contact
There is no fee. Dogs on leash are allowed. Maps are available for purchase at the Tonto National Forest Supervisor's Office. For more information, contact the Tonto National Forest Supervisor's Office, 2324 East McDowell Road, Phoenix, AZ 85006, 602/225-5200, www.fs.usda.gov/main/tonto.

12 DUTCHMAN'S AND BLUFF SPRING LOOP
Superstition Wilderness

Level: Strenuous

Total Distance: 9 miles round-trip

Hiking Time: 5 hours

Elevation Gain: 1,500 feet

Summary: This lengthy loop explores the south side of the Superstition Wilderness for stunning views.

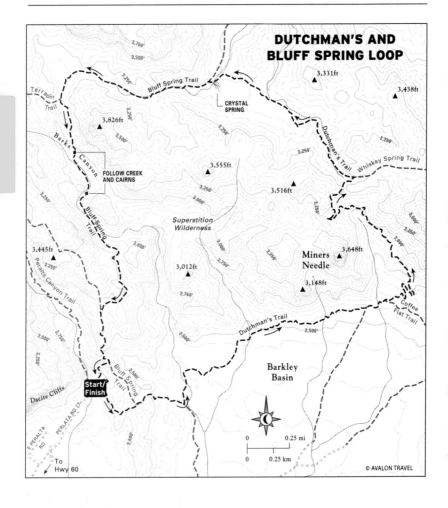

This loop guarantees some of the best desert views in the Superstition Wilderness.

It's really sort of silly how gorgeous the Superstition Wilderness is. If you thought the Peralta Trail to Fremont Saddle was awesome, this 9-mile loop gives you even more of the good stuff. Located just southeast of Peralta Canyon and Weaver's Needle, the Dutchman's and Bluff Spring Loop encompasses the Miners Needle (a smaller rock spire) and then returns via Barks Canyon. It's 9 miles of classic views of the Superstition Wilderness, filled with barrel cacti, flourishing pincushion cacti, blooming agave, and gobs of prickly pear, all against the scraggly igneous rock.

To get started, enter at the main trailhead on the north side of the Peralta trailhead parking lot. Within the first few feet, veer right at the signed trail junction to follow the arrows for the Bluff Spring and Dutchman's Trails. After just another few steps, the Bluff Spring Trail breaks away to the north. Ignore it to continue along the Dutchman's Trail heading east/northeast. After 1 mile, cross a creek bed and begin an 890-foot climb with varying degrees of intensity throughout the next 3 miles.

The rocky spire of Miners Needle comes into view from the north, and at 2.3 miles in, you're right at its southern base. Pass by the Coffee Flat Trail at 2.6 miles, then wiggle through a short series of switchbacks before the trail makes a turn to the northwest. Here, keep glancing at the Miners Needle and catch a glimpse of the small hole (the "eye") on the tip of the spire. At approximately 4 miles, the trail leads to the west side of Miners Needle. Follow cairns as it makes a sharp right turn and then leads north to an unnamed saddle at 4.2 miles, where the sign for Whiskey Spring Trail sits. Continue north along the Dutchman's Trail, which veers northwest. For the next couple miles, you're able to rest your lungs as the trail flattens and weaves through a field of low-lying vegetation.

At 5.6 miles, abandon the Dutchman's Trail to follow the Bluff Spring Trail heading west. At 5.9 miles, the trail briefly follows a small tributary, with cairns leading the way. Shortly after the trail veers south, you encounter the sign for Terrapin Trail at 6.6 miles. Ignore it and continue heading south along the Bluff Spring Trail. At approximately 7 miles, the trail follows an unnamed creek (this is actually the north end of the creek you passed over at the beginning of the hike). Things get a little tricky because you must vigilantly follow the cairns. At 7.3 miles, look on the east side of the bank for the trail as it finally breaks away from the creek for good.

At about 7.8 miles, the sights are totally mind-blowing. You're treated to a bird's-eye view of Barks Canyon below. From here, the Bluff Spring Trail heads south and makes a dramatic descent of 550 feet over 1.2 miles into the canyon and back to the Peralta trailhead. Amazing, sweeping, punch-you-in-the-face beautiful views of the Superstition Wilderness to the north and east are slowly revealed along the way. Make sure you look up from your feet frequently to enjoy them.

Options

To enjoy the most scenic portion of this hike, opt for taking the loop in the opposite direction and cut it short at 1 mile. Start the hike the same way, following the arrows for the Bluff Spring and Dutchman's Trails, but after that, instead of taking Dutchman's Trail east, take a left turn to follow Bluff Spring Trail north. It's a hard-earned climb of 550 feet along the Barks Canyon walls. At about 1 mile, you enjoy those punch-you-in-the-face beautiful views. From there, simply turn back and retrace your steps for a total of 2 miles on this up-and-back hike.

Directions

From downtown Phoenix, take I-10 east for approximately 5 miles. Take a slight right onto eastbound US-60 and go east for 32.6 miles. Turn left onto Peralta Road, heading northeast for 7.5 miles as the street turns to a well-graded dirt road and ends at the Peralta trailhead parking lot. The Peralta Trail trailhead (which connects to the Bluff Spring and Dutchman's Trails) is on the north end of the lot. **GPS Coordinates:** 33.3976 N, 111.3478 W

Information and Contact

There is no fee. Dogs on leash are allowed. Maps are available for purchase at the Tonto National Forest Supervisor's Office. For more information, contact the Tonto National Forest Supervisor's Office, 2324 East McDowell Road, Phoenix, AZ 85006, 602/225-5200, www.fs.usda.gov/main/tonto.

13 ROGERS CANYON TRAIL
Superstition Wilderness

BEST Historical Hikes, Solitude

Level: Strenuous

Total Distance: 8 miles round-trip

Hiking Time: 5 hours

Elevation Gain: 1,200 feet

Summary: Talk about remote. The Rogers Canyon trailhead sits tucked away in the Superstition Mountains, then takes you 4 miles into a canyon with ancient cliff-dwelling ruins.

Tucked far inside the wilderness, the starting elevation for this canyon hike is 4,880 feet, which allows for higher country vegetation, like oak, juniper, and Arizona sycamore trees (not to mention incredible views of the Superstition Wilderness on the way up). At this altitude, you should plan for temperatures down to 20 degrees lower than the weather forecast in the city. The hike itself provides incredible scenery as you trace an anonymous creek for a 4-mile descent into

Rogers Canyon is a classic example of the beauty and history available in the Superstition Wilderness.

Rogers Canyon. The first leg ends with a very rare opportunity to wander in and among cliff dwelling ruins. The hike, though lengthy, is easy to follow with manageable elevation gain on the way out only (remember, it's a canyon).

While the hike may be doable for most, getting to the trailhead can be a challenge. The trip includes over 20 miles of bumpy and hairy forest roads that eventually creep up the side of Iron Mountain to reach Rogers Trough trailhead. A high-clearance and four-wheel-drive vehicle is a must, and having an experienced off-road driver behind the wheel is your safest bet. Pushing your two-wheel-drive SUV on these roads is risky, and if it's been raining, be sure to reschedule no matter which vehicle you're planning to drive.

Okay, let's get to the hike already! To start, set out from the Rogers Trough trailhead, heading northwest to follow the Reavis Ranch Trail (the trail has a few wiggles but quickly turns to adopt a northwest direction) for the first 1.5 miles. When the Reavis Ranch Trail splits off to the northeast, you follow the Rogers Canyon Trail sign to head northwest (look for the trail sign hidden in a thicket of bushy vegetation).

At 1.7 miles, the trail reaches a creek bed and follows it for the remainder of the trail. Depending on the time of year and recent rain activity, you may see pools of water or ice from time to time. Follow the well-worn and narrow path as it meanders from one side of the creek bed to the other. Be on the lookout for cairns to guide you, and if you suddenly suspect you've gone off-trail via

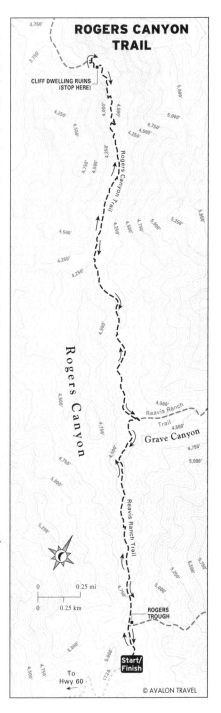

a deceiving trail blaze, chances are, you're right. When in doubt, stop, backtrack, and look for cairns. Keep in mind that the Rogers Canyon Trail closely follows the creek bed and heads northwest all the way to the ruins.

At 3.5 miles, be sure to pay close attention and veer near the creek bed, avoiding any deceiving trailblazing that travels up the canyon wall. When you're getting close to the 4-mile mark, be sure to glance on the right side of the canyon to catch a glimpse of the cliff dwellings. At 4 miles, you should see the walls of each cliff dwelling-hut from across the creek. Cross the creek and follow a small group of switchbacks up the side of the cliff to the lower landing of the ruins. A sign indicates that the homes were built by the Salado people approximately 600 years ago. Tread lightly as you explore, and be respectful of this treasured site. When ready, turn back and descend the cliff back to the creek. This spot, near the water and at the foot of the ruins, is the perfect setting for a peaceful lunch.

After grub time is over, turn around and follow the trail for the 4 miles back to Rogers Trough trailhead. Oh, and you hopefully scarfed a nutritious lunch, because you need some energy to climb the 1,200 feet of elevation as you make your way out of Rogers Canyon.

Options

Stopping at the ruins is just fine, but there's another beautiful site not far beyond. After reaching the ruins, continue for 0.5 mile until you reach **Angel Basin**, a large, flat area at the juncture of Rogers Canyon and Frog Tanks Trails. The area is said to be idyllic, open, and peaceful. If temperatures are mild, other backpackers will also be camping in this popular area. Adding this leg makes for a hike that totals 9 miles.

Directions

From downtown Phoenix, take I-10 east for approximately 5 miles. Take a slight right onto eastbound US-60 and go east for 42.8 miles. Turn left onto Queen Valley Road, heading northeast for 1.9 miles. Make a slight right onto Hewitt Station Road and go northeast for 4.8 miles. Turn left onto Forest Road 172 and remain on the winding dirt road for 14.1 miles. Turn right onto Forest Road 172A and follow the bumpy dirt road for 18.1 miles, following signs for Rogers Trough trailhead.

Note: Less than 0.5 mile from the trailhead there is a hairpin turn followed by a very steep pass. Some opt to park here and hike the rest of the way to Rogers Trough trailhead, which is a large dirt clearing. The Reavis Ranch Trail trailhead is located on the north end of the lot.

GPS Coordinates: 33.4222 N, 111.1735 W

Information and Contact

There is no fee. Dogs on leash are allowed. Maps are available for purchase at the

Tonto National Forest Supervisor's Office. For more information, contact the Tonto National Forest Supervisor's Office, 2324 East McDowell Road, Phoenix, AZ 85006, 602/225-5200, www.fs.usda.gov/main/tonto.

14 MAIN TRAIL
Boyce Thompson Arboretum

BEST(**Wildflowers**

Level: Easy

Total Distance: 1.7 miles round-trip

Hiking Time: 1 hour

Elevation Gain: 250 feet

Summary: Visit one of the state's most incredible landscapes on the Main Trail in Boyce Thompson Arboretum, a park dedicated to the conservation of arid-land plants.

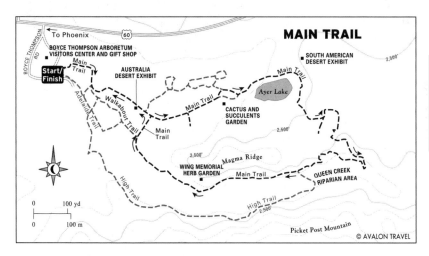

You undoubtedly pass by thousands of cacti on every hike, and chances are, you can only identify a small percentage of the prickly plants. So if you're interested in gaining the ability to utter words in addition to "saguaro" and "barrel" when describing the landscape, this is the hike for you (and any kids you might know, because it's educational).

Boyce Thompson Arboretum State Park offers 320 acres of land dedicated to cultivating arid-weather plants and educating visitors. The park has fantastic gardens and unspoiled examples of native Sonoran Desert plant life and wildflowers (acacia, desert honeysuckle, milkweed, Arizona walnut, lavender, sage, mesquite, willow, rosewood—too many to name here), with Picket Post Mountain as its backdrop to the south. The park's trails (over half of which are wheelchair-accessible) welcome hikers of varying fitness levels.

The Main Trail offers stunning views of the Boyce Thompson Arboretum.

Enter the park on the east side of the large parking lot. Pass by the gift shop and through the entryway heading east along the main walkway. After 0.3 mile, follow signs for the Main Trail and veer left to take the loop clockwise. Within the next 0.3 mile, you pass by the Cactus and Succulents Garden, a cluster of boojum trees, and Ayer Lake to the south. Feel free to stop and explore to your heart's content. At the east end of Ayer Lake, notice a turnoff to the South American Desert Exhibit. Again, explore if you wish. As you move ahead on the Main Trail, you soon pass the Upland Sonoran Natural Area to the north. And see the massive rock to the south? That's the Magma Ridge.

Close to 1 mile along, you gain a clear view of Picket Post Mountain looming to the south of the entire park. When the trail turns west, you begin to weave through the Queen Creek Riparian Area. At 1.3 miles, you pass the Wing Memorial Herb Garden on the north, followed by a eucalyptus forest filled with the towering trees. At 1.5 miles, the trail curves north to close the loop (close to the Australia Desert Exhibit).

Clearly, this loop offers just the overview of the many discoveries along the Main Trail at Boyce Thompson Arboretum. Bring the kids, the grandparents, and the dog for this outing.

Options

To experience the entirety of the park's trails, consider hiking them all. Take your pick of combinations, as each is rather short and can be easily added to the Main

Trail. Chances are, you'll wander through many of them without even knowing it as you explore the park. The other trails include the **High Trail** (0.45 mile), **Curandero Trail** (0.3 mile), **Chihuahuan Desert Exhibit Trail** (0.27 mile), and the **South American Desert Trail** (0.2 mile). Doing all trails totals 2.7 miles. Pick up a map at the park entrance gift shop to plan your preferred route.

Directions

From downtown Phoenix, take I-10 east for approximately 5 miles. Take a slight right onto eastbound US-60 and go east for 51.7 miles. Turn right onto Boyce Thompson Road and continue south for 500 feet. Pay the fee at the park gate. The Boyce Thompson Arboretum parking lot is on the left. The main entrance and trailhead is on the east side of the lot.

GPS Coordinates: 33.2798 N, 111.1596 W

Information and Contact

There is a fee of $9 per person. Dogs on leash are allowed. Maps are available at the Boyce Thompson Arboretum Gift Shop. The park is open daily (6am-3pm May-Aug.; 8am-4pm Sept.-Apr.). For more information, contact the Boyce Thompson Arboretum, 37615 U.S. Highway 60, Superior, AZ 85173, 520/689-2723, http://arboretum.ag.arizona.edu.

NORTH VALLEY

© LILIA MENCONI

The North Valley's scattered trails are accessed in a plethora of preserves. The McDowell Mountains loom about 20 miles northeast of Phoenix with endless loops, lookouts, summits, and ridges. At Fountain Hills Lake Overlook Trail, kids can watch one of the world's tallest fountains shoot a stream of water 550 feet in the air. Cave Creek Regional Park, 30 miles north of Phoenix, includes the Go John Trail, a favorite loop for hikers and equestrians alike. Hikers can escape into the Tonto National Forest and hit the Four Peaks Wilderness. Spur Cross Ranch Conservation Area offers a family-friendly hike in a riparian wonderland. Deem Hills Recreation Area and Thunderbird Conservation Park are only four miles away from each another. It's tough to know where to start. And that's a great problem to have.

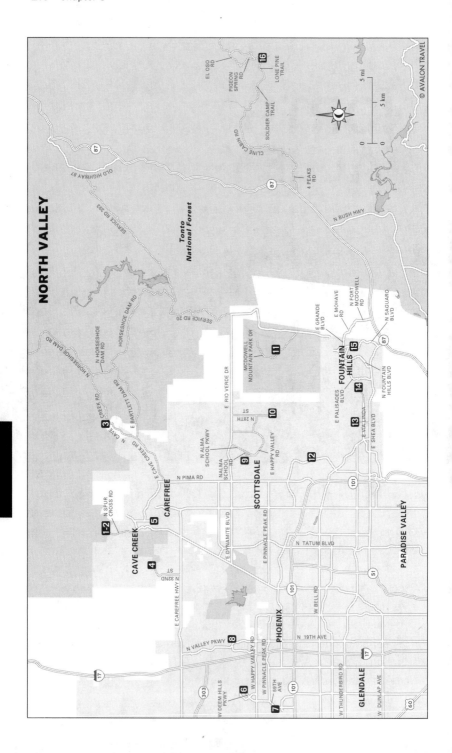

TRAIL NAME	FEATURES	LEVEL	DISTANCE	TIME	ELEVATION	PAGE
1 Spur Cross and Elephant Mountain Loop BEST		Strenuous	6.9 mi rt	4 hr	1,600 ft	212
2 Dragonfly Trail BEST		Easy	1.7 mi rt	1 hr	225 ft	216
3 Sears-Kay Ruin Loop BEST		Easy	1 mi rt	30 min	400 ft	219
4 Go John Trail		Moderate	5.9 mi rt	3 hr	900 ft	222
5 Black Mountain Summit Trail		Moderate	2.2 mi rt	1.5 hr	1,275 ft	225
6 Circumference and Ridgeline Loop		Easy/Moderate	3.9 mi rt	2 hr	700 ft	228
7 Thunderbird H-1 to H-3 Loop: Coach Whip to Cholla Loop		Easy	3.3 mi rt	1.5 hr	700 ft	231
8 Dixie Mountain Loop		Moderate	5.7 mi rt	3 hr	1,350 ft	234
9 Pinnacle Peak Trail		Easy/Moderate	2.9 mi rt	1.5 hr	1,000 ft	238
10 Tom's Thumb Trail		Moderate	4.1 mi rt	2.5 hr	1,325 ft	241
11 Pemberton and Tonto Tank Loop BEST		Moderate	9.2 mi rt	5 hr	600 ft	245
12 Gateway Loop Trail		Easy/Moderate	4.4 mi rt	2 hr	700 ft	248
13 Lost Dog Wash Trail		Easy	4.4 mi rt	2 hr	375 ft	252
14 Sunrise Trail		Moderate	3.7 mi rt	2.5 hr	1,100 ft	255
15 Fountain Lake Overlook Loop BEST		Easy	2.6 mi rt	1 hr	300 ft	258
16 Brown's Trail BEST		Moderate	4 mi rt	2.5 hr	1,100 ft	261

1 SPUR CROSS AND ELEPHANT MOUNTAIN LOOP

Spur Cross Ranch Conservation Area

BEST Solitude

Level: Strenuous

Total Distance: 6.9 miles round-trip

Hiking Time: 4 hours

Elevation Gain: 1,600 feet

Summary: Explore the Spur Cross Ranch Conservation Area with this lengthy loop.

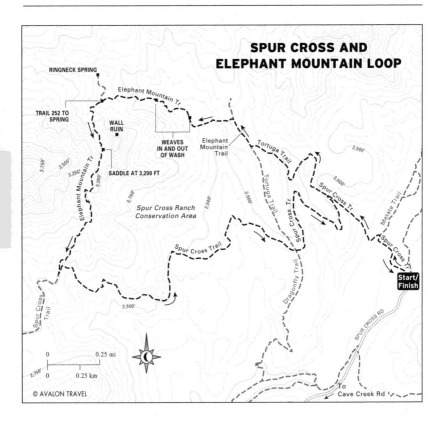

After visiting so many of the other regional parks with their fancy bathrooms, picnic tables, and running water, Spur Cross Ranch Conservation Area is just kind of...cute. Still in its infancy as the one of the newest additions to the Maricopa County Regional Parks System, there's a respectable humility to the dirt road, minimal trailheads, and well-maintained portable bathrooms. With a visit during its humble beginnings, you can be one of the first in The Valley to travel these new trails just north of Cave Creek's main drag.

Climb the "elephant" on this hike.

This loop (a combination of three trails) creates a 6.9-mile, lasso-shaped route that travels the heart of the Conservation Area's land. This trek crosses Cave Creek (the body of water, not the town), climbs up and over Elephant Mountain, and offers a visit to a working water spring *and* an ancient ruin. Heck yeah!

To begin, walk from the Spur Cross Ranch gravel parking lot north to the park's entrance, pay the entrance fee at the station, then continue north to a large clearing with portable bathrooms and a small nature center. Find the Spur Cross trailhead to the northwest of the main kiosk. The Spur Cross Trail immediately splits, so be sure to veer left to follow the Spur Cross Trail northwest. At 0.2 mile, cross over the (most likely) dry bed of Cave Creek and ignore the turnoff for Metate Trail as you begin a subtle ascent.

Continue hiking along the ascent on Spur Cross Trail, heading northwest until reaching the intersection with Tortuga Trail at 0.6 mile. This is the beginning of the loop. Start the north side of the loop by veering right to follow the Tortuga Trail as it continues northwest. At 1.1 miles, and after a 250-foot climb, you plunge into a dry gorge. As you climb out of the gorge, look for the signed Elephant Mountain Trail at 1.5 miles. Hop on the Elephant Mountain Trail, which continues northwest. After a brief 0.2 mile, the trail splits. Ignore the signed turnoff leading to the Tonto National Forest, and instead, veer left to continue along Elephant Mountain Trail heading west. Almost immediately, the trail makes a steep descent into the Boca Grande Wash and follows the wash for the next 0.3 mile. Be on the lookout for footsteps, cairns, and branches flagged with bright pink plastic ties as the trail meanders in and out of the sandy wash. The final exit of the wash occurs at 2.1 mile and is marked by a brown post.

From the end of the wash, climb a steep shale ascent for just 0.1 mile. This is the start of the main climb up the northeastern slope of Elephant Mountain. When the trail briefly mellows out at 2.4 miles, look for a small trail marker and a narrow trail that descends north. Take it! After a short 25 feet or so, you find the Ringneck Spring, which is now an old-timey water pump and metal bucket. The water is supposedly clean (maybe let the dog test it). Anyway, it's a short detour, which leads to the rare novelty of a water source in the desert. When ready, turn around and retrace your steps back to the Elephant Mountain Trail and turn right to head southwest.

Welcome to the final climb of the day! Grunt your way up the 350 feet to the Elephant Mountain saddle at an elevation of 3,215 feet. Take in the breeze and glance west to see the (what's thought to be) Hohokam ruin of a wall. To the southeast, notice the riparian cottonwood trees poking out from the Jewel of the Creek Preserve. Then continue south along the Elephant Mountain Trail for a sweet, sweet (and steep) descent of 775 feet along the south side of Elephant Mountain.

At 3.5 miles total, the steep stuff is over and so is the Elephant Mountain Trail. Hop on the Spur Cross Trail, which forces a sharp left turn to head north, then immediately east. The rest of the hike is super-easy and flat. Ignore the turnoff to Dragonfly and Tortuga Trails at 5.3 miles. At 6 miles, you once again ignore the Tortuga Trail (this is where you started the loop). Take a right turn instead to head east along the Spur Cross Trail, taking the familiar route back over Cave Creek and to the Spur Cross trailhead. Haul south along the dirt road to the gravel parking lot and congratulate yourself—someday, you can say you knew Spur Cross Conservation Area "way back when."

Options

Cut this hike into a short lasso-shaped loop that skips the climb to Elephant Mountain by combining the Tortuga Trail with the Spur Cross Trail. Begin this hike following the Spur Cross Trail to the northwest. At 0.6 mile, veer right to follow the Tortuga Trail, which continues northwest. At 1.3 miles, the trail splits. Take a sharp left turn to continue along the Tortuga Trail (ignoring the Elephant Mountain Trail) and head southeast. After 0.5 mile, the Tortuga Trail runs back into the Spur Cross Trail. Turn left onto the Spur Cross Trail as it zigzags its way back to its original juncture with Tortuga Trail. Continue along the Spur Cross Trail heading southeast, crossing Cave Creek to the Spur Cross Trail trailhead. This option totals 3.6 miles.

Directions

From downtown Phoenix, take AZ-51 north for approximately 16 miles. Take exit 15B on the left to merge onto westbound AZ-101 Loop for 1.7 miles. Take exit 28 for Cave Creek Road and turn right onto Cave Creek Road, heading north for

12.3 miles. Turn left onto Spur Cross Road and head north for 0.2 mile. Turn right onto Grapevine Road and go east for 160 feet. Take the first left onto Spur Cross Road and follow it north for 4 miles. The Spur Cross Ranch Conservation Area gravel parking lot is on the right (east). Park, then walk north along the dirt road. Pass through the park gate and pay the fee at the self-pay station. After 0.2 mile, find the Spur Cross Trail trailhead to the northwest.

GPS Coordinates: 33.8864 N, 111.9518 W

Information and Contact

There is a fee of $3 per person. An annual pass is available for $75. Dogs on leash are allowed. Maps are available at the entrance or online. The park is open daily (6am-8pm Sun.-Thurs., 6am-10pm Fri.-Sat.). For more information, contact the Spur Cross Ranch Conservation Area, 44000 North Spur Cross Road, Cave Creek, AZ 85331, 480/488-6601, www.maricopa.gov/parks/spur_cross.

2 DRAGONFLY TRAIL
Spur Cross Ranch Conservation Area, Jewel of the Creek Preserve

BEST Kid-Friendly Hikes

Level: Easy

Total Distance: 1.7 miles round-trip

Hiking Time: 1 hour

Elevation Gain: 225 feet

Summary: By far, this is one of the finest family hikes in the North Valley. Creeks, caves, cattails, and cottonwood trees—it's got it all.

This might possibly be the perfect family hike. This short, well-marked loop travels along and crosses over Cave Creek, in the stunning Jewel of the Creek Preserve. With water running in the creek year-round (albeit slow and spotty in the summer), the landscape brags a thick rash of bloated saguaro cacti that litter the surrounding hills of a riparian landscape rich with towering cottonwood and willow trees. Wildflowers like the common sunflower and desert tobacco blooms can be spotted in the dead of summer. Kids will go nuts as they cross over the water on rickety footbridges, track javelina prints in the mud, peer into

This riparian hike along Cave Creek comes with actual caves and is great for the entire family.

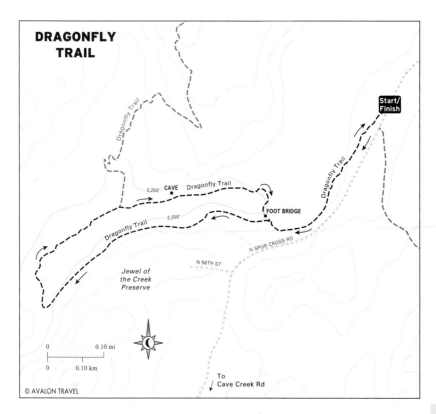

DRAGONFLY
TRAIL

Dragonfly Trail

Start/
Finish

Dragonfly Trail

2,250' CAVE Dragonfly Trail

FOOT BRIDGE

2,250'

Dragonfly Trail

N SPUR CROSS RD

N 56TH ST

Jewel of
the Creek
Preserve

0   0.10 mi

0   0.10 km

To
Cave Creek Rd

© AVALON TRAVEL

a small cave, and grab at cattails that grow like crazy in this desert wetland. Yep, it's pretty awesome.

Start the trail at the gate located on the south side of the small parking area. The entire hike is well-marked with signs for the Dragonfly Trail. For the first 0.4 mile, the trail descends, heading southwest until it curves into the marshy land close to the creek. You see a small footbridge here; ignore it for now (you cross it on the way back) and continue along the trail as it follows the south side of the creek. Admire the towering trees and continue until the trail makes an abrupt right turn at 0.8 mile to the north. Here, you make your first crossing of the creek. Depending on the time of year, you might be crossing a muddy creek bed or a simple footbridge. Once you cross to the other side, the trail is easy to find as it heads northeast and follows the other side of the creek.

Here's where the real excitement begins. With Elephant Mountain and the Tonto National Forest to the north, it's obvious that critters rely on this water source. You'll undoubtedly spy javelina or other animal tracks in the mud as you move along the path. At 1.1 miles, the Dragonfly Trail splits in two. Ignore the trail that heads north and continue east along the waterway. Soon after, you stumble upon a small cave on the north side of the trail.

At 1.4 miles, the trail turns south and crosses Cave Creek at another small footbridge. Step over to this familiar territory (this is the bridge you ignored earlier). Retrace your steps along the trail, heading east as it ascends a mere 100 feet back to the trailhead.

After a round of high-fives with the family, start thinking about the next hike. Your kids will be eager to get back out there.

Options

For a longer loop, consider adding the entirety of the Dragonfly Trail. This time, take the left turn at 1.1 miles to travel the Dragonfly Trail when it splits from the creek and heads north. After 0.9 mile, take a right and head east along the Spur Cross Trail for 1.4 miles until it ends at the Spur Cross trailhead. Take the trail south for another 0.5 mile as it becomes Spur Cross Road. The parking area and trailhead for the Dragonfly Trail is on the right. This trek equals a grand total of approximately 3.8 miles.

Directions

From downtown Phoenix, take I-10 east toward Tucson for 2.2 miles. Take exit 147B to merge onto northbound AZ-51 for 15.5 miles. Take exit 15B on the left to merge onto the AZ-101 Loop and go west for 1.7 miles. Take exit 28 for Cave Creek Road. Turn right onto Cave Creek Road, heading northeast for 12.3 miles. Turn left onto Spur Cross Road and go north for 0.2 mile. Turn right onto Grapevine Road and head east for 160 feet. Take the first left onto Spur Cross Road and go north for 4 miles. The Spur Cross Ranch Conservation Area gravel parking lot is on the right (east). Park, then walk north along the dirt road. Pass through the park gate and pay the fee at the self-pay station. Then turn around and walk south along Spur Cross Ranch Road for approximately 0.3 mile to the Dragonfly Trail trailhead and small parking lot on the west side of the road.
GPS Coordinates: 33.8843 N, 111.9546 W

Information and Contact

There is a fee of $3 per person. An annual pass is available for $75. Dogs on leash are allowed. Maps are available at the entrance or online. The park is open daily (6am-8pm Sun.-Thurs., 6am-10pm Fri.-Sat.). For more information, contact the Spur Cross Ranch Conservation Area, 44000 North Spur Cross Road, Cave Creek, AZ 85331, 480/488-6601, www.maricopa.gov/parks/spur_cross.

3 SEARS-KAY RUIN LOOP

Tonto National Forest, Cave Creek Ranger District

BEST(**Historical Hikes, Kid-Friendly Hikes**

Level: Easy

Total Distance: 1 mile round-trip

Hiking Time: 30 minutes

Elevation Gain: 400 feet

Summary: A short climb leads to prehistoric ruins that are sure to boggle any mind.

What a gem! This oft-overlooked trail is short, easy, beautiful, and jam-packed with an inspiring history lesson. No, wait, it's a prehistory lesson...pre! Amazing.

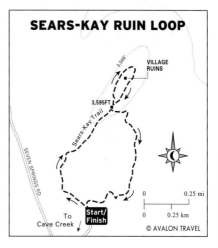

Why all the enthusiasm? Though petroglyphs are commonplace on Phoenix-area trails, here is an actual ruin of a small Hohokam village perched on a hilltop ridge. What remains today are rock-piles outlining 40 rooms spread among five buildings. The site's origins reach back—way back—to an estimated 900 years ago. That's 300 years before Columbus landed, y'all!

The Hohokam are ancient peoples who occupied this site between 1050 and 1200 CE. For 1000 years, the Hohokam thrived as farmers, craftsmen and traders. For reasons unknown to historians, the society began building defensive forts around 1050 CE. The Sears-Kay ruins prove that communities chose to inhabit tall perches (like this site atop a small mountain) from which they could see far and wide over the surrounding lowland desert—an important strategy.

Start the loop at the Sears-Kay trailhead at the northwest end of the parking area. Veer left to take this loop clockwise. It's a very short 0.3 mile up the hill to the first set of ruins. With interpretive informational plaques at every turn, you'll know more about Sears-Kay than you ever thought you might. Cautiously peer and tread lightly next to the piled rocks that outline the 900-year-old homes. Continue

Walk gently among the 900-year-old remnants of the prehistoric Hohokam homes.

on the trail to the north as it wraps around and into the main area of ruins. Again, maintain respect as you walk the same paths as these ancient people walked. Read each plaque to learn about the Hohokam diet, architecture, and general way of life.

Head south, exploring the ruins, until you see a connecting path on the south end of this upper landing. Climb down to the lower landing and look to your left (east) to find the trail marker for the other side of this loop. Avoid any trailblazed paths from the north end of the main ruins—it's not the way to go.

Follow the Sears-Kay Ruin Trail east and then south as it leads the remaining 0.3 mile down the hill and back to the parking lot. This completes your prehistory lesson.

Options
The Sears-Kay Loop is the lone hike in the immediate area. For more hikes in Cave Creek, most flock to **Cave Creek Regional Park** (37900 North Cave Creek Parkway, Cave Creek, AZ 85331, 623/465-0431, www.maricopa.gove/parks/cave_creek) or the **Spur Cross Ranch Conservation Area** (44000 North Spur Cross Road, Cave Creek, AZ 85331, 480/488-6601, www.maricopa.gov/parks/spur_cross). Both offer many miles of intersecting trail options.

Directions
From downtown Phoenix, take I-10 east toward Tucson for approximately 2 miles. Take exit 147B to merge onto AZ-51. Take AZ-51 north for 15.5 miles. Take exit

15A to merge onto the AZ-101 Loop. Take the AZ-101 Loop east for 4.3 miles. Take exit 34 for Scottsdale Road. Turn left onto Scottsdale Road and follow it north for 5.8 miles. Turn right, heading east onto Dynamite Boulevard. Take Dynamite Boulevard for 2 miles and turn left onto Pima Road. Take Pima Road north for 5.3 miles and then turn right, heading northeast, onto Cave Creek Road. Take Cave Creek Road for 6.8 miles. Continue on to Seven Springs Road, and after 0.2 mile turn right, heading northeast onto Sears Kay Ruins Road. The street ends at the Sears Kay Ruins parking lot. The Sears Kay Ruin Loop trailhead is on the northwest end of the lot.

GPS Coordinates: 33.8855 N, 111.816 W

Information and Contact

No fees or passes are required. Dogs on leash are allowed. For more information, contact the Tonto National Forest Cave Creek Ranger District, 40202 North Cave Creek Road, Scottsdale, AZ 85262, 480/595-3300, www.fs.usda.gov/recarea/tonto.

▣ GO JOHN TRAIL
Cave Creek Regional Park

Level: Moderate

Total Distance: 5.9 miles round-trip

Hiking Time: 3 hours

Elevation Gain: 900 feet

Summary: Welcome to the most popular trail in Cave Creek Regional Park!

If you're a fan of loop trails, this should be on your to-do list. And then you'll probably keep it on the list because it's a good candidate for repeat hikes. The Go John Trail offers a loop that makes for a comprehensive tour of the entire park. With a few scattered elevation increases that are spread over its 5.9 miles, you feel like you got your exercise without any grueling, painful climbing.

Cave Creek Regional Park lies close to the west border of Tonto National Forest. With very few surrounding residences or neighborhoods as a distraction, it's surely one of the more private desert hikes close to the city. The Go John Trail dominates the Cave Creek Regional Park as it makes a wide loop that stretches from the main recreation area and then practically touches the east, north, and west boundaries of the park.

Serenity is possible on the Go John Trail.

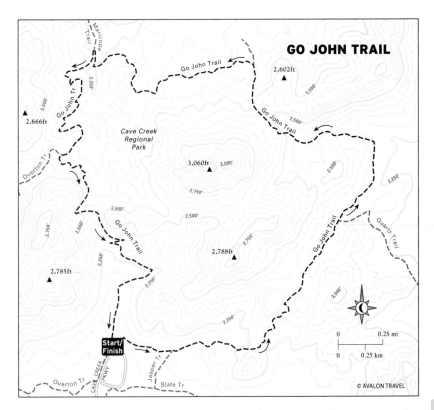

For this hike, the loop is traveled counterclockwise. Begin from the Go John trailhead and head east. At 0.7 mile, the trail veers left to the northeast. Views of distant and scattered residences of the town of Cave Creek can be seen in the distance. The first mile steadily climbs 260 feet along a wide path. The terrain mellows as the trail narrows, until 1.7 miles when the second climb of the day begins. You climb another approximate 260 feet over 0.7 mile as Go John Trail heads west. This is the most intense elevation increase of the day, which, to most, won't feel like much of a challenge.

The trail meanders to the west, walking up and down some rocky hills; this portion feels very remote as endless miles of desert stretch north into the Tonto National Forest with Spur Cross Ranch Conservation Area to the northeast. Ignore a small trail heading north at 2.8 miles. At 3.7 miles, veer right (north) to avoid a now-defunct hiking trail to the south. At 3.8 miles, make a sharp turn south and continue along the Go John Trail as it wiggles its way south for the final leg of the loop. There's another slight climb here that travels 250 feet in approximately 1 mile. Ignore a turnoff to the Overton Trail at 4.5 miles by veering left and remaining south for the 1.4 miles of an easy descent back to the Go John trailhead.

Congrats. You did it. Go John? More like Go *you*!

Options
To shorten the Go John Trail, consider starting the loop clockwise. From the Go John trailhead, start on the west side of the Go John Trail loop by veering left to head north. You climb approximately 390 feet in the first mile. Continue following the Go John Trail as it makes a small descent in the next 0.3 mile, where it meets with the Overton Trail to the west. This is a great place to turn around and retrace your steps south back to the Go John trailhead. This option makes for a 2.6-mile, out-and-back hike.

Directions
From downtown Phoenix, take I-17 north for approximately 24 miles. Take exit 223A for Carefree Highway for 0.5 mile. Take a right onto Carefree Highway, heading east for 7 miles. Turn left onto 32nd Street and continue north for 1.7 miles; 32nd Street becomes Cave Creek Parkway. Continue onto Cave Creek Parkway and head northeast for 0.9 mile. Pass through the park gate and pay the entrance fee. Take a left onto Overton Trail, heading north for 0.2 mile, and then turn left into the Go John Trail parking lot. Enter Go John Trail via the trailhead on the northeast side of the lot.
GPS Coordinates: 33.8327 N, 112.0010 W

Information and Contact
There is a $6 fee per vehicle. Dogs on leash are allowed. The park is open daily (6am-8pm Sun.-Thurs., 6am-10pm Fri.-Sat.). For more information, contact Cave Creek Regional Park, 37900 North Cave Creek Parkway, Cave Creek, AZ 85331, 623/465-0431, www.maricopa.gove/parks/cave_creek/.

5 BLACK MOUNTAIN SUMMIT TRAIL

Black Mountain Summit Preserve

Level: Moderate

Total Distance: 2.2 miles round-trip

Hiking Time: 1.5 hours

Elevation Gain: 1,275 feet

Summary: To a Cave Creeker, Black Mountain is like Phoenix's Piestewa Peak or Camelback Mountain.

Just a hop and a skip from Cave Creek's main drag, the Black Mountain Summit Trail is an absolute must for valley hikers who dig other summit trails, like Piestewa, Camelback, or Lookout. Only when it comes to Black Mountain, you won't have to deal with the parking problems and hordes of weekend hikers getting in your way. The narrow trail is a straight shot up to the summit at 3,400 feet. Dramatic views to neighboring Cave Creek Regional Park and Spur Cross Ranch Conservation Area to the north provide the wow factor. And distant ranges like the Superstition Mountains to the east are visible on clear days.

Navigate this craggy path to a dramatic view.

Black Mountain sits alone just south of the touristy area of Cave Creek. A handful of houses lie along the base of the mountain, but, all in all, the mountain is largely untouched. The trail is described as "primitive"; basically, this means that it's narrow, craggy, steep, and lacks trail markers. You won't have to guess long to figure out where the mountain's name comes from. From its western side, the dark basalt rock dominates the mountain's terrain. First-timers on this trail may experience a few fake-outs—just when you convince yourself that the top of that ridge has to be the summit, you pop up and over the terrain to learn you still have a ways to go. Oh well—that's what you're here for, right?

From the Black Mountain parking lot, head south along the paved Schoolhouse

Road. The pavement soon breaks away into a gravel drive. (Steer clear of the private driveways on either side of the road.) At just under 0.4 mile, you find the Black Mountain Summit trailhead sign, which leads to a narrow dirt path. Take a deep breath and start climbing.

The trail continues straight south for the next 0.5 mile until it begins a slight curve to the southeast at 0.9 mile. So slight, in fact, that you barely feel it. You'll inevitably come across some trailblazed paths that faintly finger off from the summit trail; stay to the south/southeast to find the correct route.

Notice the lush variety of barrel cacti and ocotillo (with leaves year-round, wow!) as you climb the black, craggy rock. The remainder of the trail is a series of rocky climbs that give your knees a run for their money. The trail frequently flattens out long enough to catch your breath before the next push.

After that final push at 1.1 miles, you are rewarded with the crazy-beautiful views from the rocky summit. Check out Cave Creek Regional Park to the west, Elephant Mountain in Spur Cross Ranch Conservation Area to the north, and the Phoenix Mountains to the south. Well done. Now turn back and return the way you came.

Options

Aside from grabbing a burger after your hike at a nearby Cave Creek restaurant, Black Mountain offers no other hikes, just the summit trail. More trails are available in **Cave Creek Regional Park** (37900 North Cave Creek Parkway, Cave Creek, AZ 85331, 623/465-0431),

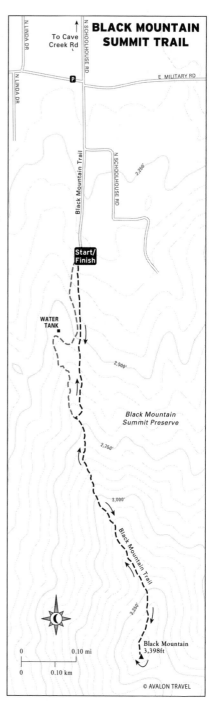

to the west of Black Mountain, and the **Spur Cross Ranch Conservation Area** (44000 North Spur Cross Road, Cave Creek, AZ 85331, 480/488-6601), to the north.

Directions

From downtown Phoenix, take AZ-51 north for approximately 16 miles. Take exit 15B on the left to merge onto the westbound AZ-101 Loop and go 1.7 miles. Take exit 28 for Cave Creek Road for 0.4 mile. Turn right onto Cave Creek Road and follow it north and then east for 12.8 miles. Turn right onto Schoolhouse Road and go south for 0.1 mile. The Black Mountain parking lot is on the right (west). Park, then walk along paved Schoolhouse Road, heading south for 0.4 mile as the road turns to gravel. Find the Black Mountain Summit trailhead sign on the left side of the road.

GPS Coordinates: 33.8299 N, 111.9436 W

Information and Contact

There is no fee. Dogs on leash are allowed. There are no maps available. For more information, contact the town of Cave Creek, 37622 North Cave Creek Road, Cave Creek, AZ 85331, 480/488-1400.

6 CIRCUMFERENCE AND RIDGELINE LOOP
Deem Hills

Level: Easy/Moderate

Total Distance: 3.9 miles round-trip

Hiking Time: 2 hours

Elevation Gain: 700 feet

Summary: Hike to the highest point in this brand-new hiking area.

If there's something to be gained from the sprawl of the city it's this: a new hiking preserve! Deem Hills was established in 2010 and offers 1,000 acres filled with saguaros, barrel cacti, brittlebrush, hackberry, creosote, teddybear cholla, and way, way, more. The name comes from Carl and Dennis Deem, who were homesteaders in the area back in the 1920s.

Today, Deem Hills is a welcome reserve and respite from suburban sprawl, complete with massive bark scorpions. You can relax. Scorpions are nocturnal, so if you see one, it's probably dead. Creepy-crawlies aside, this combination of the Circumference and Ridgeline Trails explores the west side of the park and climbs to the highest available point in the park.

Check out the far-reaching Central Arizona Project canal from Deem Hills.

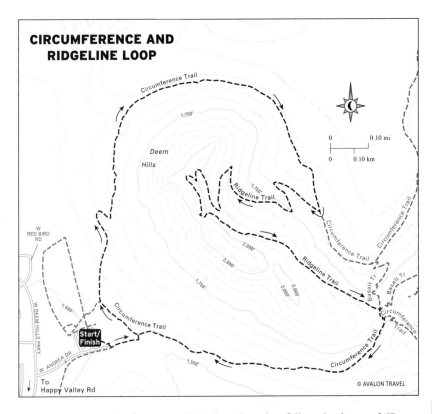

CIRCUMFERENCE AND RIDGELINE LOOP

Circumference Trail

1,750'

Deem
Hills

Ridgeline Trail

1,750'

2,000'

2,000'

Ridgeline Trail

Circumference Trail

Circumference Trail

Basalt Tr

Basalt Tr

Circumference Trail

Circumference Trail

1,750'

W
RED BIRD
RD

W DEEM HILLS PKWY

1,500'

Circumference Trail

Start/
Finish

W. ANDREA DR

1,500'

Circumference Trail

To
Happy Valley Rd

© AVALON TRAVEL

0   0.10 mi

0   0.10 km

From the east side of Deem Hills Park parking lot, follow the dirt road (Deem Hills Parkway) east for a hundred feet or so until you find the turnoff for the Circumference Trail trailhead to the left. For this hike, take the trail clockwise by making another left turn at the fork (to head northwest) located just a few feet from the trailhead. By the way, you return to this point to close the loop at the end of the hike.

Follow the gentle incline as it curves around the mountain to the northeast. The trail turns south at 1.2 miles and toward the heart of Deem Hills. At 1.5 miles, take a sharp right (northwest) to connect with the Ridgeline Trail. Let the climbing begin. Zigzag your way up a series of switchbacks and inclines until you reach the highest point, which is at 2.4 miles and approximately 3,000 feet. From this point, the trail levels out and then begins its descent heading southeast. When you hit the juncture of the Basalt Trail, you've also reached the third mile of the hike. Continue south along the Ridgeline Trail and you immediately encounter the Circumference Trail. Turn right (southwest) to return along the Circumference Trail as it descends and leads back to the Circumference Trail trailhead. Once you return to the trailhead at 3.8 miles, turn right onto the dirt road of Deem

Hills Parkway. Follow the dirt road west for a short 0.3 mile to the Deem Hills Park parking lot.

Options

For a shorter, less-strenuous hike, forgo the Ridgeline Trail. At 1.5 miles, ignore the connection to the Ridgeline Trail and continue south for another 0.2 mile. Hop off the Circumference Trail and turn right (south) onto the Basalt Trail for 0.1 mile. This connects to the other side of the Circumference Trail. Turn right (southwest) and it leads back to the parking lot for a grand total of 3 miles.

Directions

From downtown Phoenix, take I-17 north for approximately 18 miles. Take exit 218 toward Happy Valley Road and merge onto Black Canyon Highway. After 0.2 mile, at the traffic circle, take the second exit, heading west onto Happy Valley Road. After 0.3 mile, at the traffic circle, continue straight to stay on Happy Valley Road. Take Happy Valley Road for 2.9 miles and turn right, heading north, onto 51st Avenue. Follow 51st Avenue as it becomes Stetson Valley Parkway. After 0.3 mile turn right onto Deem Hills Parkway. Follow Deem Hills Parkway northeast for 0.5 mile and veer right, heading east. After 0.2 mile the Deem Hills parking lot is to the left. Park, then walk 0.3 mile east along the dirt portion of Deem Hills Parkway to find the Circumference Trail trailhead to the north.
GPS Coordinates: 33.7274 N, 112.166 W

Information and Contact

There is no fee. Dogs on leash are allowed. Maps are available online at www.phoenix.gov/parks. For more information, contact the City of Phoenix Parks and Recreation Main Office, Phoenix City Hall, 200 West Washington Street, 16th Floor, Phoenix, AZ 85003, 602/262-6862, www.phoenix.gov/parks.

7 THUNDERBIRD H-1 TO H-3 LOOP: COACH WHIP TO CHOLLA LOOP

Thunderbird Conservation Park, Glendale

Level: Easy

Total Distance: 3.3 miles round-trip

Hiking Time: 1.5 hours

Elevation Gain: 700 feet

Summary: This popular trail sits in the heart of North Valley's suburbia and provides a gentle climb to sweeping views of the city's pulse.

There are many different ways to experience Thunderbird Conservation Park, with its amphitheater, ramadas, and approximately 15 miles of multi-use trails. The trails (which used to be split among five totally exciting trail names; H-1, H-2, H-3, H-4, and H-5) just received a makeover in 2013 with some cute, desert-y names, like Desert Iguana, Sunrise, and Arrowhead Point. The former "H" in question honors Robert Hedgpeth, an early homesteader in the area. Sorry, Robert, you've been replaced.

The park is run by the City of Glendale and has experienced quite an influx

© LILIA MENCONI

The Thunderbird Conservation Park hikes are very popular with suburban residents.

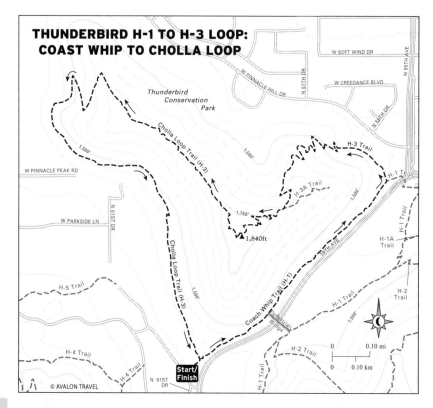

of popularity in recent years. It's really no wonder given the convenient location, easy accessibility to trails, and beautiful views.

And that pretty much sums up what the H-1 to H-3 (Coach Whip to Cholla Loop) hike is all about. You can take your pick of trail combinations in this park, but this loop walks around the west side of Hedgpeth Hills, up to the summit at approximately 1,840 feet, along a ridge, and back around the west side of the hills. All along, you enjoy incredible views to the suburban landscape that hugs the mountain ranges to the north.

To begin the loop, enter at the Coach Whip Trail trailhead across the road from the "A" parking lot. Follow Coach Whip Trail to the right (northeast) to experience the trail counterclockwise and so you can quickly bypass the zooming cars along 59th Avenue. It's a very gentle grade up the side of the hill for the first mile.

After mile 1 is complete, veer left (west) to join the Cholla Loop Trail. Be ready for a little cardio exercise, as the trail turns to a few slightly rocky switchbacks for a 400-foot elevation gain in just 0.5 mile. At 1.5 miles, you reach the summit at approximately 1,830 feet. Take in this 360-degree view of the suburban delight that is Glendale, Arizona.

Continue along the Cholla Loop Trail for an easy descent along the ridge, heading northwest. At just over 2 miles, the trail leads you to the west, then south. The rest of the hike continues south, back to the car. It's easy to follow, easy to walk, and easy to lose track of time. Before you know it, you're back at the "A" parking lot and heading home.

Options

If you're not interested in a whole lot of climbing, consider skipping the Cholla Loop. Start the hike, but instead of turning left to join the Cholla Loop at 1 mile, continue along the Coach Whip Trail, which veers northeast, then crosses Pinnacle Peak Road and quickly turns around to head south. After about 0.5 mile, veer right to take the pedestrian bridge across 59th Avenue heading northwest. Connect to the Coach Whip Trail on the other side of the bridge and turn left to follow the Coach Whip Trail southwest, back to the parking lot. This option totals approximately 2 miles.

Directions

From downtown Phoenix, take I-17 north for approximately 15 miles. Take exit 214C for the AZ-101 Loop, keeping left at the fork to merge onto westbound AZ-101 Loop. Take the AZ-101 Loop west for approximately 4 miles and take exit 19 for 59th Avenue. Merge onto Beardsley Road, and after 450 feet turn right onto 59th Avenue. Take 59th Avenue north for 1.5 miles, then turn left, heading west, onto 60th Avenue. After 200 feet, turn right onto 61st Drive and head north. Find the "A" parking lot to the left (west) with the H-1 Trail trailhead on the east side of the road.
GPS Coordinates: 33.6908 N, 112.1898 W

Information and Contact

There is no fee. Dogs on leash are allowed. Maps are available online. The park is open daily (sunrise-sunset). For more information, contact Glendale Parks and Recreation Department, Glendale Adult Center, 5970 West Brown Street, Glendale, AZ 85301, 623/930-2820, www.glendaleaz.com/parksandrecreation/ThunderbirdPark.cfm.

8 DIXIE MOUNTAIN LOOP
Sonoran Preserve

Level: Moderate

Total Distance: 5.7 miles round-trip

Hiking Time: 3 hours

Elevation Gain: 1,350 feet

Summary: The Dixie Mountain Loop connects two summit spurs, cuts through a cholla forest, and walks by a rusting truck skeleton stuck in a wash.

The city of Phoenix, like any other American city, may have its problems. But when it comes to providing hiking trails, the city's really got the right idea. And when the city is supported by enthusiastic citizens who vote for things like the Parks and Preserves Initiative (which set aside the Sonoran Preserve for 14 miles of hiking trails), you gotta feel pretty good about this place. Nice work, Phoenix.

The Sonoran Preserve is located in the transition zone to the Upland Arizona area of the Sonoran Desert. With slightly higher elevations, the area experiences approximately 5 more inches of rain per year than the Central Valley. This means you see bloated barrel cacti and saguaros among a lush thicket of teddybear cholla,

Hikers check out the "roadside attraction" on the Dixie Mountain Loop.

© LILIA MENCONI

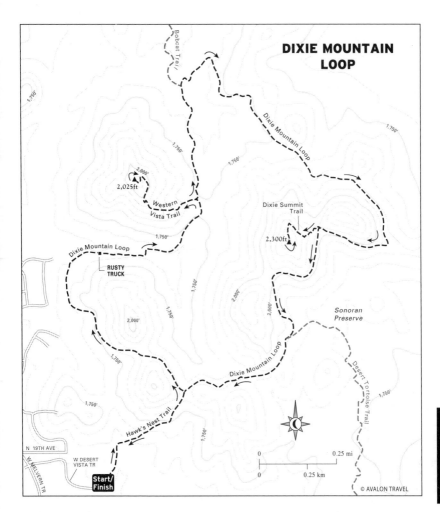

DIXIE MOUNTAIN LOOP

with green grass and rashes of wildflowers blanketing the floor. The Dixie Mountain Loop tours the north area of the preserve and connects to two short summit spurs offering fantastic views that stretch across The Valley.

To start the hike, find the Hawk's Nest Trail on the northeast corner of the Desert Vista trailhead parking lot. Follow the Hawk's Nest Trail northeast for 0.4 mile as you pass the Desert Tortoise Trail on the right. At 0.4 mile, turn left to join the Dixie Mountain Loop heading northwest. This begins the loop, which is traveled clockwise.

The trail skirts between two small mountains and curves north at 0.9 mile. At 1.1 miles, the Dixie Mountain Loop veers east to follow a wash. Keep your eyes peeled and you should quickly spot the rusted shell of a truck that somehow took a nosedive into the wash bed. Follow as the trail curves north once again. At 1.6 miles, you encounter the Western Vista Trail (marked with a "W"). Turn left to follow this small spur as it climbs 300 feet in 0.3 mile. The spur tops out at 2,025 feet with a smashing view to Deem Hills, west of I-17. Retrace your steps along the spur to rejoin the Dixie Mountain Loop, and take a left to follow it north.

At 2.7 miles, pass the connection to the Bobcat Trail and continue along the Dixie Mountain Loop as it heads northeast and then makes a sharp turn south at 2.9 miles. From here, the trail makes a subtle ascent of 275 feet over the next 0.8 mile. At 4 miles, take the turnoff to the right and climb up the Dixie Summit Trail to complete the second (and final) summit climb of the hike. This one's going to be painful but quick—175 feet of switchbacks in just 0.2 mile. Grit your teeth and get it done to enjoy the Dixie Mountain Summit with a 360-degree view of all the usual suspects: Camelback Mountain, Piestewa Peak, and South Mountain to the south; Four Peaks to the east; and Deem Hills (again) to the west.

Once you summit, take the Dixie Summit Trail back to the Dixie Mountain Loop and take a right turn to follow it south. The rest of the hike is a piece of cake. Make a gentle descent of 200 feet until 5.4 miles, when you run back into Hawk's Nest Trail. You have now closed the loop. Take a left to follow the Hawk's Nest Trail heading southwest for the 0.4 mile to return to the Desert Vista trailhead.

Options

If you're short on time and can't complete the whole loop, it's fairly easy to adjust the combination of trails to create a 3-mile summit hike. Follow the Hawk's Nest Trail from the Desert Vista trailhead northeast for 0.4 mile. This time, turn right on the Dixie Mountain Loop, heading northeast until you find the Dixie Summit Trail junction at 1.3 miles. Turn left to follow the Dixie Summit Trail west for the climb to the summit, which ends at 1.5 miles. Enjoy the view, then simply retrace your steps back to the Desert Vista trailhead.

Directions

From downtown Phoenix, take I-17 north for approximately 18 miles. Take exit 219 for Jomax Road and take a right onto Jomax Road, heading east for 1.1 mile. Turn left onto North Valley Parkway and go 0.9 mile north. Turn right onto Copperhead Trail and head east for 0.1 mile. Take the first left onto Mel Vern Trail and go north for 0.2 mile. Turn right onto Desert Vista Trail for 0.1 mile. Turn left into the Desert Vista trailhead parking lot (1901 W. Desert Vista Trail, open 6am to sunset). The Hawk's Nest trailhead is on the northeast corner of the lot.
GPS Coordinates: 33.7407 N, 112.0946 W

Information and Contact

There is no fee. Dogs on leash are allowed. Maps are available online at www.

phoenix.gov/parks. For more information, contact City of Phoenix Parks and Recreation Main Office, Phoenix City Hall, 200 West Washington Street, 16th Floor, Phoenix, AZ 85003, 602/262-6862, www.phoenix.gov/parks.

9 PINNACLE PEAK TRAIL

Pinnacle Peak Park, Scottsdale

Level: Easy/Moderate

Total Distance: 2.9 miles round-trip

Hiking Time: 1.5 hours

Elevation Gain: 1,000 feet

Summary: This beautiful hike is like the Rolls Royce of trails.

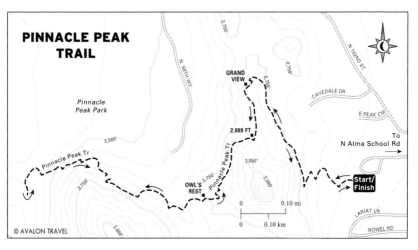

Don't you hate it when you reach a viewpoint on a trail and you don't exactly know which mountains you are admiring in the distance? Not a problem on the Pinnacle Peak Trail. The park is impeccably maintained and allows hikers to relish the incredible scenery on this interpretive trail.

Pinnacle Peak Park opened to the public in 2002 and has been wildly popular ever since. The trail caters to hikers, rock climbers, and equestrians (sorry, no doggies). Since the park is surrounded by private land, you won't make a total escape from signs of humanity. In fact, you'll do just the opposite as you drool over the pristine backyard pools of the neighboring homes while you work up a sweat. Still, the area is filled with plenty of wildlife. Look for bird nests wedged between cholla cactus needles and scurrying lizards of every variety. And there's no better way to view the majesty of the extensive McDowell Mountains that seemingly surround Pinnacle Peak to the northeast. Heck, on a clear day, this vantage point allows views all the way to Camelback Mountain to the south

© LILIA MENCONI

This impeccably maintained trail is a local favorite for hikers and climbers alike.

and Four Peaks to the east. Not too shabby.

The Pinnacle Peak Trail is masterfully designed and presents no issues as you follow it up the east side of the peak. You're treated to many interpretive plaques about the surrounding flora, such as buckhorn cholla and saguaro. There are opportunities for rock climbers to head off trail for vertical crawls along the granite rock faces. Hikers stay on the main trail.

Start the hike from the main Pinnacle Peak trailhead, just west of the visitor center. The trail initially shoots west to clear a handful of switchbacks. At 0.3 mile, the trail heads north; as soon as it curves to the south at 0.5 mile, you see the Grand View resting area. Here's where etched stones label the surrounding mountains. Look to the southwest for a clear shot to Pinnacle Peak itself—a domineering collection of granite boulders. At this point, you've climbed about 200 feet.

Moving south, notice a sign marking the highest point of the trail at 2,889 feet. Soon after, at 0.7 mile, you encounter Owl's Rest, yet another viewing pavilion. Check out Camelback Mountain to the south from here.

As the trail moves south, you make an easy descent to the low-lying saddle. At approximately 1 mile, begin a somewhat-brutal climb up a series of switchbacks heading southwest. The path then leads around the north side of the mountain. Once the trail curves south at about 1.4 miles, it begins its final descent to its west end, marked by a small trailhead in a residential area.

Now, experience the Pinnacle Peak Trail "in reverse" as you turn around and zigzag your way back the way you came.

Options

This is the only proper trail in the park, and any trailblazing is strictly prohibited. However, rock climbers with appropriate equipment can scale the granite boulders at-will. Check with the **Friends of Pinnacle Peak Park** (480/312-0990) for information about moonlit and guided hikes to experience this area from different perspectives.

Directions

From downtown Phoenix, take AZ-51 north for approximately 16 miles. Take exit 15A to merge onto the AZ-101 Loop. Take the loop east for 5.4 miles. Take exit 35 for Hayden Road. Turn left, heading north, onto Hayden Road. Take Hayden Road for 9.3 miles and turn right onto Thompson Peak Parkway. Take Thompson Peak Parkway east for about 1 mile and turn left, heading north, onto Pima Road. Take Pima Road for 2.5 miles and turn right onto Happy Valley Road. Take Happy Valley Road east for 2 miles and turn left, heading north, onto Alma School Road. Take Alma School Road for 1 mile and turn left, heading northwest onto Pinnacle Peak Parkway. Continue on Pinnacle Peak Parkway as it becomes 102nd Way/Jomax Road. After 0.3 mile turn left, heading west to enter the Pinnacle Peak parking lot. The Pinnacle Peak trailhead is on the west side of the visitor center. **GPS Coordinates:** 33.7277 N, 111.8608 W

Information and Contact

There is no fee. Dogs are not allowed. Maps are available at the Pinnacle Peak Park office. The park is open daily (5:30am-7:15pm). For more information, contact Pinnacle Peak Park, 26802 North 102nd Way, Scottsdale, AZ 85262, 480/312-0990, www.scottsdaleaz.gov/parks/pinnacle.

10 TOM'S THUMB TRAIL

McDowell Sonoran Preserve, Scottsdale

Level: Moderate

Total Distance: 4.1 miles round-trip

Hiking Time: 2.5 hours

Elevation Gain: 1,325 feet

Summary: Travel this beautiful new trail to one of The Valley's favorite spots, Tom's Thumb.

The journey to Tom's Thumb—a protruding mass of rock along one of the many ridges in the McDowell Sonoran Preserve—used to be a rugged trek through a tricky trail. Today, with the spankin' new trailhead and well-maintained Tom's Thumb Trail, hikers can easily reach an entry point and navigate their way to this favorite landmark of the McDowell Mountains.

The entire 2.05-mile trail up to the gigantic "thumb" is well-marked and beautifully cleared. With an elevation gain of 1,350 feet, you'll be feeling the burn and will get a fantastic workout. Oh, and, of course, some killer views of Four Peaks and the Superstition Mountains to the east as well as the vast, minimally populated desert land to the north.

Everyone looks small next to Tom's Thumb.

Start the hike on the Tom's Thumb Trail, which begins at the southwest corner of the shaded Tom's Thumb trailhead structure. A number of trail intersections connect to this trail. All are clearly labeled, so simply remain on the Tom's Thumb Trail to stay the course (until 1.8 miles when you take the route to Tom's Thumb).

The first 0.5 mile of the trail offers a very subtle incline as you head south to approach the north side of the McDowell Mountains. Soon after the half-mile mark, however, the first of a series of switchbacks hits. Let the grunting continue for another 0.8 mile as you climb up approximately 750 feet. At 1.3 miles, pass up

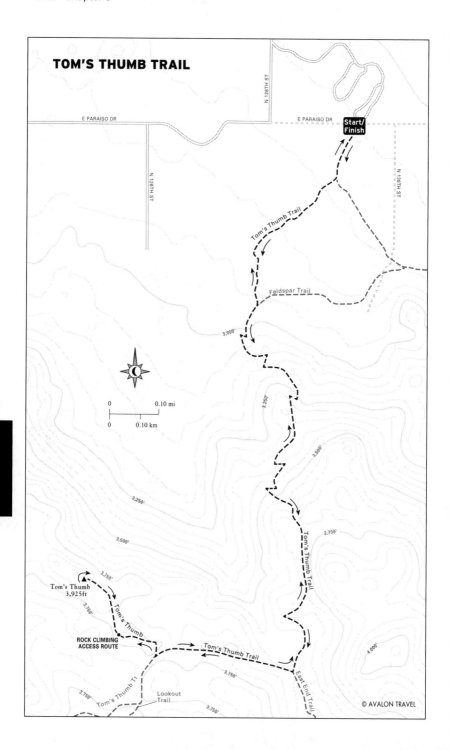

TOM'S THUMB TRAIL

E PARAISO DR

N 128TH ST

N 126TH ST

E PARAISO DR

N 130TH ST

Start/
Finish

Tom's Thumb Trail

Feldspar Trail

3,000'

3,250'

3,500'

3,750'

3,250'

3,500'

3,750'

Tom's Thumb Trail

4,000'

Tom's Thumb
3,925ft

Tom's Thumb

ROCK CLIMBING
ACCESS ROUTE

Tom's Thumb Trail

Tom's Thumb Tr

Lookout
Trail

East End Trail

3,750'

3,750'

3,750'

3,750'

0   0.10 mi

0   0.10 km

© AVALON TRAVEL

and over a ridge to find yourself in the midst of the jagged McDowell Mountains. Begin a small, relaxing descent as you travel farther south into the heart of the mountain range.

At 1.5 miles, notice a well-signed intersection with the East End Trail. Follow the right turnoff to the Tom's Thumb Trail, which heads west. Just 0.3 mile from the turnoff, notice a sign that reads "Rock Climbing Access Route." Follow this route to the northwest. This portion of the trail narrows and can be a little tricky to follow as it wiggles around the south side of some massive rock formations and then returns to its northwest direction. After a quick hop through a shady squeeze between two piles of boulders, Tom's Thumb suddenly becomes visible at 1.9 miles. From there, it's just a short, flat walk to the base of the thumb (you won't even notice, you'll be so excited by this sight).

Take some photos, eat a snack, and genuflect to the wonders of geology as you gaze up its impossibly slick surface. Once you've had enough, simply retrace your path for a pleasant descent back to the Tom's Thumb trailhead.

Options

To add another dramatic view to this hike, you can head to "The Lookout." After you return to Tom's Thumb Trail from the Rock Climbing Access Route, turn south instead of east. Follow Tom's Thumb Trail south for 0.1 mile until you find the **Lookout Trail.** Turn south onto the Lookout Trail for 0.5 mile until you reach The Lookout at 3,858 feet high. Soak in the view of Drinkwater and McDowell Peaks to the south, then simply turn around and follow the Lookout Trail back to Tom's Thumb Trail. Turn to the east on Tom's Thumb Trail and you're back on your way to the Tom's Thumb trailhead. This addition makes for a hike that totals 5.3 miles.

Directions

From downtown Phoenix, take I-10 east toward Tucson for 2.2 miles. Take exit 147B to merge onto AZ-51 and go north for 15.5 miles. Take exit 15A to merge onto the eastbound AZ-101 Loop and follow it for 6.3 miles. Take exit 34 for Scottsdale Road and follow north for 5.8 miles. Turn right onto Dynamite Boulevard and go 7.1 miles as it becomes Rio Verde Drive. Turn right onto 128th Street and head south for approximately 3 miles. Veer left into the Tom's Thumb trailhead entrance gate (23015 N. 128th St.). Follow the road for another 0.25 mile to the east-most parking lot. The Tom's Thumb trailhead is on the southwest corner of the large shaded structure.

GPS Coordinates: 33.6942 N, 111.8017 W

Information and Contact

There is no fee. Dogs on leash are allowed. Maps are available at the trailhead.

The park is open daily (sunrise-sunset). For more information, contact the City of Scottsdale McDowell Sonoran Preserve, 480/312-7013, ww.scottsdaleaz.gov/preserve, or the City of Scottsdale Parks and Recreation, 7447 East Indian School Road, Suite 300, Scottsdale, AZ 85251, 480/312-2337, www.scottsdaleaz.gov.

11 PEMBERTON AND TONTO TANK LOOP
McDowell Mountain Regional Park, Scottsdale

BEST(**Wildflowers**

Level: Moderate

Total Distance: 9.2 miles round-trip

Hiking Time: 5 hours

Elevation Gain: 600 feet

Summary: Bring a chatty friend because this moderate (but lengthy) walk through the desert offers ample opportunity for great conversation.

Some may think this trail is too boring for hikers—turns out, they're completely wrong. This 9.2-mile loop combines the Pemberton and Tonto Tank Trails in the McDowell Mountain Regional Park for a barely there elevation gain of about 600 feet stretched over the first 5.6 miles. It's flat, exposed, and long. But with a good pal in tow, the Four Peaks and Superstition Mountains clearly visible to the east, and the McDowell Mountains dominating the horizon to the west, this loop is anything but boring. Not to mention, when wildflower season kicks up, this flat desert landscape is bursting with color.

With Four Peaks visible in the distance, it's time to take a photo.

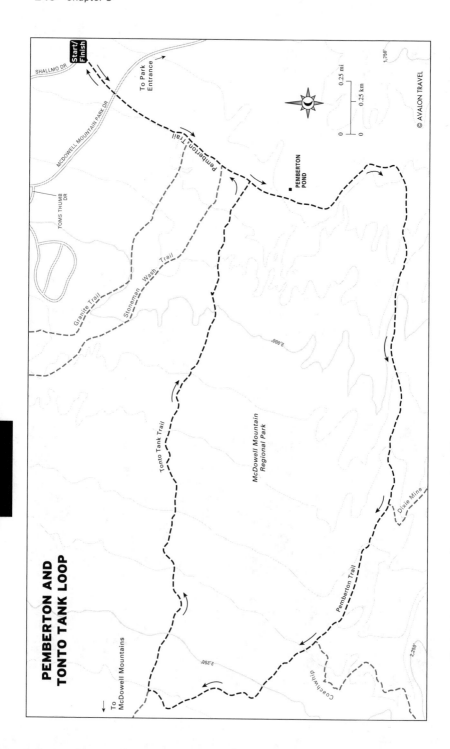

PEMBERTON AND
TONTO TANK LOOP

To
McDowell Mountains

McDowell Mountain
Regional Park

Tonto Tank Trail

Granite Trail

Stoneman Wash Trail

Pemberton Trail

SHALLMO DR

Start/
Finish

To Park
Entrance

McDOWELL MOUNTAIN PARK DR

TOMS THUMB DR

PEMBERTON POND

Pemberton Trail

Dixie Mine

Coachwhip

1,750'

2,000'

2,250'

2,250'

0.25 mi
0.25 km
0
0

© AVALON TRAVEL

Start from the Pemberton Trail trailhead and head southwest along Pemberton Trail. At 0.3 mile, cross the paved McDowell Mountain Park Drive and continue southwest for the next 1.7 miles, remaining on the Pemberton Trail as you ignore all other connecting trails. At 2 miles, the Pemberton Trail curves west. You're now walking toward the east end of the McDowell Mountain range. At 4.3 miles, continue along the Pemberton Trail as it curves north.

Take a right turn at 5.5 miles to follow the Tonto Trail heading east. Enjoy the easy terrain for the next 2.7 miles as you view Four Peaks and the Superstition Mountains to the east. Hang a left at 8.3 miles to close the loop and return to Pemberton Trail. This time, head north for the short 0.9 mile of trail as you retrace your steps back to the Pemberton Trail trailhead.

That's it—9.2 miles never felt so easy.

Options

This 9.2-mile loop is so low impact, why not go for more? Try skipping the return route along Tonto Trail and opt for the entire Pemberton Trail. Pass by Tonto Trail at 5.5 miles and continue north along Pemberton Trail. At 9.3 miles, the trail turns east for the 6.1 miles back to the Pemberton Trail trailhead. This large loop totals a whopping 15.4 miles.

Directions

From downtown Phoenix, take the AZ-202 Loop east for approximately 16 miles. Take exit 16 for Gilbert Road for 0.4 mile. Turn left onto Gilbert Road and follow it north for 2.7 miles. Turn right onto AZ-87 (Beeline Highway) and go northeast for 6.7 miles. Turn left onto Shea Boulevard, heading northwest for 0.6 mile. Turn right onto Saguaro Boulevard and go north for 3.9 miles. Turn right onto Fountain Hills Boulevard and go north for 0.6 mile. Fountain Hills Boulevard becomes McDowell Mountain Road. Continue northeast onto McDowell Mountain Road for 3.6 miles. Turn left onto McDowell Mountain Park Drive. Pass through the park gate and pay the fee. Continue on McDowell Mountain Park Drive, heading northwest for 3.1 miles. Turn right onto Shallmo Drive and head southeast for 0.8 mile. The Pemberton Trail trailhead parking lot and staging area is on the left. Find the Pemberton Trail trailhead on the south side of the lot.

GPS Coordinates: 33.6902 N, 111.7186 W

Information and Contact

There is a $6 fee per vehicle. Dogs on leash are allowed. The park is open daily (6am-8pm Sun.-Thurs., 6am-10pm Fri.-Sat.). For more information, contact McDowell Mountain Regional Park, 16300 McDowell Mountain Park Drive, Scottsdale, AZ 85255, 480/471-0173, www.maricopa.gov/parks/mcdowell.

12 GATEWAY LOOP TRAIL

McDowell Sonoran Preserve, Scottsdale

Level: Easy/Moderate

Total Distance: 4.4 miles round-trip

Hiking Time: 2 hours

Elevation Gain: 700 feet

Summary: This hike on the west-end entrance of the massive McDowell Mountains proves that the place is great from every angle.

No matter where you enter the McDowell Mountains for a hike, you just can't go wrong. Such is the case with the Gateway Loop, arguably the most popular hike on the west side of the preserve. It has all the ingredients of your typical McDowell Mountain hike—smashing scenery, multiple route options, easy navigation, and plenty of opportunity to work up a sweat. What sets the Gateway Loop apart is the killer view of Tom's Thumb, a rock formation to the northeast that is revealed right from the start at the Gateway Access Area parking lot.

This 4.4-mile, lasso-shaped loop (traveled counterclockwise) starts by tracing the south side of a McDowell mountain ridge, travels north to the Gateway Saddle,

Few can resist snapping photos of the beautiful desert on the Gateway Loop Trail.

© LILIA MENCONI

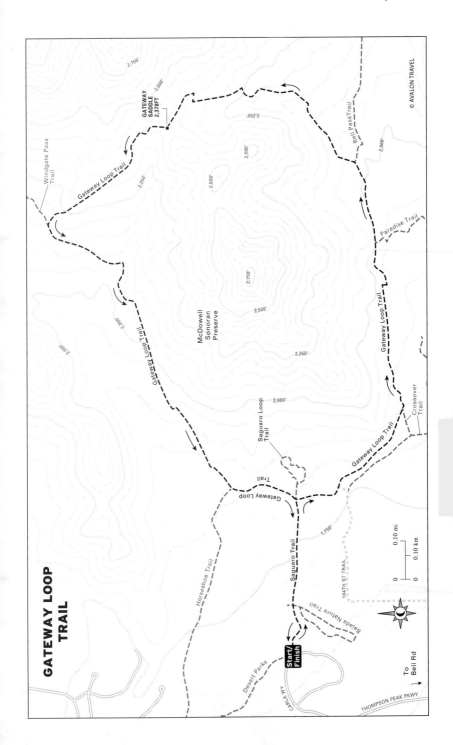

GATEWAY LOOP TRAIL

GATEWAY SADDLE 2,378FT

Gateway Loop Trail

Windgate Pass Trail

Bell Pass Trail

Paradise Trail

Gateway Loop Trail

McDowell Sonoran Preserve

Saguaro Loop Trail

Crossover Trail

Gateway Loop Trail

Horseshoe Trail

Gateway Loop Trail

104TH ST TRAIL

Saguaro Trail

Bajada Nature Trail

Desert Parks

Start/ Finish

CARLA WY

THOMPSON PEAK PKWY

To Bell Rd

© AVALON TRAVEL

2,750'
2,500'
2,250'
2,500'
2,500'
2,500'
2,750'
2,500'
2,250'
2,000'
2,000'
2,000'
2,000'
2,250'
1,750'

0   0.10 mi
0   0.10 km

and ends with a calming descent west to close the loop. With only 700 feet of elevation gain, it's a manageable challenge for the family.

To begin, head east out of the Gateway Access Area parking lot, past the large shade structure, and over a small metal footbridge. Within a few feet, you encounter a circular clearing. Follow the trail signs to continue east on the Saguaro Trail toward the Gateway Loop Trail. At 0.4 mile, you reach the intersection with the Gateway Loop Trail, with an option to follow it north or south. Take a right turn to the south to save the most rewarding views for the end.

The next 0.5 mile is an easy walk to the east with a mere 56-foot elevation gain. At approximately 0.9 mile, pass by a turnoff to the Crossover Trail. Continue along the Gateway Loop Trail as it veers north and starts its climb to the Gateway Saddle (ignore the Bell Pass Trail at 1.5 miles). After sweating your way up the remaining 460 feet, find a sign for the Gateway Saddle at 2,375 feet. At just 2.3 miles in, you're done with the toughest part of the entire hike. Sweet!

From the saddle, you can easily see the North Valley's suburbia stretch for miles when you look west. But the real treat is revealed when you continue along the Gateway Loop Trail as it travels north and begins its descent. Keep an eye out for sneak peeks of Tom's Thumb on a distant McDowell mountain ridge to the northeast.

At 2.8 miles, pass by the Windgate Pass Trail and continue following the Gateway Loop Trail as it makes a sharp left turn and heads south, then west toward this open land filled with endless paloverde trees. Pass by the Horseshoe Trail to the north at 3.7 miles and then veer south along the Gateway Loop Trail. At 4 miles, close the loop at the signed juncture (this should look familiar). Turn right to head west for 0.4 mile along the Saguaro Trail, back to the Gateway Access Area parking lot.

Options

To make a much longer loop totaling 9.5 miles, opt for the **Bell Pass Trail,** which heads east and wraps all the way around the east side of Drinkwater and McDowell Peaks. At 1.5 miles into the original hike, you encounter the turnoff for Bell Pass Trail. Follow Bell Pass Trail east for 2 miles as it curves north and reaches Bell Pass at 3,204 feet. Continue along Bell Pass Trail for another 1.3 miles as it passes Prospector Trail and comes to an end at the intersection with Windgate Pass Trail. Turn left to follow Windgate Pass Trail west for 3.1 miles, ignoring the turnoff for Tom's Thumb Trail. At 7.9 miles total, you finally reach the north end of the Gateway Loop Trail. Veer right to follow the Gateway Loop Trail west, then south for 1.2 miles. Turn right (west) at Saguaro Trail for the 0.4-mile return to the Gateway Access Area parking lot.

Directions

From downtown Phoenix, take AZ-51 north for approximately 16 miles. Take

exit 15A to merge onto the AZ-101 Loop, heading east for 6.3 miles. Take exit 36 for Princess Drive (Pima Road). After 0.5 mile, merge onto Pima Road and continue 358 feet. Make a slight right to remain on Pima Road for 0.4 mile. Take the first left onto Bell Road and go east for 1.7 miles. Turn left onto Thompson Peak Parkway and follow it north for 0.6 mile. Take the first right onto McDowell Foothills Drive, heading east for 0.3 mile until it ends at the Gateway Access Area parking lot (18333 N. Thompson Peak Pkwy.). Find the Gateway trailhead on the east side of the parking lot, past the building.
GPS Coordinates: 33.6495 N, 111.8590 W

Information and Contact

There is no fee. Dogs on leash are allowed. Maps are available at the trailhead. The park is open daily (sunrise-sunset). For more information, contact the City of Scottsdale McDowell Sonoran Preserve, 480/312-7013, ww.scottsdaleaz.gov/preserve, or the City of Scottsdale Parks and Recreation, 7447 East Indian School Road, Suite 300, Scottsdale, AZ 85251, 480/312-2337, www.scottsdaleaz.gov.

13 LOST DOG WASH TRAIL

McDowell Sonoran Preserve, Scottsdale

Level: Easy

Total Distance: 4.4 miles round-trip

Hiking Time: 2 hours

Elevation Gain: 375 feet

Summary: The Lost Dog Wash Trail to Taliesin Lookout is not only great for kids but offers an art history lesson to boot.

Man, there are just too many trails to hike in the McDowell Sonoran Preserve (and that's just the way I like it).

This out-and-back jaunt from the Lost Dog Wash trailhead ends at the Taliesin Lookout. One of America's most-famous architects, Frank Lloyd Wright, established Taliesin as a resource of study and schooling in the arts for a group of apprentices in 1937. Nestled in the foothills of the McDowell Mountains, the school flourished, and Taliesin still offers arts education today. The school's structure uses architectural elements inspired by the natural surroundings. In other words, it blends in. So, when you're looking for it from Taliesin Lookout, it's the structure you didn't see at first glance.

© LILIA MENCONI

The McDowell Mountains always promise a beautiful sunset.

Start this hike from the Lost Dog trailhead and follow signs for the Lost Dog Wash Trail. Once on the trail, there's not much to this hike. The first 0.5 mile begins heading northeast and then curves to the northwest. Simply continue northwest, remaining on the Lost Dog Wash Trail for the next 1.6 miles. Ignore turnoffs to Ringtail and Old Jeep Trails, which both lead east. The entire hike slowly gains elevation, and at 2.1 miles, you reach a small saddle on the north side of Maricopa Hill. Follow the sign to Taliesin Lookout, which is a small spur to the southeast. Here, ignore the eyesore of residences to the west (boo!) and focus on the inspired design of Taliesin to the southeast (yay!).

From Taliesin Lookout, simply turn back and retrace your steps, heading southeast along the Lost Dog Wash Trail for the 2.2 miles back to the Lost Dog Wash trailhead.

Options

To add distance and some different scenery, consider using the Old Jeep and Ringtail Trails to create a lasso-shaped loop. From Taliesin Lookout, turn around and retrace the path along Lost Dog Wash Trail for 0.5 mile, heading southeast until the junction with Old Jeep Trail. Follow Old Jeep Trail east and then south for 1.4 miles until the junction with Ringtail Trail. Hop on Ringtail Trail heading southwest, and in 0.2 mile you reach the Lost Dog Overlook at 2,000 feet. Continue along the Ringtail Trail for another 0.5 mile until it reunites with the Lost Dog

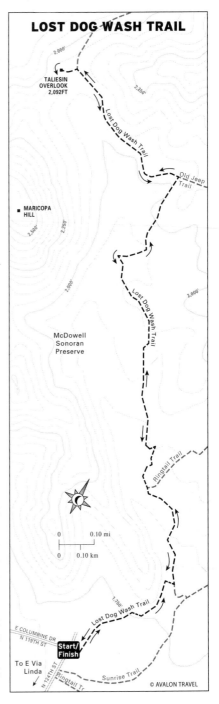

LOST DOG WASH TRAIL

Wash Trail. Follow the Lost Dog Wash Trail 0.5 mile south, back to the Lost Dog Wash trailhead and parking lot. This option totals 5.5 miles.

Also consider taking a tour of **Taliesin West** (12345 North Taliesin Drive, Scottsdale, 480/860-2700, www.franklloydwright.org, daily 9am-4pm, $32), because it really is spectacular.

Directions

From downtown Phoenix, take AZ-202 for approximately 10 miles east. Take exit 9 to merge onto AZ-101, heading north for 11.1 miles. Take exit 41 for Shea Boulevard and turn right onto Shea Boulevard, heading east for 4 miles. Turn left onto 124th Street and follow it north for approximately 1 mile until the road ends at the Lost Dog Wash parking lot (12601 N. 124th St.). The Lost Dog Wash Trail trailhead is on the north side of the lot.

GPS Coordinates: 33.6 N, 111.8128 W

Information and Contact

There is no fee. Dogs on leash are allowed. Maps are available at the trailhead. The park is open daily (sunrise-sunset). For more information, contact the City of Scottsdale McDowell Sonoran Preserve, 480/312-7013, ww.scottsdaleaz.gov/preserve, or the City of Scottsdale Parks and Recreation, 7447 East Indian School Road, Suite 300, Scottsdale, AZ 85251, 480/312-2337, www.scottsdaleaz.gov.

14 SUNRISE TRAIL

McDowell Sonoran Preserve, Scottsdale

Level: Moderate

Total Distance: 3.7 miles round-trip

Hiking Time: 2.5 hours

Elevation Gain: 1,100 feet

Summary: Don't miss climbing the Sunrise Trail, one of the best hikes in town!

The McDowell Sonoran Preserve is new, slick, clean, and super awesome. Of all the trails, the Sunrise Trail offers some of the most breathtaking views. On a clear day, the Superstition Mountains' Flatiron and Weaver's Needle are easily visible to the southeast. The Four Peaks are easy to spot to the northeast, and you might even catch the world-famous fountain in Fountain Hills spewing water to the east. The Sunrise Trail is a straight shot to the northwest as you escape the neighboring suburbs and climb along the slopes of Sunrise Peak.

Wildlife is abundant in this area. Don't be surprised if you spot black-tailed jackrabbits scurrying away as you cruise along the trail. Even rare sightings of desert tortoises have taken place in this area, so keep your eyes open and you

© LILIA MENCONI

The Sunrise Trail offers unbeatable views to the east.

might get lucky enough to see one in the wild.

To begin the hike, enter the trail at the circular Sunrise Access Area trailhead and follow the signed Sunrise Trail heading northwest. For the first 0.3 mile, you walk behind the Hidden Hills neighborhood (and try not look into peoples' backyards). Thankfully, after this short distance, it's desert land all the way.

Huff and puff your way up about 500 feet for the next mile or so until you reach the Scenic View at 1.2 miles. This signed perch indicates an elevation of 2,460 feet. It's a great spot to catch your breath, ooh and ah at the sight of the Superstition Mountains to the southeast, then get back to climbing.

The trail keeps heading northwest, and along this stretch glance to the east to see the world-famous Fountain Hills fountain blasting its waters up to 550 feet in the air at the top of each hour. At 1.5 miles, you encounter a small handful of switchbacks. Once they let up at 1.7 miles, you discover signs for a trail spur leading to Sunrise Peak. Veer left to follow the spur. It's just a short 0.1 mile west to Sunrise Peak, where you can enjoy a 360-degree view of the McDowell Mountains to the north and west, Four Peaks to the east, Superstitions to the southeast, and, on a clear day, possibly Camelback Mountain to the southwest (this laundry list of sights is why Sunrise Trail is highly recommended).

That's all there is to it! Now that the tough part is over, simply follow the spur back to the Sunrise Trail and head southeast for an easy descent.

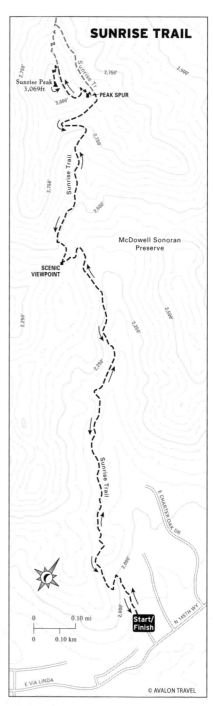

Options

For a longer hike, opt to continue west from Sunrise Peak to hike the entire Sunrise Trail. Taken end-to-end (one-way) this option totals 4.8 miles. After returning from the spur to Sunrise Peak, turn left to follow the Sunrise Trail west. Ignore any turnoffs to other trails for the next 2.2 miles until you encounter a three-way juncture. The Sunrise Trail ends here. To avoid the crowds at the nearby Lost Dog Wash trailhead, take the Ringtail Trail south for 0.6 mile to the Ringtail trailhead and parking lot, where your pre-arranged pickup ride (or parked second vehicle) awaits.

Directions

From downtown Phoenix, take the AZ-202 Loop east for approximately 10 miles. Take exit 9 to merge onto northbound AZ-101 Loop and go for 11.1 miles. Take exit 41 for Shea Boulevard, keeping right at the fork and following signs for Shea Boulevard. Turn right onto Shea Boulevard and go east for 5.9 miles. Turn left onto 136th Street, heading north for 0.5 mile. Turn right onto Via Linda and go east for 1.4 miles. The Sunrise trailhead parking lot (12101 N. 145th Way) is on the left (west) side of the road. Find the Sunrise trailhead on the west side of the lot.
GPS Coordinates: 33.5963 N, 111.7683 W

Information and Contact

There is no fee. Dogs on leash are allowed. Maps are available at the trailhead. The park is open daily (sunrise-sunset). For more information, contact the City of Scottsdale McDowell Sonoran Preserve, 480/312-7013, ww.scottsdaleaz.gov/ preserve, or the City of Scottsdale Parks and Recreation, 7447 East Indian School Road, Suite 300, Scottsdale, AZ 85251, 480/312-2337, www.scottsdaleaz.gov.

15 FOUNTAIN LAKE OVERLOOK LOOP

Fountain Park, Fountain Hills

🏢 🚶 ⚙️ 🏕️ 👫 ♿

Level: Easy

Total Distance: 2.6 miles round-trip

Hiking Time: 1 hour

Elevation Gain: 300 feet

Summary: Enjoy this lakeside trail to check out one of the world's tallest fountains.

Fountain Park is like a little taste of Disneyland in the desert. The lake, fountain, and surrounding community were established in 1970 and designed by none other than Charles Wood Jr., the man responsible for the design of Disneyland in California.

This makes a lot of sense when you see the imaginative centerpiece of the community—its man-made fountain. About 7,000 gallons of water per minute gushes 560 feet in the air as it's driven by 600 horsepower (450kW) turbine pumps. The impressive piece of engineering held the title of World's Tallest Fountain for over

© LILIA MENCONI

Aptly named, the Lake Overlook Trail offers stellar views of Fountain Lake.

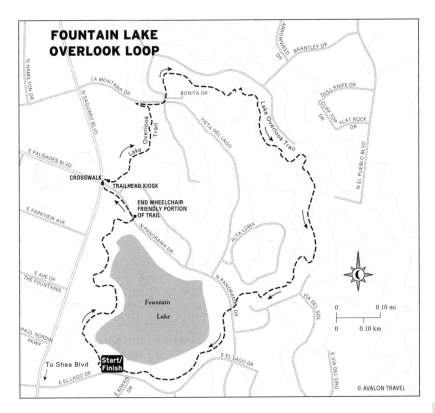

a decade. Today, it's a cherished oddity in the northeast valley. The fountain only runs for the first 15 minutes of every hour 9am-9pm, and though it can be seen from many hiking trails in the area, this trail offers the very best view.

This hike begins along the paved path in Fountain Park, crosses a road, and climbs a ridgeline trail wedged in the desert land between local private residences. Take the trail clockwise by starting from the Fountain Park parking lot and heading north on the sidewalk. This easy portion is wheelchair-friendly and lasts a mere 0.5 mile. At the northernmost edge of the walkway and lake, pass the amphitheater and turn left (northwest) to follow the sidewalk along Panorama Drive. Look for signs across the street for the Lake Overlook Trail trailhead. Cross the street at the crosswalk and step onto the dirt path, which heads northeast and continues to skirt the properties of nearby condominiums.

After 0.4 mile of desert hiking, you reach La Montana Drive. Turn right and follow the sidewalk, then make an immediate left turn (north) onto Bonita Drive. Signs for the Lake Overlook Trail are on the east side of the road.

Follow the clearly defined trail to travel up, along, and down the ridge of this small mountain. The Fort McDowell Yavapai Nation spreads to the east, and you, of course, catch some great views of Fountain Lake to the southwest. If you're hiking at the top of the hour, you may catch an eyeful of the fountain's tall spray.

Once you reach the end of the dirt path, you spill out onto the southeast side of the lake. Cross Panorama Drive once more, then hop back on the sidewalk that encircles the south side of the water. Follow the sidewalk, heading west for a mere 0.4 mile back to the Fountain Park parking lot.

Options

To shorten your walk and make it 100 percent wheelchair-friendly, skip the Lake Overlook Trail and stick to the paved Fountain Lake Loop. It can be a perfect 1.2-mile walk for strollers or little ones, since it has interpretive signage and plenty of opportunity for duck feeding. The park also offers a playground, a lively splash zone, an 18-hole disc golf course, and a Veterans Memorial.

Directions

From downtown Phoenix, take AZ-202 for approximately 16 miles east. Take exit 16 for Gilbert Road and turn left onto Gilbert Road, heading north for 2.7 miles. Turn right onto AZ-87 (Beeline Highway) and go 6.7 miles heading northeast. Turn left onto Shea Boulevard and go west for 0.6 mile. Turn right onto Saguaro Boulevard and head north for 2.4 miles. Take a right (east) onto El Lago Drive, then make an immediate left into the Fountain Park parking lot. The hike begins on the lake's sidewalk off the north side of the lot.
GPS Coordinates: 33.6016 N, 111.7138 W

Information and Contact

There is no fee. Dogs on leash are allowed. Maps are available at the Lake Overlook trailhead. The park is open daily (9am-9pm). For more information, contact Fountain Park, 12925 N. Saguaro Blvd., or the Town of Fountain Hills, 16705 East Avenue of the Fountains, Fountain Hills, AZ 85268, 480/816-5100, www.fh.az.gov.

16 BROWN'S TRAIL

Tonto National Forest, Four Peaks Wilderness

BEST Summit Views

Level: Moderate

Total Distance: 4 miles round-trip

Hiking Time: 2.5 hours

Elevation Gain: 1,100 feet

Summary: This hike takes you up and up to the saddle near the tallest peak in Maricopa County.

Oh, Four Peaks, you always have to remind Phoenix of your presence, don't you? With your tallest four summits in all of Maricopa County constantly looming over the citizens of The Valley, the folks with any inkling toward conquering adventure can't resist you for long.

You know this. This is what it feels like to be a Phoenix hiker. The Four Peaks, located on the south end of the Mazatzal Mountains, are easy to spot from most of The Valley. Often snowcapped in winter, they're impossible to miss and are the object of many hikers' fantasies.

These two hikers are happy (and chilly) at the saddle which sits below Brown's Peak.

But they're not impossible to reach. In fact, the trail to Brown's saddle (at the foot of Brown's Peak, which is the northernmost and tallest of the four) is not that difficult. Only 2 miles up in cool weather with plenty of shade provided by the surrounding piñon and oak trees (all in recovery from the devastating 1996 Lone fire), this trail can be accomplished with relative ease.

Your real challenge is getting to the Lone Pine trailhead from which Brown's Trail begins. You have two driving options. The shorter of the two (via Forest Road 168) promises what's often reported as an extremely rugged dirt road that requires a four-wheel-drive, high-clearance vehicle. The long way (via Highway 188) requires a high clearance vehicle (at least). Either way, plan for many miles of dirt roads, blind turns, and harrowing maneuvers.

To begin the hike, follow the signs for Brown's Trail on the south side of the parking area at the Lone Pine trailhead. Please note that even though the trail has a clearly labeled sign, it's easy to confuse which direction you should travel. Word to the wise: Brown's Trail heads south from the parking area. Do not take the Four Peaks Trail, which heads east, requiring a left-hand turn from the trailhead.

Now, just remain on Brown's Trail heading southeast for the rest of the hike. You're climbing all the way in a one-shot haul to the saddle. And that's all there is to it.

The well-maintained path is easy to follow. Enjoy the view of Roosevelt Lake to the east as you gain elevation and zigzag your way up the scattered switchbacks. At 1.7 miles, pass by the Amethyst Trail, which joins the Brown's Trail from the left (northeast). At mile 2, you reach the saddle, where a fire pit and large log make for a convenient lunching area. From this vantage point at 6,900 feet, you can see south all the way to the Superstition Mountains. The aged and rocky Brown's Peak dominates your view to the southeast, with the remaining unnamed peaks, well, peeking out from behind it.

Congratulations, you answered the call. Now return the way you came for an easy 2-mile descent heading northwest back to the car.

Options

Disappointed with the lack of a summit

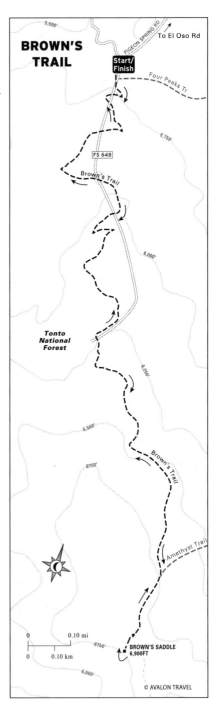

experience? Fair enough. Reaching **Brown's Peak** at 7,657 feet is doable but requires nerves of steel and some serious scrambling skills. This option is *not* for 'fraidy-cats. From Brown's Saddle, follow a faint trail southeast, toward Brown's Peak. Once you reach the near-vertical rock, look for cairns, footsteps, brief pathways, or any other indication of a trail forged by others who came before you. It's really a matter of taking your best guess as to the safest path to the summit, because there are multiple ways to scale this climb and no official trail. This climb only adds 0.5 mile, but you climb a whopping 757 feet. Good luck and be safe!

Directions

From downtown Phoenix, take I-10 east toward Tucson for approximately 2 miles. Take exit 147A to merge onto eastbound AZ-202 Loop and follow it for 16.2 miles. Take exit 16 for Gilbert Road for 0.4 mile. Turn left onto Gilbert Road, heading north for 2.7 miles. Turn right onto AZ-87 (Beeline Highway) and go northeast for approximately 53 miles. Turn right onto AZ-188 and go 20.6 miles heading south. Turn right (west) onto El Oso Road (Forest Road 143) and follow it for 8.5 miles as the dirt road climbs and twists, generally heading southwest. Turn left onto Pigeon Spring Road (Forest Road 648) to head southeast, following signs to the Lone Pine trailhead for 1 mile. Keep left at the fork to continue following Pigeon Spring Road (Forest Road 648) for another 1.4 miles heading south. The road seemingly ends in a dirt clearing, which is the Lone Pine trailhead parking lot. Find the Brown's Trail trailhead on the south end of the lot.

GPS Coordinates: 33.7053 N, 111.3380 W

Information and Contact

No fees or passes are required. Dogs on leash area allowed. For more information, contact the Tonto National Forest Cave Creek Ranger District at 40202 North Cave Creek Road, Scottsdale, AZ 85262, 480/595-3300, www.fs.usda.gov/recarea/tonto.

HIGH COUNTRY

© LOUIS KUMMERER

Summer is the time to crank up the air conditioner

and stay indoors. Luckily for you, there are options. Escape to the north, where Arizona's high country offers lush, forested landscapes and cooler summer temperatures. Check out Prescott National Forest, where tangles of trails wind through thick forests of aspen and ponderosa pine trees. Or buzz up to the northeast for a visit to "rim country" to explore the famous Mogollon Rim. With a general elevation of 4,500 feet, Sedona is surrounded by dramatic rock formations, canyons, and mesas. Venturing in and among these mars-like red rocks is a cherished activity. Flagstaff boasts the coolest temperatures in summer, with lush meadows, green forests, and wildflowers galore. If nothing else, these northern jaunts act as an escape hatch for weather-weary hikers in Phoenix.

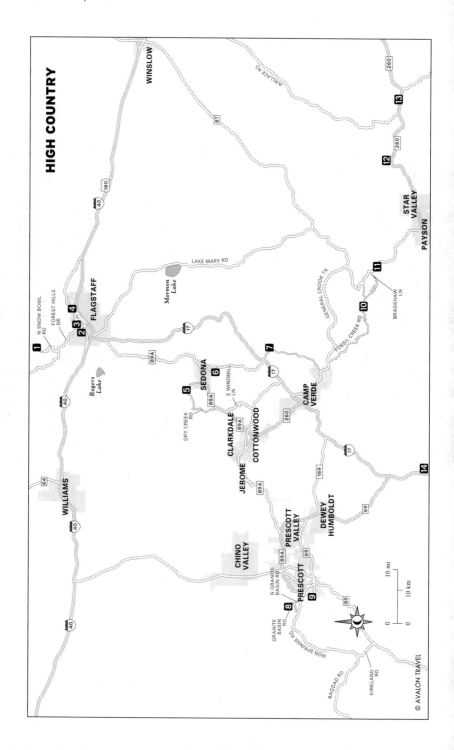

TRAIL NAME	FEATURES	LEVEL	DISTANCE	TIME	ELEVATION	PAGE
1 Humphreys Peak Summit Trail BEST		Butt-kicker	9.6 mi rt	6.5 hr	3,333 ft	268
2 Mars Hill Trail		Easy	3.4 mi rt	2 hr	500 ft	272
3 Buffalo Park Loop BEST		Easy	2 mi rt	1 hr	150 ft	274
4 Fat Man's Loop BEST		Easy	2.5 mi rt	1 hr	600 ft	277
5 Boynton Canyon Trail		Easy/Moderate	6.6 mi rt	2.5 hr	500 ft	280
6 Cathedral Rock Trail BEST		Easy/Moderate	1.6 mi rt	1 hr	800 ft	284
7 Bell Trail to Wet Beaver Creek BEST		Moderate	6.6 mi rt	3.5 hr	700 ft	287
8 Granite Mountain Trail		Strenuous	8.2 mi rt	4.5 hr	1,600 ft	290
9 Thumb Butte Loop		Easy/Moderate	2 mi rt	1 hr	800 ft	293
10 Fossil Springs Trail BEST		Strenuous	8 mi rt	5 hr	1,700 ft	297
11 Highline to Donahue Trail BEST		Moderate	4.8 mi rt	2.5 hr	1,350 ft	301
12 Horton Creek Trail BEST		Moderate	7.2 mi rt	3.5 hr	1,200 ft	304
13 Rim Lakes Vista and General Crook Loop BEST		Easy/Moderate	4.4 mi rt	2 hr	350 ft	307
14 Badger Springs Trail		Easy	1.6 mi rt	45 min	250 ft	310

1 HUMPHREYS PEAK SUMMIT TRAIL

Coconino National Forest, Kachina Peaks Wilderness, Flagstaff

BEST **Butt-Kickers**

Level: Butt-kicker

Total Distance: 9.6 miles round-trip

Hiking Time: 6.5 hours

Elevation Gain: 3,333 feet

Summary: It's only natural that the highest point in the state requires a challenging trek. This one's pretty hard-core.

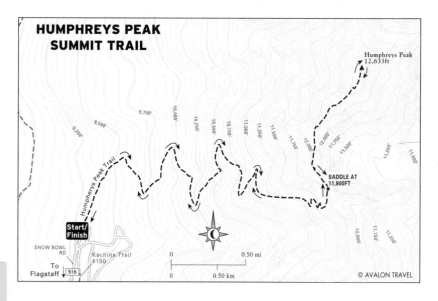

Buckle up for this one because you're in for it. Humphreys Peak is the highest point in Arizona and lives in the San Francisco Peaks on the north side of Flagstaff. The range got its name from the claim that one can see all the way to San Francisco from these heights. While that may be an exaggeration, reaching the highest point in Arizona is no easy task. It takes many hikers multiple attempts to get to Humphreys Peak at 12,633 feet, so don't be discouraged if plans hit a snag your first time. You and your party just have to get lucky with the weather and the effects of high altitude.

That said, you have the best chance with proper preparation. The trail begins

© LILIA MENCONI

Hikers are one with the weather at this high altitude.

at an impressive elevation of 9,300 feet, so it's best to spend the prior night in Flagstaff to help your body adjust to the higher altitude. Altitude sickness (splitting headache, dizziness, and nausea) is no joke, and it can ruin your ambition. In some cases, it can even lead to a life-threatening situation. Start the trail early in the morning to give yourself plenty of time for the 3,333-foot climb, which can easily take four hours or more just to ascend. Once on the trail, take it slow and steady.

Your second major obstacle is the weather. You're climbing high enough to pass the tree line and enter tundra. That's not a misprint—tundra—the only tundra in Arizona. This means the weather can turn on you quickly. For the final mile, cold winds are a constant, even in the dead of summer. It's not uncommon to experience heavy rain or hail, so bring warm clothes and rain gear. And, of course, lightning is a major concern. For the final mile of the hike, you are totally exposed. If you're on the way up and the weather looks iffy, be prepared to put summit aspirations on hold. At the first sign of a thunderstorm, get to lower ground and in the tree line as quickly as possible. Crouch down on the balls of your feet among low-lying bushes or trees. And try not to get lulled into a false sense of security by other hikers who are willing to take the risk. Assume they don't know what they're doing and make the safer choice. It will give you a reason to come back another day.

All those warnings aside, this is hands-down one of the greatest hikes in all the state. Most of the hike promises glorious summer temperatures in the 60s and 70s as you move your way up and through a thick alpine forest, across dramatic rock slides, and among sights of avalanche tracks on the slopes—not to mention, the most awe-inspiring views, said to stretch 100 miles in every direction at the peak (the views on the way up aren't too shabby, either). Throughout the hike, you see Flagstaff to the south, the entire San Francisco mountain range in every direction, and basically the entire state of Arizona. Oh, and don't forget the magnificent, satisfying, and delicious bragging rights.

The trail itself is easy to follow. From the parking lot, look for signs for Humphreys Peak Summit Trail at the north end. The first 0.5 mile is an easy walk across a beautiful meadow, bursting with purple silverstem lupine and white chaparral fleabane wildflowers. The trail leads right into the thick forest, where you remain for the next 3 miles as the path slowly creates a series of long switchbacks. So long, in fact, that you hardly notice the zigzagging at all as you make your way east. At 3.1 miles, the large switchbacks are complete and the trail heads straight east.

At 11,400 feet (approximately 3.75 miles into the hike), the trees begin to thin out and you are in the midst of a handful of switchbacks (still heading east). The next 400 feet to the saddle are hard fought. Take your time and breathe as the switchbacks subside and you continue a brutal stretch heading north. At 11,800 feet (4 miles), you reach the saddle between Humphreys (to the north) and Agassiz (to the south) Peaks. Since so many hikers are bottle-necked during that last challenging climb, it can be a party scene at the saddle as folks celebrate this accomplishment. To continue towards the summit, turn left (north), following the signs to Humphreys Peak. From the saddle to the summit, the trail climbs 833 feet in 0.8 mile. At this altitude, it takes an intense effort, to say the least. Again, slow your pace and breathe.

Soon after the saddle, pass through the very last bit of trees—a lone outcrop of gnarled and twisted bristlecone pine. The rest of the trail is totally exposed and occasionally marked with wooden posts. With scree underfoot, it may be tricky to find the correct trail at times. Do the best you can and remember that the trail generally heads north. Be prepared for a handful of soul-crushing fake summits before you reach the actual end, marked with a circle of rocks and a signpost for Humphreys Peak. Take a photo, give a friend a high-five, or cry if you need to. You made it.

The return trip requires you to retrace your steps for the long 4.8 miles back, during which you no doubt gain even more appreciation for the ground you've covered.

Let the bragging begin!

Options

To shorten the hike, the saddle is a great goal and one heck of an accomplishment in itself. Follow the Humphreys Trail for 4 miles until you reach the saddle, for an elevation gain of 2,500 feet. These views of Flagstaff to the south and the surrounding San Francisco Mountains are nothing to shake a stick at. Soak it up and then start the return descent for an up-and-back hike that totals 8 miles.

Directions

From downtown Phoenix, take I-17 north for approximately 140 miles to Flagstaff. Once in Flagstaff, continue on I-17 as it turns to Milton Road and veers right (east). Immediately after the road curves east, turn left onto Humphreys Street for 0.6 mile north. Turn left on Columbus Avenue, heading west, and follow the signs for westbound US-180. Take US-180 west (Fort Valley Rd.) for 6.6 miles, then turn right onto Snow Bowl Road, heading north. Follow Snow Bowl Road for 6.5 miles and look for signs for the Humphreys Peak Summit Trail trailhead parking lot to the left (north). The trailhead is on the north side of the lot.
GPS Coordinates: 35.3310 N, 111.7117 W

Information and Contact

There are no fees or passes required. Dogs on leash are allowed. Maps are available at any Coconino National Forest Information Center or Ranger District office. For more information, contact the Coconino Forest Supervisor's Office, 1824 South Thompson Street, Flagstaff, AZ 86001, 928/527-3600, www.fs.usda.gov/coconino.

2 MARS HILL TRAIL

Coconino National Forest, Flagstaff Urban Trails System

Level: Easy

Total Distance: 3.4 miles round-trip

Hiking Time: 2 hours

Elevation Gain: 500 feet

Summary: Perfect for the nuclear family—take the kids and the dog on this trail.

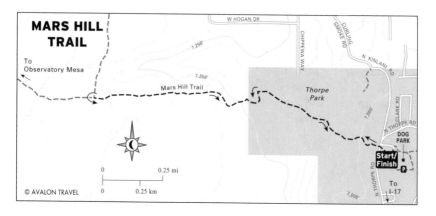

The family dog will go crazy for this trail. Not only is it a wide path with a subtle incline for maximum doggie energy burning, but the Mars Hill Trail trailhead is located at **Thorpe Park** (191 North Thorpe Rd., Flagstaff, www.flagstaff.az.gov). And Thorpe Park has an off-leash dog park complete with ramps, tunnels, and plenty of other rambunctious canine friends available for some serious romping.

For humans, the trail offers a lovely stroll up the east slope of Mars Hill, through a ponderosa pine forest. You might spy locals flinging Frisbees at the disc golf course or college kids jogging up the hill. It's the same hill, in fact, on which the Lowell Observatory is located. The observatory discovered Pluto in 1930. And while Arizonans are feeling the sting of the recent downgrade of Pluto from planet to "dwarf planet," the hill still makes for a great hike.

From the parking lot, head west to cross Thorpe Road. Begin the hike at the signed Mars Hill Trail trailhead and follow the path west. With just a few curves, the trail remains westward as it climbs a gradual 500 feet. At approximately 1.7 miles, the trail runs into a gate. Beyond the gate lies an intersection with two forest roads. Turn around here and return the way you came. It's that easy.

© LILA MENCONI

A wide path with ponderosa pines is perfect for the family dog.

And if your dog is still ready for some action when you return, let him burn it all off at the dog park.

Options

As far as hiking goes, the Mars Hill Trail is about all you can get out of this area. To add to this hike, take a tour of the **Lowell Observatory** (1400 West Mars Hill Rd., Flagstaff, 928/774-3358, www.lowell.edu, open daily). No reservations are needed.

Directions

From downtown Phoenix, take I-17 north for approximately 140 miles to Flagstaff. From I-17, continue north onto Milton Road and go 1.5 miles. Turn left onto Santa Fe Avenue, heading west. After 0.3 mile, turn right onto Thorpe Road and head north. After 0.4 mile, turn right (east) into the Thorpe Park parking lot. The Mars Hill Trail trailhead is on the north side of the parking lot. **GPS Coordinates:** 35.2066 N, 111.6578 W

Information and Contact

There are no fees or passes required. Dogs on leash are allowed. Maps are available at any Coconino National Forest Information Center or at the Flagstaff Visitor Center, 1 East Route 66, Flagstaff, AZ 86001, 928/774-9541. For more information, contact Coconino Forest Supervisor's Office, 1824 South Thompson Street, Flagstaff, AZ 86001, 928/527-3600, www.fs.usda.gov/coconino.

3 BUFFALO PARK LOOP
Coconino National Forest, Flagstaff Urban Trails System

BEST **Kid-Friendly Hikes**

Level: Easy

Total Distance: 2 miles round-trip

Hiking Time: 1 hour

Elevation Gain: 150 feet

Summary: Extremely easy, extremely beautiful, and extremely worth it.

Buffalo Park is Flagstaff at its best. This easy 2-mile loop is one of the most popular urban trails in town. Buffalo Park was originally a private wildlife park, and the ticket booth and buffalo statue remain at its entrance. Most of the trail wanders through native grassland speckled with clusters of yellow common sunflowers framed by dramatic views of the San Francisco Peaks, Dry Lake Hills, and Mount Elden to the north. With a mostly flat (93 percent of the packed-dirt trail has grades of less than 5 percent) 2-mile loop on top of McMillan Mesa, this stunning setting offers Flagstaffians a nice family stroll or an intense, multi-lap jog.

© LILIA MENCONI

Buffalo Park is just about the most ridiculously beautiful thing you'll ever see.

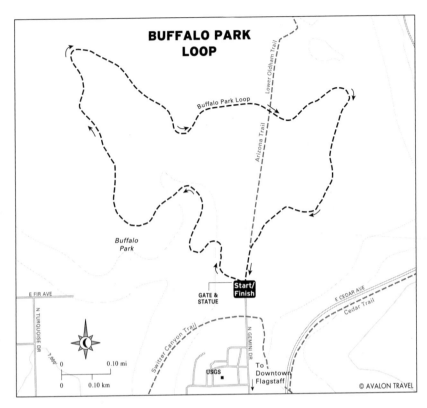

To start the clockwise loop, take an immediate left after entering the park. The first 0.5 mile rolls through a shallow, wooded ravine. Notice the workout stations with climbing ropes, wall climbs, and pull-up bars along the trail as it wiggles its way to the northwest. At approximately 1 mile, the trail turns right and heads east. Continue east and ignore the intersection with the park's central walkway to the south and the Lower Oldham Trail to the north. The Buffalo Park Trail then curves right (south). After just 0.5 mile more, the trail finds its way back to the entrance of the park.

Options

Buffalo Park can act as your starting point for any number of trail combinations that cruise in and among Elden Mountain and the Dry Lake Hills trail systems. To access more trails, follow the Buffalo Park Loop until the intersection with **Lower Oldham Trail**. Take a left turn on Lower Oldham Trail to head north. After approximately 0.5 mile, Lower Oldham Trail connects to Pipeline Trail, which heads east for 3 miles until it connects to Fat Man's Loop. Turn around here to create a 10-mile trek on this out-and-back journey.

Directions

From downtown Phoenix, take I-17 north for approximately 140 miles to Flagstaff. Once in Flagstaff, continue north on I-17 as it turns to Milton Road and veers right, heading east. Immediately after the road curves east, turn left onto Humphreys Street for 0.6 mile northeast. Turn right (southeast) on Columbus Avenue and follow it briefly until the first left (northeast) onto Beaver Street. Follow Beaver Street north for 0.3 mile and take the second right onto Forest Avenue, heading east, and follow it for 0.9 mile as Forest Avenue veers north. Turn left onto Gemini Road and follow it north for 0.3 mile. The road ends at the Buffalo Park parking lot. The Buffalo Park entrance and the Buffalo Park Trail trailhead are at the north end of the lot.

GPS Coordinates: 35.2180 N, 111.6328 W

Information and Contact

There are no fees or passes required. Dogs on leash are allowed. Maps are available at any Coconino National Forest Information Center or at the Flagstaff Visitor Center, 1 East Route 66, Flagstaff, AZ 86001, 928/774-9541. For more information, contact Coconino Forest Supervisor's Office, 1824 South Thompson Street, Flagstaff, AZ 86001, 928/527-3600, www.fs.usda.gov/coconino.

4 FAT MAN'S LOOP

Coconino National Forest, Flagstaff

BEST☾ **Wildflowers**

Level: Easy

Total Distance: 2.5 miles round-trip

Hiking Time: 1 hour

Elevation Gain: 600 feet

Summary: Take the entire family on this easy loop that climbs to some nice views and requires a bit of a squeeze through two boulders.

This easy hike is the perfect solution for Phoenix families starved of fresh air. In the cool climate of Flagstaff, kids and parents can gladly gulp pine-rich oxygen as they complete this loop. With a bit of a climb, a lovely view, and wildflowers galore, the summer heat seems worlds away.

The trail starts with an easy warm-up in the pine forest meadow at the base of Mount Elden. Following the loop clockwise, the trail quickly climbs its 500 feet and then flattens as it continues along the side of the mountain. All along, notice bursts of color as clusters of white southwestern thornapple and yellow broom snakeweed wildflowers bombard the trail.

Start the hike at the signed trailhead on the northeast corner of the Mount Elden trailhead parking lot. Begin by following the Elden Lookout Trail to the northwest for 0.2 mile until you reach a three-trail juncture. Follow the signs for Fat Man's Loop to continue straight (northwest). Pass the turnoff for the Pipeline Trail to the west and start the ascent at approximately 0.4 mile. The climbing portion of this trail leads north and only lasts for about half a mile. The elevation tops out at the signed intersection with the Sunset and Elden Lookout Trails. Ignore the turnoff and continue along Fat Man's

© LILIA MENCONI

Squeeze through this on your way around this loop.

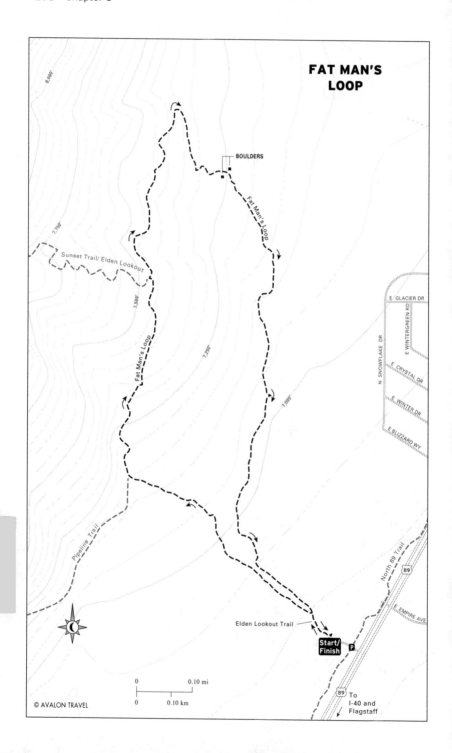

FAT MAN'S LOOP

BOULDERS

Fat Man's Loop

Sunset Trail/ Elden Lookout

Fat Man's Loop

Pipeline Trail

Elden Lookout Trail

Start/ Finish

E. GLACIER DR

E. WINTERGREEN RD

N. SNOWFLAKE DR

E. CRYSTAL DR

E. WINTER DR

E. BLIZZARD WY

North 89 Trail

89

E. EMPIRE AVE

89 To I-40 and Flagstaff

0   0.10 mi

0   0.10 km

© AVALON TRAVEL

Loop, heading north. At 1.3 miles, the trail makes a sharp right turn to the south and begins its descent. You quickly encounter two boulders that your party has to squeeze between. Luckily, you'd have to be quite large not to be able to clear it.

The Fat Man's Loop continues south. Be sure to ignore signs for the Christmas Tree and Sandy Seep Trails. Follow the trail markers as Fat Man's Loop veers to the southwest until collides with the three-way intersection (this is where you started the loop) at 2.3 miles. From there, turn left to retrace your steps along the Elden Lookout Trail south for the short 0.2 mile back to the Mount Elden parking lot.

Options

For a longer, more challenging climb, take the **Elden Lookout Trail**, which reaches Mount Elden's summit, 2,300 feet above Flagstaff. Follow the Fat Man's Loop hike for the first mile. When Fat Man's Loop reaches the Sunset and Elden Lookout Trail junction, turn left to follow the Elden Lookout Trail, which heads northwest. This steep climb is moderated by occasional switchbacks and leads up a staircase of petrified lava. Pass through an area devastated by a 1977 fire before you reach Elden's Lookout, the current fire watch tower in the area. Turn around here and retrace your steps southeast along the Elden Lookout Trail to return to the juncture with Fat Man's Loop. Turn left (north) onto Fat Man's Loop and finish out the hike. This option totals 5.7 miles.

Directions

From downtown Phoenix, take I-17 north for approximately 140 miles to Flagstaff. Take exit 340A to merge onto I-40 east toward Albuquerque. Continue on I-40 for 5.6 miles, then take exit 201 toward US-89 north for 0.3 mile. Take the first left turn onto Country Club Drive for 0.5 mile, heading west. Take a right turn onto northbound US-89. After 0.8 mile, look for Mount Elden trailhead signs and turn left (northwest) into the Mount Elden trailhead parking lot. The Elden Lookout Trail trailhead (which leads to Fat Man's Loop) is on the northeast corner of the lot. **GPS Coordinates:** 35.2304 N, 111.5794 W

Information and Contact

There are no fees or passes required. Dogs on leash are allowed. Maps are available at any Coconino National Forest Information Center or Ranger District office. For more information, contact the Coconino Forest Supervisor's Office, 1824 South Thompson Street, Flagstaff, AZ 86001, 928/527-3600, www.fs.usda.gov/coconino.

5 BOYNTON CANYON TRAIL

Coconino National Forest, Red Rock Secret Mountain Wilderness

Level: Easy/Moderate

Total Distance: 6.6 miles round-trip

Hiking Time: 2.5 hours

Elevation Gain: 500 feet

Summary: An easy, mostly flat stroll has a small elevation climb among the breathtaking sedimentary rock walls of Boynton Canyon.

This trail starts in the red dust of the Sedona desert and quickly leads you into a shaded, quiet canyon. You're soon surrounded by high forest vegetation like Arizona alder, ash, and cypress trees. It's rumored that this entire trail is one of Sedona's vortex sites, in which spiritual energies collide. No matter your disposition, the beauty and relative peace of the trail makes you wonder if there's something to the theory.

On the beginning section of the flat, dusty trail, you encounter incredible views of the canyon walls to the north of alternating fuchsia, terra cotta, and cream layers

The spire on the right, called Kachina Woman, is a vortex site that many believe yields spiritual powers.

© LILIA MENCONI

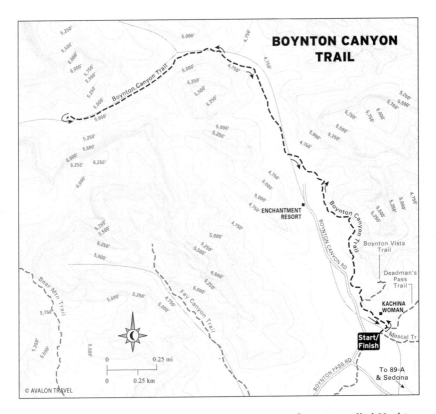

of sediment. Look to the northeast (right) to see a 300-foot spire called Kachina Woman, for obvious reasons. Ancient ruins of cliff dwellings are in the area but require some off-trail exploration for an up-close look. The park officially marks the trail as a 2-mile jaunt (1 mile in, 1 mile out), but GPS indicates a much longer trail of 6.6 miles total.

Start the hike at the Boynton Canyon trailhead on the west side of the parking lot, across from the restroom facilities. A kiosk with a detailed map clearly marks the beginning of your journey.

Within the first 0.25 mile, notice two opportunities for other trails that head east (right). Follow the Boynton Canyon Trail signs, which keep you veering left to the northwest. You may encounter other small offshoots during the early part of this hike, but if you continue to the northwest (and follow other hikers' footprints in the dirt) you'll easily find the correct path. At about 0.5 mile, notice the rooftops of the Enchantment Resort to the west. Here, the path becomes slightly rocky, so try to keep one eye on your footwork. At 0.75 mile, the resort is no longer visible and you feel cut off from the world.

With a very slow elevation gain, mile 1 is easily reached. There's no landmark indicating this point, and the trail clearly continues to cut through the canyon. If you choose to move on, you'll soon follow a well-worn trail that follows a creek bed (dry in the summer). Notice rocks with moss, hear wind rustle the pine trees, and spy a few fluffy squirrels.

Since you're no longer on the official trail after the first mile, the path becomes narrow and you may have to dodge a few branches as you wiggle through heading northwest. The canyon wall to the east starts closing in around mile 2.5. It's obvious that fewer folks make it all the way to this point, so there's no crime in turning back at any time. If you do take it to the very end (at 3.3 miles), the trail peters out at the canyon wall. A small climb offers a nice view of the distance you just completed.

Navigation back to the trailhead is as easy as the trip into the canyon. Simply turn around and follow the Boynton Canyon Trail in the opposite direction (southeast). And be sure you've had your fill of the scenery, because your quick pace makes this final leg fly by.

Options

If you really love the vibe of the Kachina Woman, you have the opportunity to reach out and touch her. At 0.3 mile, hang a right turn (east) onto the **Vista Trail.** Take the rocky incline for 0.5 mile to encounter the base of this spire. This area is supposedly the most powerful point of the energy vortex, so you may find some others meditating or praying. Taking this trail out and back totals 1.6 miles.

Directions

From downtown Phoenix, take I-17 north for approximately 95 miles. Take exit 298 for AZ-179 north toward Sedona. Keep straight (north) on AZ-179 for 14.2 miles through multiple traffic circles. Turn left onto AZ-89A and drive 3 miles west. Turn right onto Dry Creek Road for 2 miles north until the road turns into Boynton Pass Road. Continue for 0.9 mile and then turn left to stay on Boynton Pass Road for another 1.6 miles, heading northwest. Turn right onto Boynton Canyon Road for 0.1 mile north. The Boynton Canyon trailhead parking lot is on the right (east). Park, then pay the fee at the automated kiosk. The trailhead is on the west side of the lot.
GPS Coordinates: 34.9075 N, 111.8487 W

Information and Contact

There is a fee of $5 per vehicle or $15 for a seven-day pass. Pay at the automated kiosk at the entrance to the parking lot with a card or cash. Dogs on leash are allowed. Maps are available at any Coconino National Forest Information Center or Ranger District office. For more information, contact Coconino Forest Supervisor's Office, 1824 South Thompson Street, Flagstaff, AZ 86001, 928/527-3600, www.fs.usda.gov/coconino.

6 CATHEDRAL ROCK TRAIL

Coconino National Forest, Sedona

BEST Climbing and Scrambling

Level: Easy/Moderate

Total Distance: 1.6 miles round-trip

Hiking Time: 1 hour

Elevation Gain: 800 feet

Summary: A super steep climb might test the nerves of some, but the views dazzle all who make it to this vortex site.

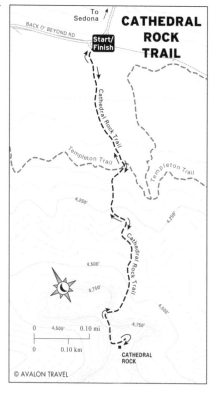

Cathedral Rock sits among a series of Sedona's famous red rock spires that jut dramatically to the sky. This trail climbs to a viewpoint near the spires and is a vortex site. Bust out your spiritual feathers and collection of power crystals for this visit, as you are treated to some special vibes. Or, at the very least, your GPS tracker might get squirrely. Whatever you might believe, this short jaunt up the rock is seriously stunning.

Be prepared to pay attention on this trail. Not only is there steep climbing ahead, but walking off-trail is strongly discouraged. The surrounding topsoil of lumpy black crust is teeming with living bacteria, moss, lichen, fungus, and liverworts. This good stuff takes decades to develop and controls erosion, stores water, fertilizes soil, and makes seeds turn to lovely plants. Okay, nature lesson is over.

Once you've secured a spot at the busy Back O' Beyond parking lot, start the hike at the clearly marked trailhead on the southwest corner of the lot. Follow the Cathedral Rock Trail as it travels southwest. You soon walk over a wash

Follow the cairns up to Cathedral Rock's saddle.

and onto a very slight incline that ends at 0.2 mile, where you encounter the slick rock. From here, the trail is clearly marked with cairns—metal cages filled with fist-sized rocks. Ignore signs for the intersecting Templeton Trail and stick by the cairns that lead up the rock.

Let the climbing begin. Use the carved footholds as you scramble up the slick stuff. Just about half a mile in, you encounter the super scary/totally awesome (depending on your temperament) portion of the trail. The chickens usually stop here while the bold move ahead. The steep stuff doesn't last long, however, and it soon turns to a moderate climb.

Keep steady feet, endure a couple more mild scrambles, and follow the cairns for the next 0.2 mile until the trail flattens. That's it. Feel free to explore the area at the Cathedral Rock spires and view some of the most mind-boggling vistas of red rock country's splendor. Rub your crystals, meditate, and get freaky-deaky as the vortex of energy washes over your chakras.

Once your renewal has transpired to your satisfaction, return the way you came and let the cairns be your guide back. Taking the wrong route down can lead to some dangerous drops that would surely spoil the serene experience.

Options

For a longer hike, combine the climb to Cathedral Rock with the **Templeton Trail** and **Baldwin Loop.** After 0.3 mile into the Cathedral Rock Trail, hang a right (west) at Templeton Trail. Follow the trail for 1 mile west, then turn left (south) on the Baldwin Loop, which lasts 2 miles. Return via the Templeton Trail (east) back to the Cathedral Rock Trail and start your climb to the spires. Return to the parking lot by following the Cathedral Rock Trail northeast. This combination totals 5.6 miles.

Directions

From downtown Phoenix, take I-17 north for approximately 95 miles. Take exit 298 for AZ-179 north toward Sedona. Continue straight (north) on AZ-179 for approximately 11 miles through a series of traffic circles. At the fifth traffic circle, take the third exit to make a left turn onto Back O' Beyond Road heading west. Continue for 3 miles west. The Back O' Beyond parking lot and Cathedral Rock Trail trailhead are to the left (south). Park and pay the fee at the automated kiosk. **GPS Coordinates:** 34.8251 N, 111.7886 W

Information and Contact

There is a fee of $5 per vehicle or $15 for a seven-day pass. Pay at the automated kiosk at the trailhead with a card or cash. Dogs on leash are allowed. Maps are available at any Coconino National Forest Information Center or Ranger District office. For more information, contact Coconino Forest Supervisor's Office, 1824 South Thompson Street, Flagstaff, AZ 86001, 928/527-3600, www.fs.usda.gov/coconino.

7 BELL TRAIL TO WET BEAVER CREEK

Coconino National Forest, Wet Beaver Creek Wilderness, south of Sedona

BEST Hikes near Water

Level: Moderate

Total Distance: 6.6 miles round-trip

Hiking Time: 3.5 hours

Elevation Gain: 700 feet

Summary: The Bell Trail delivers incredible canyon scenery with a refreshing swim in Wet Beaver Creek.

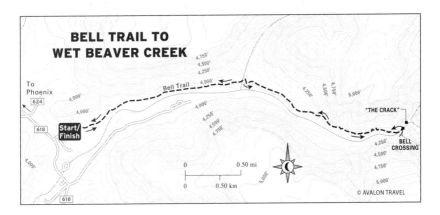

Turns out, cows can clear a decent trail. As with many of the trails in these parts, a rancher created this trail to move cattle. His name was Charles Bell, and in the 1930s, he forged this path to get livestock from the Verde Valley up to the Mogollon Rim for cooler summer temperatures. Today, the Bell Trail is still used to move cattle and is also used to move Phoenicians to the refreshing Wet Beaver Creek. The trail follows alongside Wet Beaver Creek for 3.3 miles into its breathtaking canyon on the southern rim of the Colorado Plateau and down to Bell Crossing. The creek offers ample opportunity for wading, rock-hopping, cliff-jumping, and swimming to your heart's delight.

From the north end of the Beaver Creek Campground parking lot, start walking along the dirt road and follow the signs to Bell Trail, heading east. This road starts on private property but very quickly turns into the Bell Trail and veers close to the creek at about 0.5 mile. A few smaller trails lead to the water's edge, where families

© LILIA MENCONI

The Bell Trail boasts incredible canyon views.

with small children often stop. Continue heading east as the prickly pear-covered mountains slowly turn to canyon walls. Ignore turnoffs to the White Mesa and Apache Maid Trails. Each is clearly signed, making for easy navigation.

At 2.4 miles, notice a fork. Veer to the left to remain on the Bell Trail, continuing east (ignore the Weir Trail to the right). The Bell Trail climbs approximately 100 more feet and then follows a narrow path along the side of the canyon. Don't pass on this opportunity for incredible views of the canyon and creek below. Once the trail begins a slight curve to the north, follow the sign to Bell Crossing. Take the sharp right turn to head south and begin a quick descent to the water. Once at the crossing (3.3 miles), feel free to wander along and in the shady creek, which is bombarded with riparian plant life. Bring water shoes for this portion as you search for deep swimming pools and a spot to enjoy some lunch.

Once you've splashed around, grubbed, and let your body bake on the rocks, return the way you came along Bell Trail. During the final couple of miles, keep your eyes peeled for petroglyphs. Your attentiveness will be rewarded!

Options

While looking for your swimming spot, keep in mind that a deep pool the locals have dubbed "The Crack" is located a mere 0.1 mile up-creek from **Bell Crossing,** to the north. To get there, you can try wandering along the banks and in the water from Bell Crossing. Or, for an easier trek, opt for a left turn back at the sign for Bell Crossing (follow the arrows for "The Crack" that are scratched into the sign) to continue along an unmarked trail. This makes for a total hike of approximately 6.8 miles.

For a short version of this hike, take the Bell Trail for about 1 mile until it bumps into Wet Beaver Creek. A small trail leads to the water's edge, where wading and fishing can take place. Opting for the abbreviated version totals just about 2 miles.

Directions
From downtown Phoenix, take I-17 north for approximately 95 miles. Take exit 298 for AZ-179 north toward Sedona and go 0.2 mile. Turn right onto National Forest Road 618 and go southeast for 2.1 miles. Follow generic trailhead signs to make a left turn (east) on an unmarked road. After less than 0.1 mile, the Beaver Creek Campground parking lot is on the right (south). Park here. The Bell Trail trailhead is on the north side of the parking lot.
GPS Coordinates: 34.6744 N, 111.7133 W

Information and Contact
There are no fees or passes required. Dogs on leash are allowed. Maps are available at any Coconino National Forest Information Center or Ranger District office. For more information, contact Coconino Forest Supervisor's Office, 1824 South Thompson Street, Flagstaff, AZ 86001, 928/527-3600, www.fs.usda.gov/coconino.

🔳 GRANITE MOUNTAIN TRAIL

Prescott National Forest, Prescott

Level: Strenuous

Total Distance: 8.2 miles round-trip

Hiking Time: 4.5 hours

Elevation Gain: 1,600 feet

Summary: It's a hiker's paradise here with plenty of mileage, beautiful wilderness, and a satisfying overlook at 7,185 feet.

Ready for the ultimate hike? This one's got it all. On this 8.2-mile round-trip hike, you spend most of the day in the Prescott National Forest, an environment rich with juniper and pine trees that dominate a floor scattered with prickly pear and agave. As you hike, spy moss-covered rocks next to trickling washes of cool water. With so much great stuff, this trail is shared with fellow hikers, rock climbers, folks on horseback, peregrine falcons, regal horned lizards, mountain lions, and gopher snakes, who are all eager to share this lush landscape with you. This hike ends at Vista Point, a clearing high above the land at a whopping 7,185 feet.

From the Metate trailhead parking lot, cross Granite Basin Road, heading

Granite Mountain is ridiculously scenic.

© LILIA MENCONI

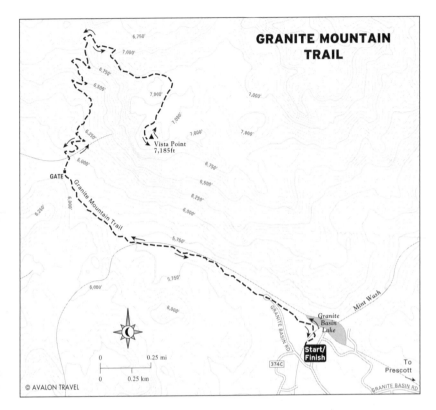

GRANITE MOUNTAIN TRAIL

Vista Point
7,185ft

GATE

Granite Mountain Trail

Granite Basin Lake

Mint Wash

Start/Finish

374C

To Prescott

GRANITE BASIN RD.

GRANITE BASIN RD.

0   0.25 mi

0   0.25 km

© AVALON TRAVEL

northwest to reach the Granite Mountain Trail (Trail 261) trailhead. Follow signs for Granite Mountain Trail as it curves north/northeast, then makes a sharp turn left to the northwest at 0.2 mile. After about 2 miles heading northwest, the trail runs into a large gate at Blair Pass. Pass by the gate and veer right to head north. From here, the trail climbs approximately 1,200 feet in 2 miles. The effort is moderated by seemingly endless switchbacks as you make your way northeast, up Granite Mountain.

After the first mile of climbing, you reach a ridge at 7,000 feet. Here, the trail flattens out and heads east for a pleasant, shaded stroll under the cover of tall trees. Soon enough, spy a sign indicating that Vista Point (your destination) is a mere quarter mile away. Expect to climb over a few rocky outcrops as the trail leads south, then curves east. Once the trail smacks into rocks and thick bushes, call it a day and enjoy the view from 7,185 feet.

After reaping your reward, retrace your steps for your return hike of 4.1 miles back to the Metate trailhead parking lot. Then stretch. You're going to need it.

Note: This hike describes the trail prior to the June 2013 Doce wildfire. Contact the Prescott National Forest for trail condition updates.

Options

For a shorter, 6-mile loop that doesn't require a hefty climb, venture through the gate at Blair Pass and take **Trail 40** to the left (west). This trail curves south and then east to make a loop around Little Granite Mountain, back to Metate trailhead. Be warned, however; Trail 40 is rugged and overgrown in areas, as it is rarely used by hikers. Long pants and sleeves are recommended to avoid getting scratched up, and your trail-reading skills will surely be tested.

Directions

From downtown Phoenix, take I-17 north for approximately 60 miles until exit 262. Take exit 262 and merge onto northbound AZ-69 toward Prescott. Continue north for 34 miles, then take the southbound AZ-89 ramp to Sheldon Street (slight right). Take Sheldon Street west for 0.8 mile. Turn right onto Montezuma Street and continue north for another 0.8 mile. The street curves left and turns into Whipple Street. Follow Whipple Street for 0.7 mile as it veers northwest and becomes Iron Springs Road. After 3 miles, take a right turn onto Granite Basin Road and follow it for approximately 4 miles, heading northeast into the Granite Basin Recreation Area. Follow signs to Metate trailhead, heading northeast and then south. The Metate trailhead parking lot is on the left (east) side of Granite Basin Road. Park and pay the fee at the self-pay station. The Granite Mountain Trail trailhead is across Granite Basin Road, to the northwest of the parking lot.
GPS Coordinates: 34.6157 N, 112.5515 W

Information and Contact

There is a fee of $5 per vehicle. An annual pass is available for $40. Dogs on leash are allowed. Maps are available at the trailhead. For more information, contact Prescott National Forest, 344 South Cortez Street, Prescott, AZ 86303, 928/443-8000, www.fs.usda.gov/prescott.

9 THUMB BUTTE LOOP
Prescott National Forest, Bradshaw Ranger District, Prescott

Level: Easy/Moderate

Total Distance: 2 miles round-trip

Hiking Time: 1 hour

Elevation Gain: 800 feet

Summary: This popular loop is a great way to view the lay of the land in Prescott and its surrounding forest.

If you've got kids and they are spending their summer complaining about the heat, here's a great way to shut them uh—er—to have some family outdoor fun in cool temperatures. Thumb Butte is the perfect out-of-town getaway to get their little lungs filled with fresh air.

At a mere 2 miles, the Thumb Butte Loop (Trail 33) is the most popular hike in the Prescott National Forest. Looming 1,000 feet above Prescott, Thumb Butte looks like a clenched fist with a protruding thumb when viewed from the north. In and among the ponderosa pine trees, alligator juniper, and prickly pear cacti, this trail travels up the butte's east side for 750 feet. Walk right past the rocky "thumb" and to a small spur in the trail that guarantees a far-reaching

Thumb's up for this quick workout on the Thumb Butte Trail.

view. The remainder of the trail is a relaxed descent along Thumb Butte's west side to close the loop.

From the Thumb Butte trailhead on the south side of Thumb Butte Road, veer left at the fork to take the loop clockwise. This direction gets the grunt work out of the way with its 750-foot climb accomplished in under 1 mile heading south (taking the opposite direction is only slightly less intense).

The first 0.7 mile of trail is steep, well-marked, and paved to prevent erosion. Interpretive plaques provide ample information about the area's history,

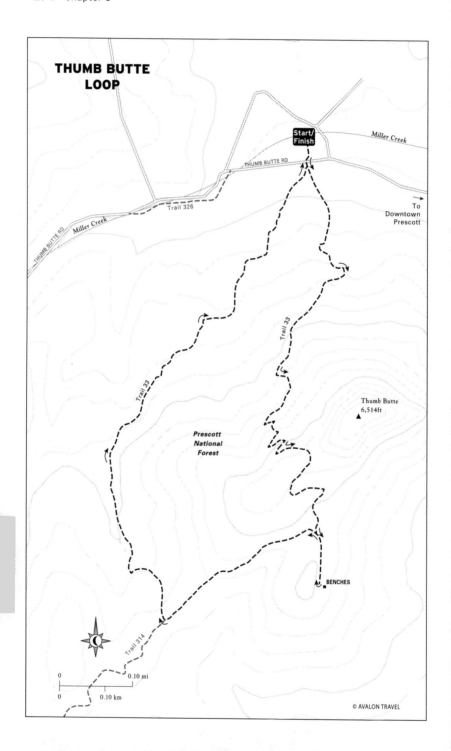

wildlife, plants, and geology. Encounter a series of intense switchbacks right before the trail mellows out at the base of the rocky protrusion on the top of Thumb Butte.

Continue south, avoiding any trailblazed paths toward the rocks. Nesting peregrine falcons populate the Thumb Butte cliff face, and the area is often closed to protect the birds. Just 0.1 mile beyond the rocky cliffs, take the well-traveled trail spur directly south and up a few steps to reach some benches. This small spur leads to a viewpoint from which you can see the San Francisco Mountains in the far distance to the northeast, the Black Hills to the east of Prescott, and the Bradshaw Mountains to the southeast.

Follow the spur path back to the loop trail and turn left (west). Enjoy an easy descent as the path curves to the northeast. It's just another 1.2 miles until the loop is closed and you're back at the trailhead.

Rest assured, your kids will thank you someday.

Options

Thumb Butte Loop is a small part of a much larger trail system in the Thumb Butte area. To create a larger loop that covers approximately 4 miles, combine Thumb Butte Loop (Trail 33) with Trails 314, 326, 392, and 367. Once you are 0.2 mile past the spur on Thumb Butte Loop, take a left turn on Trail 314, which juts to the southwest. After 0.5 mile, turn left (south) to join Trail 326. Follow it for another 0.5 mile to the intersection with Trail 392. Turn right (west) onto Trail 392 for 1.1 miles as it curves north, then east, and meets back up with Trail 367. Turn right onto Trail 367, which walks northwest along Country Road 65. After 0.6 mile, the trail meets back up with Trail 326. Veer left to continue walking alongside the road. In 0.2 mile, enter the Thumb Butte Loop parking lot from the southwest.

Directions

From downtown Phoenix, take I-17 north for approximately 60 miles until exit 262. Take exit 262 and merge onto northbound AZ-69 toward Prescott. Continue north for 34 miles, then take the southbound AZ-89 ramp to Sheldon Street (slight right). Take Sheldon Street west for 0.8 mile. Turn right onto Montezuma Street and continue north for 0.2 mile. Take the second right onto Gurley Street and go west for 3.5 miles (Gurley Street turns into Thumb Butte Road). The Thumb Butte picnic area and trailhead parking lot are on the right (north). Park here and pay the fee at the self-pay station. The Thumb Butte Loop trailhead is across the street, to the south.

GPS Coordinates: 34.5516 N, 112.5209 W

Information and Contact

There is a fee of $5 per vehicle. An annual pass is available for $40. Dogs on leash are allowed. Maps are available at the trailhead. For more information, contact Prescott National Forest, 344 South Cortez Street, Prescott, AZ 86303, 928/443-8000, www.fs.usda.gov/prescott.

10 FOSSIL SPRINGS TRAIL

Tonto and Coconino National Forests, near Strawberry

BEST **Hikes near Water**

Level: Strenuous

Total Distance: 8 miles round-trip

Hiking Time: 5 hours

Elevation Gain: 1,700 feet

Summary: This outrageously popular trail leads to one of the best swimming holes around.

You'll feel like an old-timey pioneer at this creek and swimming hole as you and your fellow swimmers strip down and dive in for a refreshing dip. Fossil Springs is a series of freshwater springs that feed into Fossil Creek. With the heavy concentration of calcium in its waters, the pebbles and debris found in the creek are coated with a rock-like substance called travertine—creating the "fossils" for which the creek is named. The springs gush 20,000 gallons per minute of 70-degree water year-round. Even though the springs are still considered "hot," the water feels fantastically cool after the four-mile descent into the canyon.

Campers and hikers take a cool dip at one of the most popular Fossil Creek swimming holes.

© LILIA MENCONI

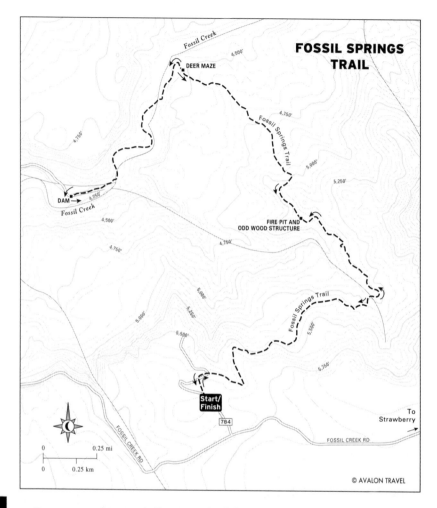

For sure your biggest challenge on this hike is parking. The Fossil Springs Trail parking lot only accommodates about 12 vehicles. This destination is wildly popular with campers, hikers, and equestrians, so plan for a weekday, if possible. Oh, and please, please plan to hike your trash out. It's definitely a big-time bummer to see so much garbage from irresponsible explorers. (Lame.)

Start from the well-marked trailhead on the northeast end of the Fossil Springs Trail parking lot to follow a nicely cleared and wide dirt path. Hang a right at the fork heading east to pass over a slightly rocky and quick shortcut. In no time, the two trails reunite. After 0.75 mile, you encounter a clearing with a few scattered fire pits. Continue north and rejoin the trail. From here, the trail turns right (east) and wiggles down, down, down. Wide on loose rock, the trail is very easy to navigate. Before you know it, you complete the first 2 miles, at which point you find another small clearing with a strange-looking wood structure and large fire pit. Continue for the next 1.5 miles as you descend farther and farther into the canyon, now heading northwest.

After a deer maze at mile 3, you soon pass an intersection with the Mail Trail. Veer left (south) to continue following the now-narrow Fossil Springs Trail through a riparian landscape. On your right, you spy a wash (usually dry in the summer). The Fossil Springs Trail cuts over the wash at 3.4 miles.

Once you've hopped across the dry wash, follow a narrow trail through some dense foliage. You know you're close when you pass by a campground and then traverse a narrow cut through wild tangles of blackberry bushes. To your left, pass the series of springs that feed the rushing creek. Once you've reached the remnants of an old dam with an accompanying kiosk, take in the views of a dramatic Fossil Creek waterfall below. Climb down to the foot of the falls for a popular swimming hole with a rope swing and plenty of people enjoying the clear, cool waters. Follow the trail farther south for more swimming areas that may offer a little privacy.

Whatever you do, don't miss this opportunity for a good swim. After four miles, you'll feel giddy with the satisfaction of splashing around in such a naturally beautiful place. It's a great time to cool off, lie on the rocks, and chow on a hefty snack.

Once you've dried off, return the way you came. Remember that easy downhill hike into the canyon? Now you get to hike up, up, up the 1,200 feet to the Fossil Springs Trail parking lot. Don't be surprised if you soon find yourself longing for another dip in the refreshing spring waters.

Options

From the Fossil Springs Trail trailhead and parking lot, your only trail option is the Fossil Springs Trail. If you're only interested in a short hike, however, this trail can easily be cut to accommodate. And since the start of the trail sits on top of the canyon, the views of the split land below are stunning from the get-go. For a short and satisfying jaunt, simply follow the Fossil Springs Trail for 2 miles to the strange-looking wood structure and fire pit. Nestled in a quiet clearing, the area makes for a fine stopping point. Turning around here and then climbing back to the Fossil Springs trailhead makes for a hike that totals 4 miles.

Directions

From downtown Phoenix, take the AZ-202 Loop approximately 13 miles east and exit on Country Club Drive. Turn left and continue for 2.7 miles, heading north until Country Club Drive becomes AZ-87. Follow AZ-87 approximately 80 miles north (through Payson and Pine). In the town of Strawberry, take a left on Fossil Creek Road and go 5 miles west. Continue as the asphalt gives way to a packed-dirt road for the final 2 miles. Look for signs for Fossil Creek trailhead parking on the right. The Fossil Creek Trail trailhead is on the northeast end of the parking lot. **GPS Coordinates:** 34.4072 N, 111.5685 W

Information and Contact

No fees or passes are necessary. Dogs on leash are allowed. Maps are available at any Coconino National Forest Information Center or Ranger District office. For more information, contact Coconino Forest Supervisor's Office, 1824 South Thompson Street, Flagstaff, AZ 86001, 928/527-3600, www.fs.usda.gov/coconino. For an updated information recording, call the Fossil Creek Hotline at 928/226-4611.

11 HIGHLINE TO DONAHUE TRAIL

Tonto and Coconino National Forest, near Pine

BEST Solitude

Level: Moderate

Total Distance: 4.8 miles round-trip

Hiking Time: 2.5 hours

Elevation Gain: 1,350 feet

Summary: Take the famous Highline Trail to Milk Ranch Point, an incredible outlook on the Mogollon Rim.

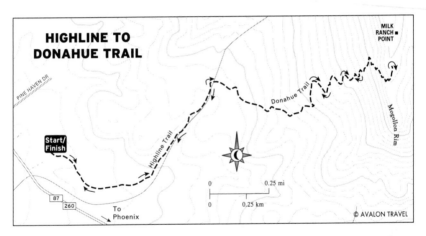

Leave it to the homesteaders to map out a satisfying trek through nature. This trail starts with a serene walk through a pine forest along a portion of the 50-mile Highline Trail before connecting with a quick climb up the Mogollon Rim. The Highline Trail was established in the late 1800s to connect the small collection of homesteads and ranches that sat below the rim. Today, the Highline Trail is shared with the massive Arizona Trail, which runs 790 miles across the entire state of Arizona. Don't panic. For this hike, you only take the Highline/Arizona trail for about 1.5 miles before connecting with the Donahue Trail. From there, it's another 1 mile up to the rim. And with so many miles to explore along the Highline/Arizona Trail, running into another hiker is a rarity.

From the parking lot for Pine trailhead, begin the hike at the southwest corner of the lot. Follow signs for the Highline Trail, which travels southwest then curves southeast for 0.5 mile. At 1 mile into the Highline Trail, it makes a turn to the

This quick hike ends near Milk Ranch Point on the top of the Mogollon Rim.

east. Cruise through the pine trees and a few washes, and breathe in the fresh air as you continue on this easy path.

At 1.5 miles, notice the sign for Donahue Trail. Take a sharp left (northeast) and start breathing—the real climbing begins here. The switchbacks start almost immediately, and you soon notice the trail becomes narrower as the elevation increases. On a couple of the switchbacks' turns, the trail may mislead you. When given the choice, opt for the sharp turn rather than the path that continues straight to avoid any fake-out trails.

After almost a mile of climbing 800 feet, the trail flattens and dissipates onto a clearing, where you can enjoy amazing views to Shannon Gulch to the southeast and Cedar Mesa to the south. Welcome to Milk Ranch Point, a flat outcrop of land extending south on the west end of the Mogollon Rim. This is the end of the hike. Once you've explored, enjoyed the scenery, and tracked a few elk prints, retrace your steps along Donahue and Highline Trails for the return trip of 2.4 miles back to the car.

Options

For an as-long-as-you-want-to-keep-walking stroll through the forest, skip the turnoff onto the Donahue Trail and continue along the Highline Trail east. This path leads 50 miles total and roughly traces the south side below the Mogollon Rim. The Pine trailhead is at the west end of the trail, and the closest landmarks along the Highline Trail (within the first 6 miles heading east) include Red Rock

Spring, Pine Spring, and Webber Creek. Follow the Highline Trail east as long as you wish and turn back whenever you want for a total mileage of your choice.

Directions

From downtown Phoenix, take the AZ-202 Loop approximately 13 miles east and exit on Country Club Drive. Turn left and continue north for 2.7 miles until Country Club Drive becomes AZ-87. After approximately 70 miles, continue north on AZ-87 and drive through Payson. After approximately 12 miles from the final traffic circle in Payson, turn right (east) at the brown sign for Pine trailhead, just south of the town of Pine. The Highline Trail trailhead is on the southeast corner of the parking lot.

GPS Coordinates: 34.3739 N, 111.4435 W

Information and Contact

No fees or passes are required. Dogs on leash are allowed. Maps are available at any Coconino National Forest Information Center or Ranger District office. For more information, contact Coconino Forest Supervisor's Office, 1824 South Thompson Street, Flagstaff, AZ 86001, 928/527-3600, www.fs.usda.gov/coconino.

12 HORTON CREEK TRAIL

Tonto National Forest, near Payson

BEST Hikes near Water

Level: Moderate

Total Distance: 7.2 miles round-trip

Hiking Time: 3.5 hours

Elevation Gain: 1,200 feet

Summary: This delightful jaunt travels along Horton Creek to end at its gushing mountain spring.

You really can't go wrong with this hike. It's not too intense but lengthy, and travels to the beautiful Horton Spring. The proper trail is a wide path that skips along the banks, but many hikers prefer to get their feet wet and travel up the creek itself. Either way, you are treated to a rich riparian landscape filled with wild grape, ferns, and lupine wildflowers. The trail climaxes at the creek's source, Horton Spring.

To find the trailhead, leave the Horton parking lot and head east to cross a one-way bridge. Below the bridge is Tonto Creek, which Horton Creek may or may not feed into, depending on the time of year. Look for signs to the Horton Campground. Enter the area and veer left to find the signed Horton Creek Trail (Trail 285) trailhead.

Behold the natural beauty of Horton Creek.

Descend a small slope and begin the hike along a narrow passage over the (most likely) dry Horton Creek, heading north. The path extends along the west side and is thick with riparian vegetation. Just when you're wishing you wore long pants, the trail opens up to a fork. A cairn in the shape of a large arrow made of logs tells you to veer left. This is the wide, easy path. Opt for the right if you're looking to skip along and in the actual water.

Taking the left side north for the first half mile or so, you easily forget that this trail is supposed to travel with the creek, because you won't hear or see it. But don't be discouraged; you soon pick up the sounds of rushing water as the trail veers closer to the water's edge. The trail frequently provides small walkways down to the creek, so there's plenty of action if this is the path you prefer.

Continue along the gentle slope for the next 2.5 miles. Once you reach the third mile, hang a sharp left, following the cairns northwest along a switchback. It may feel counterintuitive to walk away from the creek, but fear not! The next time you see water, it's gushing out of the land. At 3.5 miles, notice the sign pointing you toward Horton Spring. Follow the trail to the right (southeast), then northeast.

A few more steps and you discover the source of the rushing waters. A worn path leads within feet of the spring, which constantly pours water down stacked boulders to create mesmerizing falls. Peer through the rocks and into the dark cavern from which the cool water flows. A shallow pool sits at the foot of the falls. Take a seat and observe the glittering trout that populate the creek. Once satisfied, return the way you came. Or, if the water looks too good to pass up, make your way along the creek and its banks.

Options
Many hikers combine this trail with the **Highline Trail** and **Derrick Trail** to create a 9-mile loop. From the spring, return to the signed trail marker and follow the arrows right (southeast) for approximately 2.5 miles along the

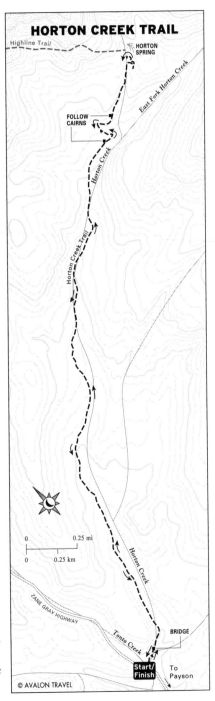

Highline Trail. Turn right (southwest) onto Derrick Trail and follow it for approximately 2.5 miles. The loop ends at the Horton Campground and Horton Creek Trail trailhead.

Directions

From downtown Phoenix, take the AZ-202 Loop approximately 13 miles east and exit on Country Club Drive. Turn left and continue for 2.7 miles, heading north until Country Club Drive becomes AZ-87. After heading north for approximately 70 miles (in Payson), turn right onto eastbound AZ-260 and travel approximately 16 miles east of Payson. Look for signs for Horton Creek and turn left onto Forest Service Road 289/Zane Gray Highway heading north. Follow it for 1 mile, past signs for the Horton Campground and Horton Creek Trail trailhead to the right, and then continue on the road to cross the single-lane bridge heading west (left). After you cross the bridge, the Horton parking lot is immediately to the left (south). Walk back across the bridge, heading east to the Horton Campground. Find the Horton Creek Trail trailhead on the northeast side of the campsite entrance.
GPS Coordinates: 34.3401 N, 111.0954 W

Information and Contact

No fees or passes are required. Dogs on leash are allowed. Maps are available at any Tonto National Forest Information Center or Ranger District office. For more information, contact Tonto National Forest Supervisor's Office, 2324 East McDowell Road, Phoenix, AZ 85006, www.fs.usda.gov/tonto.

13 RIM LAKES VISTA AND GENERAL CROOK LOOP

Apache-Sitgreaves National Forest, near Payson

BEST◗ Historical Hikes

Level: Easy/Moderate

Total Distance: 4.4 miles round-trip

Hiking Time: 2 hours

Elevation Gain: 350 feet

Summary: Start this easy loop with an incredible walk right along the edge of the Mogollon Rim, then continue strolling through the forest.

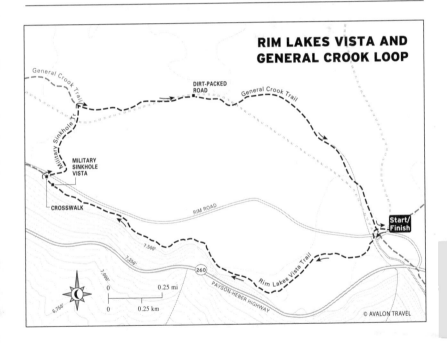

Taking in views at the 7,800-foot elevation of the Mogollon Rim is a deeply satisfying experience—especially when you don't have to climb for it. Instead, your car does the heavy lifting when you drive up to the Vista parking lot, conveniently perched at the top of the Mogollon Rim. After walking along the rim itself and feeling the juice from such crazy-beautiful views, you connect to the General

At the edge of the Mogollon Rim, the sights are stupendous.

© LILIA MENCONI

Crook Trail, which leads through the forest and back to the trailhead.

A hero in his time, General George Crook came to the Arizona Territory in 1871 and operated as Commander of the Military Department of Arizona. During an 11-day journey from Fort Apache to Fort Whipple, Crook paved this trail, and it soon became the third major road to be built in northern Arizona. The road was used to resupply Fort Apache as troops patrolled reservation borders—all in an effort to subdue the neighboring Apache tribes. Today, hikers may feel less obliged to view Crook as an outright hero, but just another influential figure during this conflicted time in U.S. history. This concludes the educational part of this hike.

From the Vista parking lot, two trails lead out. The General Crook Trail trailhead is on the northeast side of the lot, and the Rim Lakes Vista Trail trailhead is on the southeast. Choose the Rim Lakes Vista Trail to take this loop clockwise (you later return to the parking lot via the General Crook Trail). The Rim Lakes Vista Trail is a well-worn path through the pine trees for the first 0.25 mile heading west, marked by blue diamonds affixed to the surrounding tree trunks. When the trail seemingly comes to an end, look to your left (south) to see a crosswalk that leads across Forest Service Road 300 and into the wilderness on the other side. At mile 1, you come to the edge of the rim. Don't be alarmed if your eyes pop at the 100-mile views to the endless mountains and canyons to the south, including the distant Four Peaks. Continue along the trail, which skirts the Mogollon Rim's edge heading west, and take your time to enjoy the spectacular vistas. AZ-260 can be heard from below, but with these spectacular sights, you hardly notice.

After another mile, begin to walk alongside Forest Service Road 300 once more. Soon enough you undoubtedly come across other folks, who opted to drive to a popular viewpoint called the Military Sinkhole Vista. After you pass by the small parking lot, it's time to cross the road once more at a crosswalk heading northeast. Here, take the Military Sinkhole Trail for a very short 0.5 mile that cuts north through the forest and hooks up with the General Crook Trail. At the signed juncture, turn right (east) to take the General Crook Trail. Following the General Crook Trail is often vague and the path is marked only by chevron-shaped plastic markers nailed into the tree trunks. The trail loosely follows a dirt-packed road, and both lead back to the parking lot, so take your pick. The General Crook Trail offers a higher serenity factor and sense of history. That said, be respectful and avoid stomping on the many saplings you encounter. You are rewarded with a cruise through a gorgeous ponderosa pine and quaking aspen forest, meadows filled with wildflowers, and an opportunity to see elk in the area (at the very least, you'll step around piles of "evidence" that they're around).

After bouncing through the forest from chevron to chevron, you emerge at the General Crook Trail trailhead at the northeast end of the Vista parking lot.

Options

For a much longer jaunt to the Woods Canyon Lake, start with the General Crook Trail, heading northeast for approximately 4 miles until it runs into the **Meadow Trail.** Turn right to follow the Meadow Trail northeast for approximately 2 more miles until you reach Woods Canyon Lake. Retrace your route back to the Vista parking lot for a total hike of approximately 12 miles.

Directions

From downtown Phoenix, take the AZ-202 Loop approximately 13 miles east and exit on Country Club Drive. Turn left and continue for 2.7 miles, heading north until Country Club Drive becomes AZ-87. After heading north for approximately 70 miles (to Payson), turn right onto eastbound AZ-260 and travel approximately 30 miles east to climb to the top of the Mogollon Rim. Just as AZ-260 reaches the top of the rim, keep a vigilant eye for an easy-to-miss left turn onto Forest Service Road 300/Rim Road. Look for the Rim Lakes Vista parking lot immediately on the right (north). The Rim Lakes Vista Trail trailhead is on the southeast corner of the parking lot.

GPS Coordinates: 34.3057 N, 110.8975 W

Information and Contact

No fees or passes are necessary. Forest Service Road 300/Rim Road may be occasionally closed. Dogs on leash are allowed. Maps are available at the Black Mesa Ranger District at 2748 East Highway 260, Overgaard, AZ 85933, 928/535-7300. For more information, contact the Apache-Sitgreaves National Forests at 30 South Chiricahua Drive, Springerville, AZ 85938, 928/333-4301, www.fs.usda.gov/asnf.

14 BADGER SPRINGS TRAIL
Agua Fria National Monument

Level: Easy

Total Distance: 1.6 miles round-trip

Hiking Time: 45 minutes

Elevation Gain: 250 feet

Summary: Mosey along the soft sand of the Badger Springs Wash for a short walk to the Agua Fria River.

Welcome to a hike in a riparian wonderland (riparian is just a fancy word for the abundance of plant life that sprouts along a water source). The Badger Springs Trail travels along the Badger Springs Wash and meets up with the Agua Fria River. It's best to travel this trail in late spring or early summer to take advantage of some wading and swimming opportunities. By late summer, expect to find the Agua Fria reduced to very slow-moving (or not-moving) water.

The river isn't the only feature this hike has to offer, however. Expect to see a fine example of ancient petroglyphs, courtesy of the late prehistoric Perry Mesa Tradition people who roamed this area between 1250 and 1450 CE. The Agua Fria National Monument

Get close to this incredible collection of petroglyphs (but don't touch).

contains 70,900 acres with 450 prehistoric sites. With the water source nearby, the area's wildlife includes coyotes, bobcats, antelope, mule deer, javelinas, snakes, lizards, and over 170 bird species. The riparian landscape offers fertile soil for wildflowers, like the common sunflower, which can grow up to 9 feet. Yes, a wonderland indeed, and perfect for the kids.

To begin the hike, find the Badger Springs Trail trailhead on the southeast corner of the Badger Springs parking area. Pass through the cattle gate and follow the trail signs leading farther southeast. At about 0.1 mile, the trail collides with the soft sand of the Badger Springs Wash. From here, it's a straight shot to the southeast as the trail weaves along, across, and through the wash bed. At 0.8 mile, find the curve of the Agua Fria River. Kick off your shoes and wade through the water. Don't forget to search for the rocky walls northeast of the shoreline for an amazing collection of petroglyphs. Admire them from a safe distance and be respectful of the ancient markings.

Once you've cooled down and explored the area, turn back and travel northwest along the Badger Springs Wash to the trailhead.

Options

For an open-ended, longer haul, follow the Agua Fria River. If you turn right along the shore, the river winds south and is flanked by the Perry Mesa to the east and the Black Mesa to the west. After approximately 14 miles, the river intersects with the highway. If you opt for a left turn, the river leads you north and intersects with Bloody Basin Road in approximately 4 miles. No matter which way you choose, beware of quicksand in the area as you create an exploratory hike with a total mileage of your choice.

Directions

From downtown Phoenix, take I-17 north approximately 50 miles out of the city. At exit 256, turn right onto Badger Springs Road, heading east. Drive through the clearing, past the Agua Fria National Monument kiosk, and onto the dirt road to the southeast. Continue

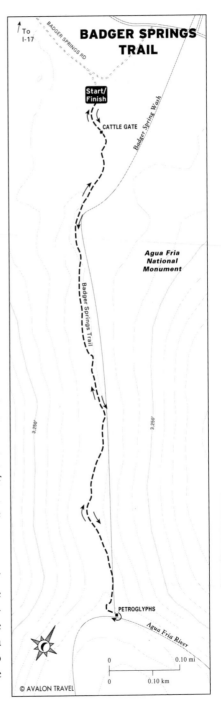

along the dirt Badger Springs Road southeast for approximately 1 mile, past the restrooms. Find parking at the next turnoff to the right (south) into a parking circle. The Badger Springs Trail trailhead is on the southeast side of the parking circle. **GPS Coordinates:** 34.2312 N, 112.1001 W

Information and Contact

No fees or passes are necessary. Dogs on leash are allowed. Maps are available at the information kiosk near the restrooms. For more information, contact the U.S. Department of the Interior Bureau of Land Management Hassayampa Field Office, 21605 North 7th Avenue, Phoenix, AZ 85027, 623/580-5500, www.blm.gov/az.

RESOURCES

© LILIA MENCONI

City, State, and National Parks

Apache-Sitgreaves National Forest
30 South Chiricahua Drive
Springerville, AZ 85938
928/333-4301
www.fs.usda.gov/asnf

Boyce Thompson Arboretum
37615 U.S. Highway 60
Superior, AZ 85173
520/689-2723
www.arboretum.ag.arizona.edu

Cave Creek Regional Park
37900 North Cave Creek Parkway
Cave Creek, AZ 85331
623/465-0431

City of Phoenix Parks and Recreation
Phoenix City Hall
200 West Washington Street
16th Floor
Phoenix, AZ 85003
602/262-6862
www.phoenix.gov/parks

City of Scottsdale McDowell Sonoran Preserve
480/312-7013
www.scottsdaleaz.gov/preserve

City of Scottsdale Parks and Recreation
7447 East Indian School Road
Suite 300
Scottsdale, AZ 85251
480/312-7275
www.scottsdaleaz.gov

Coconino Forest Supervisor's Office
1824 South Thompson Street
Flagstaff, AZ 86001
928/527-3600
www.fs.usda.gov/coconino

Estrella Mountain Regional Park
14805 West Vineyard Avenue
Goodyear, AZ 85338
623/932-3811
www.maricopa.gov/parks/estrella

Flagstaff Visitor Center
1 East Route 66
Flagstaff, AZ 86001
928/774-9541

Glendale Parks and Recreation Department
Glendale Adult Center
5970 West Brown Street
Glendale, AZ 85301
623/930-2820
www.glendaleaz.com/
parksandrecreation/ThunderbirdPark

Lost Dutchman State Park
6109 North Apache Trail
Apache Junction, AZ 85119
480/982-4485
www.azstateparks.com/parks/LODU

McDowell Mountain Regional Park
16300 McDowell Mountain Park Drive
Scottsdale, AZ 85255
480/471-0173

Picacho Peak State Park
(I-10 Exit 219)
P.O. Box 907

Eloy, AZ 85131
520/466-3183

Pinnacle Peak Park
26802 North 102nd Way
Scottsdale, AZ 85262
480/312-0990
www.scottsdaleaz.gov/parks/pinnacle

Prescott National Forest
344 South Cortez Street
Prescott, AZ 86303
928/443-8000
www.fs.usda.gov/Prescott

San Tan Mountain Regional Park
6533 West Phillips Road
Queen Creek, AZ 85242
480/655-5554
www.maricopa.gov/parks/santan

**Spur Cross Ranch
Conservation Area**
44000 North Spur Cross Road
Cave Creek, AZ 85331
480/488-6601
www.maricopa.gov/parks/spur_cross

Tonto National Forest
Supervisor's Office
2324 East McDowell Road
Phoenix, AZ 85006
602/225-5200
www.fs.usda.gov/tonto

U.S. Department of the Interior
Bureau of Land Management
Hassayampa Field Office
21605 North 7th Avenue
Phoenix, AZ
623/580-5500

www.blm.gov/az

**Usery Mountain Regional Park
Nature Center**
3939 North Usery Pass Road
Mesa, AZ 85207
480/984-0032
www.maricopa.gov/parks/usery

**White Tank Mountain
Regional Park**
20304 West White Tank Mountain
Road
Waddell, AZ 85355
623/935-2505
www.maricopa.gov/parks/white_tank

Map Sources
Green Trails Maps
P.O. Box 77734
Seattle, WA 98177
www.greentrailsmaps.com

National Geographic Maps
212 Beaver Brook Canyon Road
Evergreen, CO 80439
800/962-1643
www.natgeomaps.com

United States Geological Survey
USGS National Center
12201 Sunrise Valley Drive
Reston, VA 20192
703/648-5953

Wide World of Maps
www.maps4u.com

2626 West Indian School Road
Phoenix, AZ 85017
602/279-2324 x4

1444 West Southern Avenue
Mesa, AZ 85202
602/844-1134 x218

17232 North Cave Creek Road
Phoenix, AZ 85032
602/795-4868

Phoenix Area Hiking Clubs
Arizona Backpacking Club
www.meetup.com/
Arizona-Backpacking

Arizona Outdoor & Travel Club
P.O. Box 21951
Mesa, AZ 85277
www.azotc.com

Arizona Trail Association (ATA)
P.O. Box 36736
Phoenix, AZ 85067
602/252-4794
www.aztrail.org

Arizona Trailblazers
www.azhikers.org

Sierra Club
Grand Canyon Chapter
202 East McDowell Road, Suite 277
Phoenix, AZ 85004
602/253-8633
www.arizona.sierraclub.org

Hiking Gear Retailers
Arizona Hiking Shack
3244 East Thomas Road
Phoenix, AZ 85018
www.hikingshack.com

LowerGear
1828 East University Drive
Tempe, AZ 85281
480/348-8917
www.lowergear.com

Recreation Equipment, Inc. (REI)
www.rei.com

12634 North Paradise Village
Parkway
Phoenix, AZ 85032
602/996-5400

1405 West Southern Avenue
Tempe, AZ 85282
480/967-5494

Suggested Reading
Epple, Lewis E., and Anne Orth. *Plants of Arizona*. Guilford, CT: Globe Pequot Press, 1997. Organized by plant or flower color, this expansive resource includes full-color photos of more than 900 plant species.

Kavanaugh, James. *Southwestern Desert Life, An Introduction to Familiar Plants and Animals*. Phoenix, AZ: Waterford Press, 2001. With full-color illustrations by Raymond Leung, this brochure-style reference piece offers a quick and accurate way to identify desert plants and animals.

Nester, Tony. *Desert Survival: Tips, Tricks, & Skills*. Flagstaff, AZ: Diamond Creek Press, 2003. Tony Nester is a desert survival expert who has made a career advising the U.S. military, National Park Service, Grand Canyon

Field Institute, and the greater public on indispensable desert survival techniques.

Telander, Todd. *Birds of Arizona.* Guilford, CT: Globe Pequot Press, 2012. Illustrated by the author, this pocket guide features full-color pencil drawings of the most common birds in Arizona.

Online Resources
Arizona Hiking
www.arizonahiking.blogspot.com

Arizona Hiking Trails
www.arizonahikingtrails.com

HikeArizona.com
www.hikearizona.com

Todd's Desert Hiking Guide
www.toddshikingguide.com

Index

AB

A Mountain: 90
Agua Fria National
    Monument: 310
Angel Basin: 203
Apache-Sitgreaves National
    Forest: 307
Arizona Canal Loop at
    Arizona Falls: 81
Badger Springs Trail: 310
Baldwin Loop: 285
Bell Crossing: 288
Bell Pass Trail: 250
Bell Trail to Wet Beaver
    Creek: 287
Black Mesa Loop: 169
Black Mountain Summit
    Preserve: 225
Black Mountain Summit
    Trail: 225
Black Rock Long Loop: 102,
    103
Black Rock Short Loop: 105
Blevins to Cat Peaks Loop:
    181
Boulder Canyon Trail: 165
Boyce Thompson
    Arboretum: 205, 207
Boynton Canyon Trail: 280
Bradshaw Ranger District:
    293
Brown's Peak: 263
Brown's Trail: 261
Buffalo Park Loop: 274
Butcher Jones Trail: 162
Butterfield to Gadsden
    Trails: 115

C

Camelback Mountain: 75, 78
Carter, Mansel: 146
Cat Peaks Pass Trail: 183
Cathedral Rock Trail: 284
Cave Creek Ranger District:
    219
Cave Creek Regional Park:
    220, 222, 226
Charles M. Christiansen
    Memorial Trail 100: 49
Chihuahuan Desert Exhibit
    Trail: 207
Cholla Trail: 77, 78

Circumference and
    Ridgeline Loop: 228
Civil War sites: 152, 156
Coach Whip to Cholla Loop:
    231
Coconino National Forest:
    268, 272, 274, 277, 280,
    284, 287, 297, 301
Cook, General George: 308
Curandero Trail: 207

DE

Deem Hills: 228
Derrick Trail: 305
Dixie Mountain Loop: 234
Dobbins Lookout: 134
Doce wildfire: 291
Double Butte Loop: 89
Dragonfly Trail: 216
Dreamy Draw Loop: 53
Dreamy Draw Recreation
    Area: 49, 52, 53
Dutchman's and Bluff Spring
    Loop: 198
Dysart Trail: 112
Echo Canyon Recreation
    Area: 75
Echo Canyon Summit Trail:
    75, 80
Elden Lookout Trail: 279
Eliot Ramada to Double
    Butte Loop: 87
Estrella Mountain Regional
    Park: 109, 112, 115

F

Fat Man's Loop: 277
Flagstaff: 268, 272, 274,
    277
Flagstaff Urban Trails
    System: 272, 274
Flatiron, The: 188
Ford Canyon Loop: 96
Fossil Springs Trail: 297
Fountain Hills: 258
Fountain Lake Overlook
    Loop: 258
Fountain Park: 258
Four Peaks Wilderness: 261
Freedom Trail 302: 62
Friends of Pinnacle Peak
    Park: 239

G

G. R. Herberger Park: 81
Gadsden Purchase: 109
Gateway Loop Trail: 248
General Crook Loop: 307
Geronimo Trail: 128
Gila to Baseline Loop: 109
Gila Trail: 111
Glendale: 231
Go John Trail: 222
Goat Camp Trail: 106
Goat Canyon Trail: 107
Goldmine and Dynamite
    Loop: 145
Granite Mountain Trail: 290

HI

Hayden Butte Preserve
    Park: 90
Hayden Butte Summit Trail:
    90
heat stroke: 21
Hidden Valley Trail: 143
Hieroglyphic Trail: 192
High Trail: 207
Highline to Donahue Trail: 301
Highline Trail: 305
Hohokam people: 25, 192,
    214, 219
Holbert Trail: 134
Hole in the Rock Trail: 84
Horton Creek Trail: 304
Humphreys Peak Summit
    Trail: 268
Hunter Trail: 155

JK

Jacob's Crosscut Trail: 186
Jewel of the Creek Preserve:
    216
Kachina Peaks Wilderness:
    268
Kachina Woman: 280
Kennedy, Marion: 146
Kiwanis Trail to Telegraph
    Pass Lookout: 137

L

L. V. Yates Trail 8: 56
Lookout Mountain
    Circumference Trail 308:
    32, 36

Lookout Mountain Preserve: 32, 36
Lookout Mountain Summit Trail 150: 32, 38
Lookout Trail: 243
Lost Dog Wash Trail: 252
Lost Dutchman State Park: 185, 188
Lost Goldmine Trail: 193
Lowell Observatory: 273
Lower Oldham Trail: 275

M
Main Trail: 205
Mars Hill Trail: 272
McDowell Mountain Regional Park: 245
McDowell Sonoran Preserve: 241, 248, 252, 255
Meadow Trail: 309
Merkle Memorial Loop Trail: 178
Milk Ranch Point: 301
Mogollon Rim: 307
Mohave Trail 200: 65
Mormon Loop Trail: 127
Mormon Trail to Hidden Valley Loop: 125

NO
National Trail: 140
North Mountain Area: 49
North Mountain National Trail 44: 46
North Mountain Park: 43, 46
North Mountain Recreation Loop: 48
North Overbank and North Terrace Loop: 122

P
Papago Park: 84, 87
Pass Mountain Trail: 172, 176
Payson: 304, 307
Pemberton and Tonto Tank Loop: 245
Peralta Trail to Fremont Saddle: 195
Peregrine Point: 164
Perry Mesa Tradition people: 310
petroglyphs: 25, 55, 100, 137, 192, 310

Phoenix Mountains Park and Recreation Area: 59, 62, 65, 68
Phoenix Mountains Preserve: 40, 43, 46, 49, 53, 56, 59, 62, 65, 68, 71
Picacho Peak State Park: 152, 155
Piestewa Nature Trail 304: 59
Piestewa Peak Summit Trail 300: 68
Pima Wash Trail: 131
Pine: 301
Pinnacle Peak Park: 238
Pinnacle Peak Trail: 238
Prescott: 290, 293
Prescott National Forest: 290, 293

QR
Quartz Ridge Trail 8A: 71
Rainbow Valley to Toothaker Loop: 112
Ranger Office Loop Trail: 85
Red Rock Secret Mountain Wilderness: 280
Ridgeline Trail: 132
Rim Lakes Vista and General Crook Loop: 307
Rio Salado Habitat Restoration Area: 122
Rogers Canyon Trail: 201

S
Saguaro Lake: 162
Salado people: 203
Salt River Project: 82
San Tan Loop: 148
San Tan Mountain Regional Park: 145, 148
Scottsdale: 238, 241, 245, 248, 252, 255
Sears-Kay Ruin Loop: 219
Sedona: 280, 284, 287
Shadow Mountain: 40
Shaw Butte Trail 306: 43
Siphon Draw Trail to The Flatiron: 188
Sonoran Preserve: 234
South American Desert Trail: 207 South Mountain Environmental Education Center: 136
South Mountain Park: 125, 128, 131, 134, 137, 140

Spur Cross and Elephant Mountain Loop: 212
Spur Cross Ranch Conservation Area: 212, 216, 220, 227
Strawberry: 297
Summit Trail 300: 64
Sunrise Trail: 255
Sunset Vista Trail: 152
Superstition Wilderness: 165, 169, 185, 188, 192, 195, 198, 201

T
Taliesin West: 254
Telegraph Pass Lookout: 137, 142
Telegraph Pass Trail: 138
Tempe: 90
Templeton Trail: 285
Thumb Butte Loop: 293
Thunderbird Conservation Park: 231
Thunderbird H-1 to H-3 Loop: Coach Whip to Cholla Loop: 231
Tom's Thumb Trail: 241
Tonto and Coconino National Forests: 297, 301
Tonto National Forest: 162, 219, 261, 297, 301, 304
Trail 202: 67
Treasure Loop Trail: 185

UVWXYZ
Usery Mountain Regional Park: 172, 175, 178, 181
Vista Trail: 180, 282
vortex sites: 280, 284
Waterfall Trail: 100
Weaver's Needle: 169, 196
Wet Beaver Creek Wilderness: 287
White Tank Mountain Regional Park: 96, 100, 103, 106
Wind Cave Trail: 175
Wright, Frank Lloyd: 252, 254

www.moon.com

DESTINATIONS | ACTIVITIES | BLOGS | MAPS | BOOKS

MOON.COM is ready to help plan your next trip! Filled with fresh trip ideas and strategies, author interviews, informative travel blogs, a detailed map library, and descriptions of all the Moon guidebooks, Moon.com is all you need to get out and explore the world—or even places in your own backyard. While at Moon.com, sign up for our monthly e-newsletter for updates on new releases, travel tips, and expert advice from our on-the-go Moon authors. As always, when you travel with Moon, expect an experience that is uncommon and truly unique.

KEEP UP WITH MOON ON FACEBOOK AND TWITTER
JOIN THE MOON PHOTO GROUP ON FLICKR

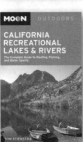
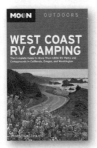

MOON TAKE A HIKE PHOENIX

Avalon Travel
a member of the Perseus Books Group
1700 Fourth Street
Berkeley, CA 94710, USA
www.moon.com

Editor and Series Manager: Sabrina Young
Copy Editor: Deana Shields
Production and Graphics Coordinator:
  Darren Alessi
Cover Designer: Darren Alessi
Map Editor: Albert Angulo
Cartographers: Albert Angulo, Chris Henrick,
  Stephanie Poulain, Brian Shotwell, Heather
  Sparks

ISBN-13: 978-1-61238-530-3
ISSN: 2330-4936

Printing History
1st Edition – November 2013
5 4 3 2 1

Front cover photo: © AgStock Images, Inc. /
  Alamy
Title page photo: © Lilia Menconi
Back cover photo: © Peter Cade / Getty Images

Printed in Canada by Friesens

Keeping Current

We are committed to making this book the most accurate and enjoyable hiking guide to
Phoenix. You can rest assured that every trail in this book has been carefully reviewed in an
effort to keep this book as up-to-date as possible. However, by the time you read this book,
some of the fees listed herein may have changed and trails may have closed unexpectedly.
If you have a favorite gem you'd like to see included in the next edition, or see anything that
needs updating, clarification, or correction, please drop us a line. Send your comments via
email to feedback@moon.com, or use the address above.